I'm Still Here

EARTHA KITT

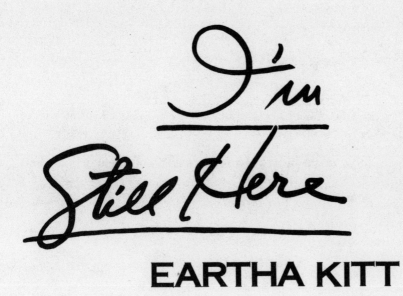

I'm Still Here

EARTHA KITT

SIDGWICK & JACKSON

LONDON

To all of you who chose to be my enemies, with loving affection; to my friends – you know who you are.

The publishers would like to thank Frances Stonor Saunders for her help in preparing the manuscript.

First published in 1989 by
Sidgwick & Jackson Limited
1 Tavistock Chambers, Bloomsbury Way
London WC1A 2SG

ISBN 0283 99772 9

Photoset in Great Britain by
Rowland Phototypesetting Limited
Bury St Edmunds, Suffolk
Printed by Billings and Sons Limited
Worcester

To Kitt and my public for keeping me here

Contents

1 'Yella Gal'

I often think of my mother. Though I do not remember what she looked like, I feel her presence with me all the time. I still feel her warmth, her beauty, as she played with Pearl, my half-sister, rolling on the ground – or on the floor when we happened to find a place where someone accepted us, which was not often. Most of the time we lived in the forest, or at least slept there covered with pine straw.

I remember a long, long period we had been travelling out. I don't know where we had come from or where we were going, only that the road was the longest road I had ever seen. The cotton was high and twilight was covering the sky's edge. As I walked alongside my mother, glancing at my half-sister in her arms, I wondered why she did not carry me sometimes. My child-like mind never realized that it would be difficult for her to carry us both; and Pearl was still a baby, while I at least could walk.

I don't remember Moma carrying anything more than us. There were no bags or sacks, no bundles of any kind; just our empty hands, Moma, Pearl, and me. There was a house further up the road that I could only just see the top of. My body was weary, my shoeless feet were in pain from the rocky dirt road, my belly cried from hunger and my throat was dry from thirst as I wondered what we were going to do as night came on. I pushed my stomach tight with my hand, trying to keep Moma from hearing the growls as I did not want her to feel that she had to comfort me. My other hand gripped hers and I felt her hand tighten in return. Though she did not say anything, I felt her gesture say, 'I know, I know.'

The cotton followed us each step of the way and I imagined the bogeyman peering from the long rows of stalked fields. Their bulbs seemed to get bigger and bigger as the night came on stronger. I wished Moma would find a place for us to sleep before the bogeyman got us. Just as dusk was beginning to hover over us, Moma turned onto a pathway leading to the house. There was smoke coming from the chimney, so obviously someone was there.

Moma knocked on the door a few times and it opened. I don't know what the face behind the voice looked like as I was busy hiding against Moma's back, not wanting to be seen. This seems to have been instinctive. Moma asked for shelter and food, pleading softly with the woman. I could hear her saying, 'Just for tonight . . . my children are hungry and tired . . .'

As I glanced up to take a quick peek at the voice's owner, she was looking around to see what was hiding: 'No, I don't want that yella gal in my house.'

Seems I had heard those words before, but this is the first time that I can remember. I felt hurt, most of all for Moma's sake. I did not think of Pearl. I don't remember ever seeing her until that God-forgiving-ever-long road. I only knew Moma was carrying a baby that must be my sister, since once in a while she would talk to it with soft comforting words.

As the door closed in our faces, Moma, Pearl, and I faced the big road again. We walked until a forest of mostly pine trees gave us shelter. Moma scratched away at the leaves and pine straw to make a nest for us to sleep in, then covered us with a blanket of pine straw. She laid Pearl down first, covered her, then me, and finally she lay down herself, cuddling us in her arms for the heat of her body to warm us. I did not sleep, it seems, for a very long time. I was scared of the bogeyman. I did not know what a bogeyman was, but I was scared of it.

Where did we come from? Why did we leave? Where are we going? As I lay on my back with these questions in my head, I looked through the pine tree tops to the sky. The stars were twinkling as though trying to give me an answer; the moon shone through the night sky making me ask more and more questions, but all of these questions without answers just haunted me.

Why was I called 'yella gal'? What did it mean? Was Pearl the same as me? I knew vaguely what Moma looked like, but I do not remember if she was like me or not. Something was wrong and it seemed to be all my fault. Was it because I was a yella gal? As I searched the sky for an answer I thought there was a bogeyman behind every tree, bush and rock. Every shadow became an image of something scary; every sound was a beast of prey that would get us before the night was over.

I did not remember any other people in the world but us and that voice we had just left. I did not remember anything before those moments. I certainly knew nothing of animals, only of scary things without an image. I must have finally scared myself to sleep since when my eyes opened there was straw on my face and Moma was gone. Pearl was just lying there with her tiny feet kicking the air in bliss. I looked around to see if Moma was anywhere nearby, but she wasn't.

The trees seemed a little more friendly to us now. I felt they knew where Moma was. I don't remember being able to talk. My questions became stronger in my head and the trees began to sway a little, as though trying to give me answers.

I could not cry – I was too scared and hungry. Pearl must have been hungry too because she started to whimper a little and then her loud crying echoed through the forest. I tried to comfort her and as my hands wiped the tears from her face, I began to notice something for the first time. She was not the same colour as me. My hands were different from her face. Pearl was black. I don't remember thinking of what colour Moma was.

I began to cry with her, 'Moma, Moma . . .', and through rays of sunlight I saw a figure coming towards us. Gradually I realized that it was Moma, with her skirt turned up to hold fruit and berries and melons she had stolen from someone's farm. I wiped my eyes quickly so that she wouldn't see I had been crying. Since I had already sensed I was a problem I did not want to give her any more trouble than was necessary. Moma came to us through the sun rays, smiling, and fussed over us as she shared her bounty as though all was right with the world. When we had eaten our fill, she cleaned us up as best she could and we started out again.

The next scene I remember is Moma talking to a black man at a biggish house with chickens, dogs, cats, a cow, mules and other animals. This is my first memory of seeing such things, but I found out later what they were. I didn't hear what Moma was talking about with the black man – perhaps I blocked it out – but I felt sure that I had either seen this man before or heard his voice somewhere. I seem to remember him as Uncle Pete, but perhaps that was something in the future.

He was extremely tall, and very firm in his discussion with Moma. She was speaking softly to him and I think I could hear sobs in her voice. I sat on the porch steps trying to attract the attention of one of the animals to play with me, but it didn't want to. The black man pointed to the barn, mumbling some words and pointing his finger, and Moma's face turned in that direction. Though her movement was slow, with me following behind her, her steps were firm and each vertebra of her back pulled her up higher and higher until she seemed the tallest woman in the world. She covered us up with whatever she found in the barn, alongside the animals, just as she did in the forest. The black man's family came to give us some bread and, I think, some milk, though maybe it was water. Then, next morning, just as the sun peeked up over the cotton fields, Moma gathered us up again and we were back out on another dirt road.

Some time later we came to a tiny cottage in the middle of a huge cotton field. Moma knocked on the door and I instinctively hid where I could not be seen. My hair was red, thick like the hair on a poodle, and long, sticking out as though I had my hand in an electric socket. Since I was not aware of a difference in people's colour at this age, I do not recall ever seeing a white person, but I was becoming aware that I was a victim of some kind of prejudice.

When the door opened I stiffened with fear, hoping with my whole body that we would be accepted, that Moma and Pearl would not be turned away again because of 'that yella gal'. I saw my mother going into the tiny house. She poked her head around the door, saw me pressed against the outside wall of the tiny cottage, and beckoned for me to follow. Like a cat I slowly moved in behind her, still trying to hide myself.

The lady lived alone, I thought. There was no one else there, just a cat sleeping on a pillow by the fireplace. We were shown to a bedroom where we began to settle down. Moma left the room and returned with a tin tub that she filled with buckets of water from a well in the yard. She bathed us and gave us some bread and milk she got from the lady's pitcher. When I peeked through the cracks of the bedroom wall, the lady was sitting in a rocking chair near the fireplace where the cat was reclining. The lady did not say very much – she just rocked and rocked.

Moma started to tidy up the tiny house, as though there was an understanding that this was to be the reason we could stay. I saw a tiny garden, but remained sitting on the side of the bed cuddling Pearl for the rest of the day because I did not want to leave the bedroom in case the lady saw that I was a yella gal and we would be on the move again. Moma moved around the house doodaddling until time for bed.

We three slept together. The lady had another room for herself. I kept waking through the night, wondering what our tomorrow would be like.

On rising, I noticed Moma was still doodaddling around, making something for us to eat; when she called us to breakfast, it was bread and milk. I gathered this was all there was, so I settled down to it. Pearl was fed by Moma putting pieces of bread in milk to soak before it was put into her mouth.

After breakfast, Moma went to the lady's room and brought her to the table. The lady carried a stick. It was then I noticed that she was about my colour, which made me feel a little more comfortable, but more so when I realized something was wrong with her. She couldn't reach what she wanted, so Moma gave her a plate of corn bread with a slice of fatback with heavy cream and a glass of clobber milk. The lady mumbled something to Moma who then brought her a cup of some black liquid – must have been coffee. Moma poured some milk in it and put the cup to her right side, placing the lady's hand on the cup. It was then I realized that the lady was blind.

I knew now that I could have fun and play without fear. Moma went off some place shortly after breakfast giving me instructions to watch over Pearl and not go away from the house. The old lady was put in her rocking chair where she stayed most of the day, mumbling to the cat and rocking to and fro. Pearl and I played on the floor beside her. From time to time I would get the old lady a cup of water, put it in her hands, and return to the floor where Pearl was sometimes sleeping, sometimes just kicking her feet in the air. I knew Moma was coming back but when and from where I could not imagine.

There were no time mechanisms around. Time was told by the sun shadows of one's self. I would stand in the yard looking at my own shadow; its height and position would tell me when the field workers would be going home. I was expecting Moma at any minute now as, according to my shadow, the sun would soon be gone and I reckoned that she must have gone somewhere to work.

This routine went on for some time: up with the rooster's crow, home for something to eat. Moma would go off, returning at dusk to feed us again, then go to bed, and so it continued. Sometimes I wandered down by the edge of the forest through the cotton fields – on Saturdays or Sundays, I guess, when Moma was in the house taking care of the old lady. I cleared the area I found and gathered some pine straw and huge low branches for my house, with old boxes and logs for my furniture. I found some string to rope it off into a sitting room, a bedroom and a kitchen. My imagination was obviously very keen – my house contained old rags for curtains, a box for a table, even corn cobs for dolls that I wrapped in rags for their clothes.

The old lady's house must have been pretty remote because I do not remember seeing anyone until one day Moma came back with some people who had a little girl, slightly bigger than I was. I don't remember what colour she was but since she came and played with me sometimes I guess no one noticed if we were different. Anyway, she hardly ever came.

After a while at the old lady's house, Moma and I planted a garden of vegetables – collard greens, cabbage, potatoes, sweet yams. I think there was a black man helping us digging the soil to prepare a garden.

Once, in the middle of the night, Pearl woke up and needed to relieve herself. Moma wasn't in the house and the old lady must have been asleep. I took Pearl outside by the edge of the garden bordering the cotton field. As Pearl relieved herself – it seemed to take for ever – I saw a huge shadow of a strange figure lying near the rose bushes. Fear struck me deeply for I knew instinctively it was not something to play with. I stood next to Pearl almost not breathing, hoping she would hurry up. Just as I got Pearl back to the steps of the tiny cottage, the figure got up and started to move towards us. Since Pearl could hardly walk I half carried, half dragged her into the house in silence as the animal lurked closer to us. As it put its feet onto the steps, I closed the door as fast as I could. The figure made a moaning sound scaring me enough to make my heart beat so hard it almost stopped. I said nothing to Pearl, just put her back to bed. Since the moon was full I could see the figure quite clearly when I looked through the window. It looked like a big fluffy mule, but I knew it wasn't. It kept walking around the house, and I wondered desperately where Moma was. The old lady was blind, she couldn't help if this thing got into the house.

Next morning I discovered some kind of tracks around the yard and prints of something huge that had been lying near the rose bushes. When I showed them to Moma she said it was a bear. Later, when I went to my play area in the woods, I found the footprints were there as well. The bear had broken the strings that separated my rooms and my furniture made from boxes was crushed. I don't remember ever going back there again.

I was always worrying that Moma might leave and never come back. I don't remember talking ever, but I was a very keen listener and silent as a cat. I listened through the cracks in the walls. One night, I awoke to hear Moma sobbing and when I peeked through the cracks of the bedroom wall, I saw her on her knees in front of the black man who helped out in the garden. A small fire was burning; the soft crackling of the burning wood accompanied Moma's sobs. Very softly her words came through the cracks: 'Please take my children.'

'No, I don't want that yella gal in my house.'

The words stung my being like a thousand bees had swarmed into my very soul. Moma continued to sob and plead.

'No, I don't want that yella gal. She would cause trouble with my children.' The black man's voice became a little louder. 'I'll take Pearl, not Eartha Mae.'

In fear, I returned to my place in the bed. I lay very still, not wanting to make trouble. I wanted to cry but couldn't. Why didn't he want me? Finally I must have gone to sleep.

When morning came fully, Moma was doodaddling with pots and tin dishes at the wooden stove. In silence I came out of the bedroom. I didn't look at her and didn't want her to see me. I was in the way, a problem to her. No one wanted us because of me, the yella gal. Moma got Pearl up, cleaned her and sat her down across from me at the table, then she sat next to Pearl as she fed her. The old lady came out of her room, leaning on her cane, and Moma crossed the floor to help her.

I looked at Pearl carefully: she was much darker than me. If I was the same colour as Pearl, Moma would not be having so much trouble. Today she seemed unusually quiet and was not fussing over us as she normally did. The joy in her was gone and she moved more slowly, not looking into our faces. Something was haunting her, making me feel as though I was uglier than ever.

Moma left the house, but soon came back to get us. She took us to the cotton field where she had been working. She laid Pearl down on a cotton sheet, then told me how to pick cotton and put my little handfuls into the cotton sack she had strung over her shoulders. Many others were doing the same, as were their children. We would start up one end of a cotton row and come down the other. When Moma thought I was tired, she would make me stay next to Pearl waiting until she and the others returned, moving us from time to time as they progressed further along the fields. The sun was hotter than fire at times and then we would all sit under trees to cool ourselves, drinking water brought from the white man's yard in pails. But the cotton pickers did not rest too long in the shade because cotton was a penny a pound and it took all day to make one dollar, even for the strongest men.

At times the crew of cotton pickers was called on to pick peaches or soy beans. This was particularly uncomfortable as the fuzz from the peaches or soy beans got into the skin when you were wiping off the sweat from the heat. I saw Moma many times in agony, almost in tears trying to comfort herself from the fuzz. I too suffered from this many times as I tried to help Moma make a dollar a day, but I always tried not to reveal my discomfort.

Some time after that night when I had seen the black man with Moma on her knees pleading for her children, he and Moma left us at a house. I don't remember how we got there, but I can picture in my head the scene as Moma and the black man walked away through an arch of roses. Moma was happy as they walked away arm in arm and I stood in the yard looking after them. A ray of sun shone through the arch on to me and I felt sure that this was the last time I would see Moma. This time I knew she would be gone forever.

I stood in silence with some kind of long stick in my hands – it must have been a broom – and the movement of my body slowly swept the leaves closer to the plants as though I had been hypnotized. My movement continued to sweep my hurt under the bushes. Now I knew Moma was gone forever. I did not cry. I could not cry. I would not cry. My soul was hurt and lost. I tried to warm myself in the rays of the sun, looking to the heavens, reaching for the arms of God to hold me: hold me, caress me, please let somebody want me.

2 *Gracie and Willie*

'Eartha Mae, come here, let me see what you look like.'

It was the voice of a black lady who held Pearl in her arms as she came onto the porch of the house where we were to stay for some time. Two teenagers followed her, wearing raggedy clothes that looked worn out from working in the fields. Gracie and Willie. They were black. They just looked at me with no words.

The house had one bedroom, a sitting room with a fireplace, a kitchen across a walkway separating it from the house itself. A set of steps led from the walkway connecting the kitchen and the house with a yard where there was a vegetable garden with a fence taller than me, much taller. All sorts of beans crawled along the fence, spreading their vines up and down in all directions. Some were long and skinny and others were fat, turning a yellowish colour. Lima beans, string beans, peas, cabbage, collards, beets, potatoes, white and red. The corn was turning yellow, ready to be eaten. Since the garden was plentiful I thought with comfort that at least I would not be hungry again.

I was holding the broom that I had taken from the front yard. This broom was my comfort in many ways. It gave me something to hold on to. I was immediately told to sweep the back yard that was to be kept without a dead leaf anywhere, as was the yard in front and at the side of the house. I don't remember what time of day this was but I kept sweeping until I was told to come into the kitchen, then I was shown my duties there. A huge black stove that burned small chipped logs was to be filled each morning and evening or whenever food had to be prepared. Big pots that I could hardly lift were to be kept clean. Tin plates and cups were to be washed after each meal. The house was to be kept clean, things kept neat. Water was to be brought from the spring in the forest in two pails, for drinking and washing.

I could not reach the top of the stove to lift down the pots that were to be washed in a tub on a table that I also could not reach. I moved a chair to the stove, removed a pot, put it on the chair, pushed the chair to the table, got on the chair, put the pot in the tub, washed it, and put it away in much the same manner. I repeated this exercise several times until it was done, dishes and all.

When the evening came, I had to make a fire in the fireplace after cleaning the ashes that were to be put around the rose bushes, depending on the time of year. Slop the pigs, feed the chickens, gather the eggs; and so it went, my life with the black lady – whom we called Aunt Rosa – her husband and her two teenage grandchildren.

Pearl was always being cuddled in the arms of one or the other. Since no one paid much attention to me, I found a corner at the side of the fireplace where I curled up when I had eventually finished all my chores. All four children were to sleep in one bed, in the same room but separated by a curtain from the bed where Aunt Rosa slept with her husband. On a table by the window was a kerosene lamp; a line was strung from wall to wall to hold whatever clothes there were.

I don't remember having anything to cover my body but a crocker sack dress made of the sacks potatoes were stacked in, and nothing on my bottom as far as I remember. The dress was very itchy, like a nest of fleas, especially when it was extremely hot.

The house was built on wooden stilts and that gave me a place to hide when company came. Since I did not want to be seen by anyone I quite often hid down there with the cats, dogs, chickens or whatever else was sitting in the shade. There were beams along the wood blocks where I would hide things I had found.

One day as I cleaned the house, I found a pack of cigarette tobacco with leaves of paper. I had seen how the men rolled the tobacco into these leaves of paper, lighting it with a match. I went under the house and did the same. It made me sick as a dog, but I remember enjoying the getting-away-with-something that I thought was to be only my secret. But one day Gracie saw the tiny puffs of smoke coming from under the house and that was the end of my secret. I was terrified that she would tell the rest of the family and I kept waiting for my punishment. At last, one day, it came.

Gracie and Willie had come back from the fields alone. I had been left with Pearl and my chores. I was doing my usual sweeping of the yards and Pearl, as always, was sleeping.

'Eartha Mae.' Willie's voice shook my soul. 'Come here.'

I walked as slowly as I could towards him, dragging my broom behind me.

'Get me a switch from that peach tree,' he said, pointing.

When I brought a very thin switch of branch from the tree, Willie said, 'You can do better than that. I want a big one. You know the kind: a nice fat one.'

My heart started to pump more and more with the weight of fear. When I returned with a bigger, fatter switch, Gracie, who had been cuddling Pearl, moved nearer to him with a burning smile on her face. I stood like a stone in front of him, my head bowed to the ground. He swished the switch in front of me after removing its leaves. I dared not look at his face. Gracie was sitting next to him now, watching.

'Pick up your rags,' he said, lifting the bottom of my crocker sack dress. I lifted the bottom a little way up my thigh. The switch struck the ground, raising dust around my feet. My heart pumped more heavily. 'More!'

As the private parts of my tiny body became exposed they both started laughing: 'Damn, you're yella all over, ain't cha?'

Willie leaned his elbows onto the upper step as he peered back in laughter. Gracie joined in.

'Turn around,' Willie suddenly said. As my body turned, the switch came across my backside with a sting that would make the devil cringe. I gritted my teeth, holding my jaw and muscles as tight as I could – no tears. The pain was too great, tears could not ease the agony.

'Yella gal likes smoking tobacco junk!' The switch went into its place again. Six.

Willie and Gracie were laughing more softly now. They must have had their fun for the day. Willie swished the switch in the air a few times, allowing the blood stains imprinted on it to dry before finally tossing it onto the woodpile. I stood there, head bowed to the ground, holding my crocker sack dress up around my waist, waiting for my next orders. Still no tears.

'She ain't gonna tell nobody. She gets the same if she does,' Willie said in the air for Gracie's ear and mine to hear. I could see their shadows move away from my area. I don't know where they went. They had obviously taken Pearl with them as she was no longer in sight.

When my hands finally let go of the hem of the crocker sack dress, I felt wet and sticky; the blood from the switch wounds was now drying, and the dress was sticking to it. I picked up my wound-healer, the broom, and continued sweeping my hurt under the rose bushes.

When the time for all to be returning from the fields came, I had gathered wood from the woodpile for the stove and the fireplace, made a fire for both, laid the table, and gone to the spring for fresh water. Since I could not sit properly now with welts swelling up, I found my little corner by the fireplace, leaning on my thigh as far over as I could so as not to show the pain.

I don't know how long Pearl and I stayed in that house but it seemed for ever. During harvesting time when food was plentiful I was given enough to eat. When the winter months came and not so much was to be had, I was given what was left. The scraps thrown to the dogs and cats was between me and them to be shared, sand and all.

I lived in silence in this house. When I wanted company I went to the forest, following and watching the forest animals – squirrels, rabbits or birds. I would also find food that was safe to eat, even grass. One we called 'sourgrass' grew tall in the fields with a purple flower which could be sucked. There were also wild hickory nuts, wild grapes we called 'bullseyes', and blackberries. Anything the animals ate, so did I.

Sometimes, just for the fun of it, Gracie and Willie would put a crocker sack over my head, tie it around my waist, then tie me to a tree and welt my bottom with a peach tree switch, laughing in meanness until the blood ran down my thighs and legs like urine.

'She ain't gonna tell nobody or she gets the same again,' Willie would say.

One day only Gracie and I were left at the house. Pearl was always sleeping. I was on the porch. I can't remember what I was doing when Gracie softly called me into the house. 'Lie down on the floor,' she said, 'on your back.' Gracie kneeled beside me. She gently rolled my crocker sack dress to my waist. She had something in her hand. It looked at first like a piece of stick but it was made of cloth. Softly she began to stroke my private area with this cloth-like stick. My body stiffened like a mummy. I couldn't understand what she was going to do as she placed her body over mine trying to move this cloth-like stick between her private parts and mine. Cringing, I closed my eyes, then I heard voices in the distance coming from the front yard – the family was back. Gracie never had a chance to complete her 'whatever', for she darted up like lightning, running to the bedroom and returning with empty hands. I ran to do my chores: wherever, whatever had to be done. This action was never referred to again.

Moma was always in my mind. I could see her face and her silhouette in the space of my eyelids in any corner, any shadow. I could hear Moma's voice in the singing of any bird, the swaying of the branches of every tree, the whistle of the wind, the sound of any raindrop. I would see her coming to get me on the path of any sun ray.

'Moma, I didn't mean to hurt you. Moma, why did you give me away?' The hurt kept haunting me with these questions.

'I'll take Pearl but I don't want that yella gal in my house. She will cause trouble with my children.' The black man's voice kept ringing in my brain.

The sight of Moma's back as she and he walked away through the cotton field arm in arm – her back seemed to have been smiling in sadness as she left me standing in the sunlight.

Once in a while the old man, Aunt Rosa's husband, went to town for supplies – Orangeburg it must have been, I learned years later. He would return so drunk the mule had to bring him home. That is the way with animals I guess: they always know the way home. The old man would roll off the wagon into the yard when the mule stopped. We would all rush out hoping for some surprises other than the regular supplies. Once he brought back a bunch of yellow stick-like things in a bunch. I did not know what to do with it when one was given to me. Willie and Gracie were tossing theirs from one hand to the other like a piece of a puzzle trying to be put in place. They too did not know what it was. They were put aside while we unpacked the wagon, carrying everything to the barn or the house to be put away. The old man was lying on the porch face-down to sleep, between bouts of vomiting that I had to wash away.

When finally I had enough time to investigate my yellow stick, I took it under the house where all my little secret findings were. The smell was very pleasant. I thought it was something to eat but when I bit into it the skin was not pleasant to my tongue. Then I noticed the inside was also yellow, slightly lighter, separated from the skin. I figured that since this was softer it must be the food part. Until this day, whenever I see one I smile in the memory of my first banana.

3 'Gonna Storm'

The first day I went to school, I was given some strange-looking clothes by the white people who owned the cotton plantation. They lived in a big white house that I never saw the whole of, with a store in the back where some supplies were kept. They had some children, but I was never aware how many. I only saw them once in a while, and this day was the once in a while. These strange clothes were put on me to wear with high boots with strings that hooked criss-crossingly, overlapping from one side to the other, and tied at the tops which came halfway up my tiny legs. Even though they were too tight I pretended to feel no pain for it was the first time I ever remember having anything on my feet. The dress I only remember as something soft and gentle, much too big, but it was a real dress. My bushy long red hair was made neat in three braids, two hanging over each ear, the other down the side of my face.

The children of the other black families got dressed in their only fineries and were walking with Gracie, Willie and me to the tiny quiet schoolhouse at St Peter's Church. A graveyard separated the school from the church. As I looked along the dirt road towards the church and the school in the distance, I saw a line of white children coming from that direction. Their voices became louder as they got nearer and became uncomfortably screeching as I saw them link themselves hand in hand. Stretching themselves across the dirt road they screamed, 'Nigger, nigger, need no school. Nigger, nigger, is a fool.' As we tried to get out of their way, we were pushed into the ditch of mud as they laughingly carried on down the road: 'Nigger, nigger, is a fool. Nigger, nigger, need no school.'

On our arrival at the school a black man was standing at the door with a long ruler in his hand. His black hair was slicked down so tight to his head he must have used a can of lard. As each of us entered the schoolroom, we had to put out a hand to be whacked. The sting was sharp, leaving wide red marks where the blood had come to the surface, giving me visible evidence of another form of meanness.

'You must never be late,' said the slick-hair man's voice.

None of us bothered to tell the slick man why we were late or why our clothes were somewhat stained with dry mud, which we tried to clean off as best we could. Since the slick man said nothing about this, neither did we. It seems that the white schoolchildren regularly did this and perhaps the slick man thought it best not to discuss it, just pretend not to notice.

A black pot-belly stove was in the centre of the floor. We grouped ourselves around it according to size since some of us, me in particular, did not know our age. I was given a small box holding a piece of corn bread, a piece of fatback and, I believe, an apple.

After scrambling through something on paper that I could not understand, I just listened and watched until a bell rang, clang! clang! clang! I moved into the graveyard with the other children. As I stood alone, not knowing what the next move was to be, some of the children gathered round me. They made a circle round me as though they were going to play 'Ring-around-the-rosie', but instead of singing they just followed each other in a silent circular movement. I was holding my box loosely in my arms when suddenly it was grabbed by one of the children, much bigger than me. They were all bigger than me. They were all darker than me.

I don't recall a feeling of fear. Since I hadn't given them a reason to hurt me I stood calmly in the circle after the box was taken. I don't think they made any sound. I saw the big girl take the top from the box and, after mustering up as big a mouthful of spit as she could, she spat into the box with laughter that could wake a bear in hibernation. Then they all started laughing as the box was handed back to me. Then the clang! clang! clang! was heard again, and we all lined up for our return to the slick man's schoolroom.

After my first day at school, I was not anxious to return and was very happy when field hands were needed by all. I don't remember going to that school more than four or five times. I was afraid of meeting the white children, afraid of the black children, and afraid of the slick man.

Each time Gracie, Willie and I were left at the house alone with Pearl, who was always sleeping, Gracie and Willie would send me for a peach tree switch. They would put a crocker sack over my head, tie it around my waist, and tie me to a tree to have their fun watching the welts swell up on my naked bottom, until the Gods asked for mercy. I never made a sound, guessing that it would please them to hear me cry and make them whip me more.

There was a pen for the hogs and the mule extending from the farm where they slept. At hog-killing time, the men would gather around the pen after separating the one to be killed from the ones to be saved. The sound of their screeching voices would ring in my head for days and nights after. A very sharp knife was jabbed into the front of the neck as the hog was straddled by one of the men who gleefully punched the death wound, leaving the hog gasping like hiccups as blood reddened the dirt beneath it. We children, with our heads hanging through the slits of the wooden fence, watched in silence. The older ones sitting on the rim yelled with laughter as the slaughter went on.

A big pot-bellied urn was placed on the fire to heat water for the hooves and other parts of the hog which were to be boiled. Some parts were to make soup, others smoked sausages – pork this, pork that, to be hung in the barn for future eating. Nothing was wasted.

An area of this particular barn was for storing food for winter or until harvest time. Sauerkraut made from cabbage or collard greens was barrelled; sweet potatoes were put in a hole in the ground lined with pine straw, covered with dirt, leaving a hole just big enough for a man's hand to reach in. This was to prevent rotting and to protect from frost.

We were very lucky this year – the little tenant farm Aunt Rosa and her husband had on rent from the white man yielded plenty of crops. The barn was full for bad times. Sugar cane syrup was on the barn shelves, corn meal was sacked, the chickens had reproduced prolifically as had the hogs. Pecans were bigger, hickory nuts were gathered and the barn was swelling in abundance. As the fields were emptied at the white man's command, we felt happy at the sight of a beautiful barn of winter comfort and gave thanks in song and prayer at St Peter's Church. All the blacks were cheerful, with big smiles when they met each other on the road or path.

Aunt Rosa's husband took the last bit of food payment to the white man, returning with his body hanging off the wagon, and dragging himself onto the porch to be sick and sleep it off until planting time came. I don't remember seeing much of him until field work was needed.

I received one of the worst beatings of my life when I was sent into the house to fetch a sweater one evening when Aunt Rosa got chilly sitting on the porch smoking her corn pipe. We were all simmering down for the coming winter; all the chores were done. I finally had a rest period and was sitting in a nook on the porch with my feet dangling over the side.

'Eartha Mae, get me that sweater hanging on the clothes line in the bedroom,' Aunt Rosa said.

There was only one sweater of hers I knew of. I went into the bedroom with tremendous joy that I was asked to do something, for it meant I got attention. It was getting a bit dark and my eyes could not place exactly where the sweater was among the rest of the family's things hanging on the line which held the clothes as well as the curtain separating the two beds. A kerosene lamp was glaring at me from the bed table, a box of matches at its side. I lit the lamp, held it near the clothes line in search of the sweater, when all of a sudden the whole line went up in flames, curtain and all. The fire starting without warning. All I could do was to crawl like an angry snake darting to safety. I started pulling at the things on the line. I was getting scared by the sound; my heart pounded like thunder as my hands grabbed at anything to smother the flames, but, in my panic, I dropped or put down the lamp and it started a fire in another area of the clothes line. I closed myself in the room to keep the smoke from warning the others, but it began to choke me as the fire could not make up its mind whether to flare up or smoke up. I was too scared to yell. Since I don't remember talking, perhaps I didn't know how to yell either.

Someone must have smelled or seen the smoke because they all came running in yelling, pulling the ropeline to the floor, chucking things out of the window, stomping on the wooden floor and finally dousing out the flames completely with water.

That punishment did not hurt at all. I took my smack with great dignity because I deserved it and was glad to be relieved of the guilt. Not too much damage was done. Some clothes were destroyed but the bedding and the house were still comfortable enough for us to sleep in.

All returned to the porch and the evening's quietness. The night sounds were coming on, which I always delighted in. I would lose myself in thought, imagining which animal or bird made which sounds. In my mind's eye I could see each and every one of them, and tried to see myself as one of them: free to fly, to crawl, to play, to sit high in a tree as I sometimes did, looking out onto the world as far as I could see. What was it like way, way out there?

My imaginings drifted back as I heard the voice of Aunt Rosa: 'It's gonna storm.' The world was silent. No wind was felt, the sky was clear, the fireflies were beginning to flirt. God began to light his candles in the sky, the world was gradually being covered by the sun's reflection; only the sounds of night remained, with Aunt Rosa's voice: 'It's gonna storm.' She had said this many times before when nothing had come of it, perhaps just for the fun of it.

Sometimes I saw Aunt Rosa's husband take a shotgun and walk through the fields into the forest. Very often he returned with a rabbit, a squirrel, a possum, or some kind of bird that would be prepared for food. I always loved these times for it became a festival with everyone participating in the preparation.

On Sundays a hen would have its neck wrung and be prepared for the preacher's visit. I was not very fond of the preacher's visits for he ate all the best parts of the chicken – or both chickens if there were two – most of the sweet potato pie, corn bread made with clobber milk, buttermilk biscuits, and collard greens. In between mouthfuls he would preach a quiet preaching that could barely be understood.

Since the children were not allowed to sit at the table with the preacher, I watched him in his gluttony swallowing all he could, trying to burp air from his walrus-like self in order to find room to devour more. Since I was always the last to get a part of whatever was left, I hated each bite that preacher took as I felt my stomach getting more angry, realizing it was not going to be getting more than scraps. It was no surprise to me when the preacher finally left that there was hardly anything left for the rest of us as he wobbled off through the cotton fields to the main road and into nowhere. Each Sunday in church when I looked at him, I would recall every piece of chicken he had chewed, cleaning the bones as efficiently as a nest of ants would do.

Sometimes Pearl and I were made to sing or recite for church services in front of all the people who were shouting their souls into the floors (that gave way from time to time), calling on the Holy Ghost to help them lead a better life. Some of them moaned and cried with prayer; some fainted and were carried out; some just bowed their heads as they rocked up and down and to and fro. Some just sat and stared at the others. Only one organ was played, louder and louder as the moaning went on and on and the preacher kept preaching. When all finally became quiet, I found myself and Pearl standing at the front. I don't recall what we sang exactly, but the silence of the people, who simply grunted in approval at times, made me feel something burning inside of me that made me happy. I felt self-conscious in front of all these people, but these were the only times I received attention.

One Sunday on our return from church I was hiding in my usual place under the house, watching spiders rise through the air on an invisible string as they wove a trap for flies, when I heard talking through the floor. Soft female tones were coming to my ears, and I became gradually aware of the words.

'That man was stabbed right there in front of us. We were coming out of the church. The blood flew everywhere.'

'You know the man?'

'Sure, I knew the man. He was playing around with that kinky girl lives over towards Abby's place. Their ol' man come home from up North. Somebody musta told him Rufus was in the church. He come straight to the church. Had this big knife in his hands, stabbed Rufus straight in the chest. Rufus had no chance, just fell down and died. The blood flew everywhere.'

'They just let him lay there till he was sure gone. Jessie sure looked mad standing over that man with that knife in his hand. Blood was all over the place.'

'Yeah, I never saw so much blood. Rufus knowed that kinky gal had a man up North. Yeah, Jessie just stood there looking at Rufus – Jessie was sure moved.'

'Where he at now?'

'Jessie looked around at us looking at him and he ran off through the graveyard into the woods.'

'Somebody go after him?'

'You know nobody gonna go after Jessie. Everybody knew what that kinky woman was doing. Rufus musta knowed he was looking for trouble.'

The voices got softer. They must have moved to another side of the room. I could not hear any more of the conversation until I saw the women's feet coming down the front porch steps, mumbling: 'Ain't no white law would catch Jessie. No white law made for black people killing each other.'

'Yeah, Jessie safe in the woods. He come back when things cool off.'

The distance took the voices with it. Aunt Rosa was left on the porch. She sat in the rocking chair and rocked, lighting her corn pipe. I crouched in silence as the smell of the tobacco in the air reached my nostrils. Aunt Rosa just rocked until the rest of the family returned from wherever they were.

Our days and nights followed the usual routine: me the first up, getting wood for the stove and fireplace. Make a fire in both, prepare for the meal of grits or corn bread and a piece of fatback with a slab of cream.

Moma was talked of once in a while. I knew she was somewhere nearby living with the black man. His six or so children were older than her, I think, or somewhere near her own age. As I listened through the cracks of the floor from under the house or from the bedroom or from anywhere I could, I learned she was going to have a baby. Why would Moma want a baby when she did not want me?

As usual, twilight time was passed sitting on the porch with Aunt Rosa smoking her corn pipe and us gazing into the nowhere around us; crickets sang their twilight melodies, an owl would hoot to a mate nearby that would answer from time to time. Our souls were at peace with the year's yield of plenty stored in the barn. All was calm and serene. The sun was at its last ebb, sinking behind the trees that were fading into the darkness.

All my chores had been done, so I too was at peace sitting gazing into the nowhere. 'Gonna storm,' Aunt Rosa would say from time to time in between the puffs of smoke crawling from her mouth like tiny clouds. This particular evening was peculiarly quiet: there was a special kind of stillness in the air.

'Gonna storm.'

4 Hard Times

Next day we spent cleaning up the leftovers in the fields. The white men in wagons driven by strong work mules came to weigh and put the cotton we had picked into crocker sack sheets. They threw the sheets of cotton onto the wagons to be taken to the mills for baling and for sale. I often waited by the wagons for the white boy to throw me some pecans, as he sometimes did.

We went home early this day. Nothing was said among the blacks as the families separated and left the fields. A silent wind passed over us, a kind of warm chill, as we moved towards our humble abodes. As we neared the house, a sudden fuss started among us. We looked over the fields behind and saw a whirlwind of yellow and brown dust with a few other colours intertwined. A very strange feeling came over me as we ran as fast as we could for cover. When we reached the house we all gathered in one corner and clung to the floor. No one spoke.

A kind of whistling came closer and closer. We clung to each other tighter and tighter. Nothing was said. No other sound could be heard. As I looked through the cracks in the floor, I could see the animals and chickens huddled under the house. No sound but the whistling coming closer, turning into a 'swissh – swissh – swissh'. I can't recall where Pearl was, but she must have been somewhere among us. She was often carried in one of the crocker sacks with only her head poking out.

Aunt Rosa's husband and Willie ran to pull in the shutters on the windows and bolt the doors before joining us on the floor. As the whirlwind came closer the whistlings and swisshings became noisier and joined with the sound of things falling and hitting against each other. The house shook like a giant was pulling it apart. Nothing was said. Suddenly it was silent.

After a while we got up from the floor and cautiously opened the door to see what had happened. The barn had completely disappeared. The garden was like an emptied graveyard where vegetables had been. The flower yard had a few rose bushes standing in loneliness. The top of the animal shelter was gone and one side had collapsed. A few hogs wandered around in shock, the mule bayed in fear, some chickens twitched in death having been thrown against the ground. Those left came out from under the house to see if the others were still alive.

All our winter supply was gone – all of it. Aunt Rosa and her husband stirred around in silence. There was nothing to say, nothing to do, save wonder how God could be so cruel. The whirlwind had made a zig-zagging path from place to place, picking up and putting down or carrying whatever it wanted, leaving a trail of things rejected as it went. A typhoon, hurricane, or whatever name it goes by, does not care where it travels or what it picks up; and it drops its bounty like feathers along the way.

This was a year I would remember forever. God seemed to have been angry with the world that year. Lightning had struck a field and burnt it to a crisp of ashes, so that nothing would grow there for some time. After the storm, there was very little to eat so all the black families on the plantation gathered together and sent the men into the forest with their shotguns to hunt food. The women had the big pot-bellied urn fired up in great expectations for when the men returned.

The five families huddled with their children around the fired pot, looking at the woods, waiting for the pangs of hunger to be eased. A rabbit or two, a squirrel perhaps, a possum, a bird, anything. Finally the figures of the men came through the edge of the forest. We poked the fire in readiness for a great feast. Onions were thrown into the boiling water, a few potatoes brought by one of the families, and whatever else could be found. As the men drew nearer, my mouth began to salivate. I could taste each and every wild animal; I imagined the men carrying them in silence, opening their hunting bags to show their catch.

A bag was put on the ground and a cute, emaciated little turtle gradually sneaked its head out in hopes of meandering on its way to safety, only to wind up in the pot-bellied urn, making me feel more sorry for it than I did for my hungry stomach. I don't remember getting even a peek of it as a cup of the boiling hot water was given to each of us.

The grown-ups would gather at times to do quilt work. A frame made from wooden slats was hung from the ceiling, piles of square-cut rags were piled in baskets on the floor, and six to eight women would work from the corner to the centre following the planned design.

'Yes, she's very sick. Nobody knows what kinda sickness it is, but she's very sick.'

I could barely hear enough to understand all that was being said. I was busy sweeping the yard when I heard 'She is very sick', and my curiosity was aroused. Watching the cow at the same time, I moved closer to the window in order to hear more clearly. Somehow I knew they were talking about Moma.

My broom moved more slowly so as not to drown out the words. They must have sensed my quiet nearness, as I was called into the house. 'Eartha Mae, bring us some water.' I was afraid to take my eyes from the cow for she might eat something to make her ill. I had already pulled her from a large bush of red berries growing in the middle of the field that I was warned might be poisonous. I never could understand why the bush was not pulled up if it was poisonous, but I didn't question the adults because I was too afraid of the back of a hand.

We had already sent the cow before this one to be slaughtered because, though we paid for a milk cow, it turned out to be a beef cow. This one was a treasure for not only was she a milk cow, giving us butter, cream and clobber milk, but she had also given us a calf.

I pulled the cow further into the field away from the garden fence where, among other things, lima beans were growing. I had been told not to let the cow eat the lima beans, as usual without any explanation. When I thought the cow was far enough into the field and unable to reach the garden fence before I could return, I ran as fast as I could and scooped a pitcher of water from the kitchen bucket that I had brought from the spring in the forest that morning. As I gave one lady a cup of water, each in turn asked for some. I went uneasily from one to the other – a cup of water for each. I looked out of the window to see if the cow was still in the area of the field where I had left her. As I passed around the quilt my heart began to thump more strongly. I could not see where the cow was. I began to feel more and more uneasy. Finally all had been given water and I ran back to the yard – dropping the pitcher and cup somewhere – to see the cow pulling and chewing at the lima beans.

'Oh God, please help me!' my soul sang as I pulled and tugged. The cow would not budge. I grabbed her head to push it away from the lima beans, but back went her head to the fence. 'Bessie, please Bessie, Bessie, Bessie, please!' I pulled and tugged. The rope around her neck had a bell – it started to clang as she yanked away from me back to the beans. I took hold of the rope; I pulled and pulled, but my tiny body was dragged after hers as she moved to a more thickly covered area of the fence. The bell was now clanging more loudly as she enjoyed her find. I prayed and cried in silence: 'Oh God, please help me, don't let anything happen to Bessie.'

The tears began to sting my cheeks, mixing with the sweat from the hot sun. I was pulling and crying and praying and begging and then Bessie stumbled backwards. She swayed, she wobbled, she slobbered. One leg collapsed and then another, then her whole body wobbled to the ground. I stood hypnotized, stunned into standing like a statue, before running to her, holding her head in my arms and trying to talk her into getting on her feet. 'Please Bessie, Bessie please!' as I saw her getting bigger and bigger.

The devil's feet ran down my back as Bessie's 'Moo-oo-oo' went across the yard. The sound of her calf in answer brought me to sobs I cannot describe – afraid for the whippings I knew I would get and afraid for the calf who, like me, might be left without a mother.

The cow's yell and moo must have brought the women from the house. I sat motionless as the cow moo-ed and the calf answered. Looking across the yard I saw the calf's little head poking through the slats of the garden fence, calling its mother as the women mumbled over the sick cow. One returned to the house bringing back baking soda that was given to the cow. I was pushed aside as this was done. A short while later, the cow laid her head down as she breathed more slowly. 'Go get Ed,' I was told. I ran without thought to Ed's house on the other side of the forest.

A lady was working in the field just at the end of the forest. I, with tearful breath, told her what had happened and asked for Uncle Ed. Around here everyone was called 'uncle' or 'aunt' or some related name. She told me Uncle Ed was not at home but that she would come and help. She and I ran back to find the cow taking her last breath and crying her last call to the calf. The calf cried louder as it pranced in agitation along the barn fence. Its little cries penetrated my entire being, and haunt me to this day.

The mumbling of the women quietened as they walked back into the silent house. Everything became so still when the cow died that I could hear the whip sounds on my backside as I waited for my punishment. I did not get a beating. The cow was buried by the men the next day in a field where corn was usually grown. The grave mound became a place of sanctuary for me. Thank goodness the calf grew to be a milk cow.

Some time later Pearl and I were in bed when Aunt Rosa and her husband returned from a visit somewhere. Gracie and Willie were in the sitting room by the fireplace when I awoke to the sound of voices. I peeked through the cracks in the wall and listened.

'She's very sick . . . no one knows what kinda sickness . . .' I could barely hear, so I pressed my ears closer to the crack. 'She sits up and talks. Sometimes she goes into the sitting room like she's getting better, but no, next thing she goes away, sleeping like she's gone . . .'

'Moma, Moma,' I thought as I watched through the wall's crack. They sat in silence as the fire burned down to a cinder.

I returned to my place in the bed, put my face into the mattress, and cried myself back to sleep feeling something terrible was wrong with Moma. The new baby must be big now. I wondered how big. What did it look like? Was Moma going to give it away like she did Pearl and me?

Some time later Pearl and I were washed in a tub and dressed in clean clothes to be taken to visit Moma. It was not too far away in the mule-drawn wagon. The cabin Moma was sick in had a sitting room, a kitchen to the side like the one we lived in, a well in the yard; I don't remember more than one bedroom but the black man had a lot of children it seemed. Where they slept, I don't know.

I remember being taken in to see Moma. She was lying on a bed in the bedroom, where a curtain served as a partition to separate her from the bed on the other side of the room. Several grown-ups were standing around her bed. Nothing was said, Moma was still. She just looked into nowhere. I stood a little distance from the bed. In silence I saw Moma helpless – no laughing or joking as I remembered, no movement. I felt her eyes caress me as she slowly turned her head towards me. I can feel her every touch in my memory: the soothing of her smile to ease our pangs of hunger, never giving the impression that life was bad, just that this *is* life. 'Moma!' I cried in my soul, but no tears reached my eyes.

Still in silence, I was taken from her bedside by some women. A voice clicked in my brain: 'Eartha Mae, you're so still – don't you wanna cry?' This voice haunted me. I did not like it. 'Eartha Mae, you're so still.' They sat me in a chair by the fireplace and they all looked at me. 'She's so still, she's not crying. She's too still,' the voice said, digging deeper and deeper into my brain. I remember the touch of her hands as she placed me in the chair – it made my skin crawl. My eyes followed the voice and I glanced up to see what its owner looked like as though I wanted to imprint it in my memory bank.

We were taken back home and life went on until one night when I was again awakened by sounds from the sitting room. Gracie and Willie were in their usual places by the fireplace. As I peeked through my usual crack in the wall, I heard their voices.

'Did you shut the kitchen door?'

'It's shut and bolted. What you so scared about?'

'The front door – the front door's not shut. Put the bolt on!'

Both of them went to the kitchen door and slid a piece of wood through a steel rod to bolt the door to the connecting wall. I saw them cross the room to do the same to the front door, but before they had a chance to do so, Aunt Rosa and her husband came in.

As they entered the front door, the back door that had just been bolted flew open, making them all huddle together near the fireplace. They whispered to one another in fear that Moma had tried to get to us first to tell us she had gone. As the whispering continued I slowly returned to my place in the bed. So Moma had gone. Suddenly, as I gazed at the ceiling, I felt her presence over me. The room was warm and serene in her comforting us. Pearl was asleep as usual. I did not want to wake her, I wanted to have Moma's presence all to myself. No one was ever to know that she and I spent her last moment together before her long journey. I went back to sleep, comforted.

Some time later we were gathered in the wagon, bathed, cleanly dressed and primped up to be taken to St Peter's Church. I stood over the empty hole in the ground as Moma's coffin was lowered into it. A huge limb from a tree shaded the area over the grave as the ceremony went on. I stood near as the preacher gave his sermon and the people swayed in sorrow. When the casket was lowered to its resting place, a ray of sunlight came through the branch. Standing in the rays of the sun, I knew she would come back on these rays for both of us.

I knew too who was responsible for Moma being taken away. That voice was still imprinted on my brain. I did not cry but just stood watching, remembering every move that each of them made and the sound of every voice, waiting to hear *that* voice again. As the dirt was shovelled onto the coffin I looked beyond the grave at the other graves, to the skyline and over the fields to the white man's plantation house, still in silence. Then I heard the voice say, 'Eartha Mae, she didn't cry, she's too still.'

We returned to our lives. In the spare time I rarely had I would be in the forest in another play area I had made for myself. I made a slingshot to kill rattlesnakes or a bird and I would cook them on a hickory wood fire. Wild nuts and berries were often my playhouse meal, or the red and yellow clay that I found by the roadside.

The young baby Moma had left, Almita, was with the black man's family. She must have been about six months or so.

'Almita sure is getting big, she's walking now,' a voice revealed one day as I hid under the floorboards of the house.

From other conversations, overheard from the living room, the kitchen, the porch or in the fields, I learned more about Moma's death. Seemingly her body had been taken from her death bed and laid out on a board the night she died, while the black man's family threw the mattress out of the window to be burned in the yard. The neighbours saw the burning in the distance, thought the house was on fire and ran over to put it out. When they saw the mattress on fire, they got suspicious and put the fire out to find voodoo-like relics in the corner and letters in the centre of the mattress.

One letter from the South complained that Moma was taking over, ruling the family and the black man with witchcraft-like power. It also accused Moma of having an affair with a neighbour. A letter from the North said, 'Never mind, when I come home I will get rid of her in a way she will never come back.'

When Moma was in her talking spans, she had apparently told some of the neighbours how it was. The sister from up North had come home; Moma and she were left in the house to prepare dinner for the others who were working in the fields. When the dinner was about ready, the sister sent Moma to the well for water. On Moma's return, two plates of food were on the table; the sister told Moma she wanted her to try a seasoning she had brought back from up North. A small package was given to Moma, the contents of which she sprinkled over her food. They both ate, each from different plates. When the meal was consumed, Moma said she felt a little ill; she went to the living room to make a fire, feeling a pain in her stomach. As it got stronger, she ran to the front door trying to get into the yard to vomit. The black man was entering the door at the same time, and Moma told him she did not feel well. He helped her to the bedroom and put her to bed, saying he would take the mule and ride into town for a doctor. Moma held herself, thinking the doctor would be along soon. The pain got stronger – perhaps she passed out. The doctor never came, neither did the husband.

Years later, when I found Pearl living in New Jersey, she confirmed this story, finishing it with 'He was in on it.'

Like a cat I heard what no one ever thought I could hear, ignoring me in my status as a nitwit.

Aunt Rosa became ill one night. She asked her two teenage grandchildren, Gracie and Willie, if they would go to the white man's house for medicine.

'I scared, the moon is full. I ain't going out there.'

'I'll go,' a tiny soft voice from my mouth said. Aunt Rosa, who could hardly hold her head up, put a quarter in my hand, opened the door, and showed me the way. Outside the door I stood still, looking around with thoughts of spirits roaming in the full moonlight. Which would be the shortest way? Each bunch of plants in the yard became a spook, each tree something to be afraid of. If I took the long way along the front of the forest, I thought, along the meadow by the old covered wall, then onto the newly made highway across the cotton field where the plantation house was, then no spooks would bother me. I planned my route. But if I take the short cut? I did not think about this long enough to change my mind with pros and cons – my feet took to the dirt.

I could see clearly in the full moonlight: across the cotton field where the lightning had struck, across the Indian clay path into the woods. I had played in these woods many times and knew just about every nook and cranny, but the shadows thrown by the moonlight made it all different. I could see imaginary spooks at every turn, every branch was going to grab me; I thought I was going to be eaten by some monster and never found.

I finally got to the graveyard where Moma was buried. A path led straight through. I stood for a moment to gather my nerves and wondered if I could see clearly enough to stay on the path and not step into a grave, never to be seen again. I could go alongside the graveyard leading me behind the church onto the highway crossing into the cotton field, and not go through the graveyard at all. But then I decided that Moma would protect me. I darted along the path that led to Moma's grave. When I reached it I stopped for prayer to help me on my way. I recognized Moma's grave and the tree with the long limbs hanging over it. The moon shone through the branches as I prayed with a slight hope that she would push away the dirt and carry me with her. I had new strength as I darted through the fields to the white man's house.

I knocked on the door. The old man came to see who it was, and looked down on my tiny figure.

'And what is such a tiny little thing doing out on a full moonlight? Ain't you scared?'

'Aunt Rosa is sick.' I held my hand out showing him the quarter and the little piece of paper it was wrapped in with the name of the medicine. We walked across the yard to the supply store. He was mumbling something I could not understand as he looked through different bottles for the correct medicine and then he gave it to me in return for the twenty-five cents.

It took me no time returning to Aunt Rosa. She patted me on the head and told me how brave I was, which made me feel very proud of myself and my great accomplishment. Happily I sat in my usual corner by the fireplace watching Aunt Rosa take her medicine with a cup of water.

When the harvest time was nearly ending the fields sometimes had patches of leftovers, scraps of cotton left in the cotton heads which the children were sent to finish collecting. One Saturday Gracie, Willie and I were sent out to finish a field. When the white man came to weigh in our pickings and pay us, I was given a whole dollar – I had picked one hundred pounds of cotton. There is no way in the world I can describe my feelings. When I saw the look on Aunt Rosa's face as I handed her my dollar, I felt like the most beautiful child in the world. I had made her happy, a feeling I wanted to keep for the rest of my life.

5   Up North

One morning when I awoke my eyes would not open. They were glued shut. Afraid to say anything that would draw attention to myself, I felt my way to the wash basin. No matter how I tried, the eyes would not open. I kept bathing them until the crust softened enough for me to pry them open with my fingers. Conjunctivitis had attacked them in the night.

When my chores were done I sat in a hiding place behind the barn turning my face to the sun, as I thought the sun healed all. While I was doing this, I saw a white man leaving the road. He crossed the field, lifted my chin in his hands, nodded his head with no words, turned and left. Could this have been my father?

We got a big package from up North one day: pink and white dresses the likes of which I had never seen before, and white shoes – shoes! Pearl and I were cleaned up (Pearl was walking now, she was big now), dressed in these up-North clothes, and taken to Sunday church. We even had little umbrellas to match. How the faces stared at us as we walked hand in hand through the churchyard crowd. Of course we were put on exhibition to entertain; we sang some little song or other.

'Most be Mamie sent them clothes,' I heard in the whisperings. I had heard that name before. Seemingly I had an aunt somewhere up North, Moma's sister. Sounded like an awful long way away, up North. Another box came another day, and a letter. The letter was read by somebody who could read. I could never understand why grown-ups would talk as though children are never supposed to hear anything. You sure have to listen hard.

'You don't wanna go up North, Eartha Mae.' Suddenly I realized that I was the centre of attention. A lot of fuss was being made over Eartha Mae. 'What you wanna go up North for?'

Things were being pulled out of the box and everyone scrambled to see what was coming next. Dark funny clothes from a strange place – but new. Stockings (I had never seen stockings before), a plaid jacket; red, blue, green, all sorts of colours; sweaters, skirts, a fawn hat like a French sailor's cap; and underwear, long underwear. What do you do with that?

All the fussing and going on with no one telling me what was happening. Buckets of hot water were poured into a tin tub. My hair was washed, combed and braided for about the third time since I had been with that family. God, was I cleaned up! Something strange was going on, of which I had no understanding.

As I was being scrubbed and rubbed in the bath, they said, 'You gonna be scared. They have them big houses up North, on top of one and the other – line upon line, on top of one and the other. Trains fly through the air, sometimes they fall down, and it's cold – you ain't never gonna git warm.'

'Eartha Mae! You gonna be scared.'

I just listened to all this attention, not wanting to be scared but wanting to go wherever it was.

Everything in the box was put on me: two pairs of long underwear, two sweaters, two skirts, the jacket, the shoes. I guess they fitted. The French sailor-type cap became too tight as they yanked and pulled to make it fit over three braids of long red hair, but I didn't feel a thing. I was numb with excitement. Somebody wanted me. Aunt Mamie up North wanted me.

Pearl wasn't going, *I* was going, *I* was the one that was wanted. A dilapidated car with no floor came to pick us up to go to the train station in Orangeburg or Columbia. I was given a shoebox containing a catfish sandwich on white bread – white bread, that was really something, white silvercup bread – a piece of sweet potato pie and an apple. The dilapidated car chugged along the road as our feet almost dangled to the ground. When I read the little train story to my daughter years later, I remembered this dilapidated car: 'I think I can, I think I can . . .'

We finally got to the station where the train was to take me up North. A tag was pinned on my jacket by a porter: 'My name is Eartha Mae Kitt. I am to be met by Mamie Kitt at Pennsylvania Station in New York.' The porter put me in a seat next to a window. I did not close my eyes the whole night; my face was glued to the window watching the objects go by, in great expectations of what was to come at the end of my mysterious journey.

'New York, Pennsylvania Station! New York, Pennsylvania Station!' the porter kept shouting as he came towards me. 'This is where you get off, little girl,' he said. He took me by the hand and led me to the platform.

We stood there in a crowd of ant-like crawling people. So many people, I never saw so many people. It was like watching an ants' nest. How can so many people be in one place at one time? What are they doing? Where are they going? I was watching the ant-like crawling people in amazement when a tall majestic figure walked out of the crowd towards me. She had black hair to her shoulders, cut straight, with bangs across her forehead, high cheek bones and big black eyes. She was a giant. Looking down on me she said, 'So this is what you look like.'

I was delighted to see that she was the same colour as me, and felt she would accept me because of this. I could be her daughter. The porter was thanked, I was taken by the hand and she led me through the people up some stairs onto the street, where I really had a culture shock. There were more people running and scrambling, pushing and shoving, like someone had thrown a dead insect into the ants' nest making them scramble for food. I kept getting out of the way – someone might step on me.

Then I heard a thundering noise. Something was making a thundering noise about my head. We were walking under it. A bridge of steel surrounded us – it carried the thundering noise. Automobiles were burping, stopping, going, screeching, screaming; red lights, green lights, blinking lights. 'They have trains that fly in the air. Sometimes they fall down on the people.' The words haunted me as I stood beside my aunt, who explained nothing. Why did we stop? I'm scared.

When I looked up, the buildings were so tall I could not see the top of them. 'People live in houses on top of one another,' I remembered being told. I watched people go in and out. Little specks of white things were coming down from the sky. I had only seen snow once down South. It was on the ground one morning when I went to get wood from the wood pile. No one told me how it got there. As I watched the white flecks coming down, my aunt must have realized this was a strange sight to me because she explained, 'It's snowing.'

We got into a big, big automobile with many other people who sat like mummies in a tomb waiting for the crypt to be opened so they could come to life again. We went to the back. I could see through the back window made of glass. I watched the cars following the big, big automobile. Then the thundering sound came again – I was a scared rat as I waited for the flying train to fall down on us. When we got off the big, big automobile we crossed the street; now the snow was slippery, and I started sliding on it in a playful manner. 'Don't do that, you'll fall,' my aunt said.

We went into a house and walked up some stairs. My aunt rang a bell, a black lady opened the door and looked down at me with a smile. 'So that's Eartha Mae!' A light went on as she put her hand on a wall. As we walked into a large hallway I saw rooms on the side but my attention was on the button the lady had touched on the wall that made light. There were no kerosene lamps and no candle could be seen. We walked along the hallway to a sitting room.

Since I had no bag – just my shoe box with catfish sandwiches on white silvercup bread, sweet potato pie and an apple still intact – I had nothing to unpack. Three grown-up ladies (two daughters and a mother) and my aunt stood me in the middle of the floor for inspection.

'She looks healthy,' they agreed. They began to peel off my clothes: the coat, the French sailor's hat, then the two sweaters, the skirts, two pairs of long underwear. As they peeled me off their laughter became so loud I was embarrassed to tears. The Eartha Mae they thought looked so healthy was skinny as the peach tree switch she was beaten with by Gracie and Willie. They re-dressed me leaving one of everything.

They talked among themselves between laughter while I tried to figure out what kind of lifestyle I was going into. Suddenly I stiffened, petrified. I needed to relieve myself. I went to a window but there was no outhouse in the alleyway. I was obviously shifting from one foot to the other as I gazed around wondering what to do. My aunt finally noticed my discomfort and she laughingly took me to a small room. Not explaining anything, she left me there after pushing a button on the wall to make light. I looked at each object in the room. One was a tub – that was easy to figure out; then a basin to wash your hands. But the other one, what could the other one be for? I looked out of the window but still couldn't see an outhouse.

I was curious about how light was made, so I decided to investigate the switch on the wall. My discomfort had subsided to some extent by this time, and I played with the light switch for a while – off, on, off, on. At least that was figured out, though I still did not understand it. It was magic. I sat on the side of the tub still trying to figure out what was for what. I was getting more and more uncomfortable when my aunt finally opened the door to see why I had been so long. When she saw me turning different colours trying to hold myself in, she shrieked with laughter and pointed to the toilet bowl. As I relieved myself I could not figure out where it was going. Like magic it will just disappear, I hoped. It didn't. I was sitting on the side of the tub again when my aunt returned. Again in laughter, she showed me a chain hanging from something above the toilet. She pulled it, and everything disappeared in a flood of water. But where does it all go? Nothing was explained.

On the way back to the sitting room where the three grown-up ladies were talking amongst themselves, I saw a bigger room with a big, big bed. I went into this room, and looking out the window at the street full of cars and people, I saw a black girl a little bigger than me coming across the street. I knew she was coming here and sure enough a short time later she was in the room.

'This is Eartha Mae, Joyce.' Joyce looked at me and smiled. We could play together and be friends, though she was not my colour. I wished she would like me.

I watched Joyce playing with some buttons on a piece of furniture.

The voices turned to music as I gazed at what Joyce was doing. Different types of voices came, then music, then voices. They explained, 'If you turn this button, people will talk to you. If you turn that button, music will play.' As they went about their ways in different parts of the house I kept my place sitting in front of this piece of box-like furniture, turning the buttons in one direction and another. Someone came by and said, 'There are little people inside. Turning the buttons to a certain point means you want them to play music, another point means you want them to talk.' I often sat by the radio for long periods of time hoping the little people would come out so I could see what they looked like.

Then came the day my aunt took me to school. I was introduced to a class of children smaller than me. I was nervous to a state of numbness. The teacher's name was Mrs Beans and she was a tiny bean-like figure. I was given some books and shown to a seat in the back of the class. I watched the kids thumbing through their books while the teacher asked from time to time for someone to read something. God, please don't let her ask me. I sat rigid in my seat, hoping I could pass the time without anyone knowing I could not read. I looked at my book as though all was well, not even knowing what page we were on.

Somehow the morning passed. A bell rang – recess. I followed the children into the schoolyard; some of them played, some of them huddled together, watching me cower alone against a wall. In my discomfort, I could feel a plan being hatched. The most unattractive girl in the bunch, the biggest and the darkest, seemed to be giving the others orders. My instincts told me she was trouble. I stayed alone until the bell rang for us to return to class. When the school hours came to an end, I was really relieved to see my aunt waiting for me at the schoolyard gate. Day by day my aunt took me to and fro until she thought I could find my way on my own.

Bit by bit I began to read numbers, then a few words, then whole sentences; I felt very proud that I was gaining more independence – all was going okay. Mrs Beans did not push me. She must have realized my ignorance and just waited until I was more at ease.

'Eartha Mae, will you read the next paragraph?' My heart leapt into my mouth, my feet would not hold me up, my blood ran hot and cold. I could not feel anything as my body slid to a standing position from the desk. I stood looking into my book like a dunce, waiting for the miraculous ability to make the words form into a picture I could understand. Mrs Beans' voice came softly to my ears in the silence of the room that made my heart pound like thunder. She read the paragraph. I became so ashamed I almost died in the thunderous beat of my heart. 'You may sit down, Eartha Mae.' A little snickering went through the room.

On my way home from school I sometimes noticed the big dark girl with a group of kids from class walking together behind me. They were stopping when I did, going when I did, giggling sometimes as they watched me, then suddenly disappearing. Then it came.

I was in the centre island of Seventh Avenue, waiting for the traffic to allow me to cross, and wham! into the traffic I went, books flying everywhere, flat on my belly as the group of kids surrounded by the big dark leader (who obviously did the pushing) were laughing their heads off. Then they disappeared. I was too scared to say anything to anyone about this but I knew I had to stay away from this gang. Finally one of the kids in the class told me this girl was a bully, and that picking on me was her form of amusement. I was to challenge her and win.

I knew nothing about fighting but one day, in the same place as before, I was waiting for the traffic to pass when they ganged up around me, waiting for the girl to attack. When she did, I found myself on the ground gasping for air as her body throttled me. Only God knows what gave me strength but after seeing blood and hearing the ringing in my ears, I realized that it was her or me. The cotton-picking strength I had in my tiny muscled body enabled me to beat the hell out of her, not knowing what I was doing but I was so mad I saw fire. She never bothered me again. I had gained respect and pulled the kids to my side – there was no more trouble.

Suddenly, with this confidence boost, I was reading and writing when called on. Gradually I was overcoming my shyness, but I could not understand why Mrs Beans did not stop me after each paragraph as she did the rest of the children. Sometimes she let me read whole pages. I was kept after school one day and Mrs Beans said she was putting me into another class. She did not explain why. Seems my whole life had been lived with no one explaining anything. I was soon put up half a grade where I remained for half a term until I was again promoted by another half grade. And so it went on until I reached Mrs Bishop's class. Mrs Bishop was a beautiful gentle mulatto lady who made me feel special. For some reason I was made to read more often than anyone else, longer and longer paragraphs. I was advancing faster than the others. I suppose she was forcing me out of being such a quiet child: since I seldom talked, this was her way of making me talk. She would keep me after school at times, just to make me talk. I was given different books to read, and she would recite to me, asking me to write down what she was saying.

Mrs Bishop somehow learned that I had not been seeing much of my aunt. Since my arrival from the South, my aunt and I had been rooming with the Wayde family and Mrs Bishop found out that I was being taunted by Mr Wayde. I don't know how she got all this out of me but somehow she did. I was afraid to be caught in the house alone as Mr Wayde often returned without warning shortly after I got in from school. He smelled. I could not stand his smell as he grabbed me, threw me on the sofa and held me down under his horrible breath. Mr Wayde also had a bad foot that made him limp, and I could smell his foot as he walked through the long hallway to the sitting room where I used to sit listening to the radio. There was nowhere to run since the sitting room was at the end of this big hallway, and our room was at the beginning of it beside the front door. Thank heavens for my cotton-picking strength that enabled me to wriggle out from under him after kicking his bad leg, agonizing him into protecting himself. Too ashamed to tell anyone, I sat in the hallway downstairs until a member of the family came.

Moma Wayde and Aunt Mamie got into an argument one evening: 'You're not paying enough attention to that child,' Moma Wayde was saying, 'That's your child, we're not supposed to take care of her . . .'

Aunt Mamie had a lover whom she often went out with at the weekends. Joyce and I were given a dime for the movies and a nickel for popcorn or whatever. We would very often stay at the cinema all day. The first movie I remember seeing was something with an octopus living in a lighthouse that killed everyone. I got so scared I ran all the way back home and hid under the bed until my aunt found me, laughing her head off as she pulled me out.

I was sitting in bed reading a book one evening when my aunt came into the room yelling, 'What have you done with my box of chocolates?' I could not imagine what chocolates she was referring to. Before I could say, 'What chocolates?' an ironing cord came down over my body like the stings of the peach tree switch. In my surprise at this beating – which left me with a black eye – I heard myself say once, 'I didn't do it.' Lash after lash in between, 'You ate them!' She found the chocolates that night where she had hidden them – no explanation – and I went to school with a black eye. Mrs Bishop just took my chin in her hand, shook her head, and said nothing.

Then I got sick: pneumonia, they said, the whooping cough, they said, can't go to school, they said, send for the doctor, they said, nothing I said. I was whooping and coughing until my chest was sore. Moma Wayde and Aunt Mamie were always arguing. It ended one night when Aunt Mamie wrapped me up in a blanket in my pyjamas with my bedroom slippers on and dragged me into the streets of snow and slush, hailed a cab (that was more than difficult to find) and moved us to an apartment on Seventh Avenue at 137th Street. We had a room in the back across from the bathroom where I would crawl to vomit up any foods given to me, or flush food I could not eat or did not like down the toilet.

It was fun in that house. Music was being played every day, there was tap dancing and singing. I was happy there. As I got strong enough to stand on my feet, I sneaked for a peek at the source of the music, tap dancing and singing. Through the crack of a huge sliding door Mr Anderson – whose apartment we were renting a room in – was teaching someone tap dancing as someone else played the piano. That's a face in the movies! I surprised myself. Bill Robinson, the Nicholas Brothers, Ethel Waters – I saw movie faces through the crack from day to day. I wanted Mr Anderson to teach me tap dancing but as soon as I got better we went to another room in another apartment on another street – 137th at Eighth Avenue, fourth floor, rooming with an old lady whom we rarely saw.

Mr Charles, Aunt Mamie's lover, was still around. He was okay, I guess, but in my mind he was going to take her away like they took my mother. Fearful that day would come, I made up my mind not to like him.

While we were still living here Relief time came. There was a war in Europe; something about a Hitler, the Germans, the Russians. The movie newsreels were always showing us people being killed by people we were not supposed to like. The Germans were killing us good Americans. People in Europe were going hungry, then we were going hungry. Relief stations came into play; the WPA was formed and the CCC. I didn't understand any of this but hunger was something I was already familiar with; to me hard work and hunger was nothing new.

Before I had worn ordinary clothes like the rest of the children at school and those I played with in the streets. Aunt Mamie was working and I was going to school as usual, until one day she took me to a Relief station. I was given two dresses, one pink with daisies, one blue with daisies. Aunt Mamie bought me one pair of shoes – brown with a white spot on the front. Then I knew we were poor, because the kids at school poked fun at me; my Relief dress gave me the stigma of poverty.

'You're poor,' one of the kids behind me in line said.

'Yeah, you're poor,' said another.

I had thought everyone was poor, except white folks. Now I thought to myself, I'm poor, I am so ashamed, and my heart cried.

I was sent to the Relief station once a month for whatever was being given out by the government. Sometimes Aunt Mamie went with me. This time I went alone, from Eighth Avenue to the last avenue on the east side of Manhattan.

'You look like a strong little girl, you can have ten pounds of apples if you can carry them,' the Relief man said.

Not wanting to disappoint him, I took a five-pound bag in each arm. Proudly I walked out of the Relief station demonstrating how strong this little girl could be. As I trod the streets on the way home, the blocks got longer and longer as the apples got heavier and heavier and I got tireder and tireder. I had no nickel to catch a bus; besides, the buses did not go across town, only up and down. As apple after apple fell to the street, I picked them up again with visions of apple pie, apple custard, baked apple, apple sauce. My aunt will be proud of me, she will pat me on the head in warmth with smiles to make me feel what a good girl I am. As I neared our apartment house on 137th Street, I glowed with excitement as I got closer and closer to the praise my aunt was going to give me.

'You stupid child,' my aunt's voice rang out as she opened the door, 'you can hardly hold one bag in your arms, why would you want two? What a stupid child.' Needless to say the apples – plain old apples – were my diet for a month, with not even one finger of a pat to make them go down more easily.

On my way to school one morning all the windows of the stores were shattered. Glass was sprangling the sidewalks, things were scattered helter-skelter from pillar to post. A storm must have hit during the night, I thought, or maybe this is what they told me down South was going to happen: 'The buildings fall down on top of people and kill them.' In wonderment I sat in the class as Mrs Bishop explained. A white policeman had walked into a bar – Small's Paradise – in Harlem and shot a black man in the stomach, for no apparent reason. The people took to violence. Every store from the east side to the west side, from 110th Street to 155th Street, was ransacked. Only those who had been fair in trade were untouched. Mrs Bishop had brought a radio from home for us to hear President Roosevelt say, 'I understand the anger, but not the looting. . . .'

Aunt Mamie put me in a Sunday school which had a choir, and I soon became a lead singer. Every Sunday I had to watch in fear as the whole church quietened down to a silence that penetrated my very bones. My aunt, sitting in a front row, held her head down. I would glance at her at times, trying to see if she was pleased. There was a recital one evening. The play we did was *Snow White and the Seven Dwarfs* and I was Snow White. Aunt Mamie had made me a dress exactly like the one in the movie. When it was over a lady came over to my aunt and said, 'Your child was born with the hand of God on her shoulder.' Aunt Mamie is proud of me, I thought. I ran after her trying to hold her hand as we walked home, hoping she would show some hint of this pride through her touch – but, as always, she didn't.

We moved from 137th Street to 1756 Madison Avenue: Mr Charles' apartment – one bedroom, one sitting room, a tiny, tiny kitchen, a tiny, tiny bathroom. Mr Charles was never there. It turned out he had gone into the army. I found this out when Aunt Mamie got sick one day and I was sent to get him from the army barracks at 110th Street.

Now I had progressed in my piano lessons, which were a part of my education from my aunt, who gave me twenty-five cents to pay for them. Every Saturday: piano lessons, clean the house from top to bottom, and be in by nine p.m. One Saturday I did not go to my piano lesson, but sneaked off to the movies instead. The teacher must have got a message to Aunt Mamie telling her and I got one of the worst beatings of my life. Mr Charles walked in just as Aunt Mamie was about to ram the piano stool down on my head while I folded myself in the corner of the bedroom. The ironing cord was not doing a sufficient job.

In silent anger I went to school the next day after ironing my blouse and skirt on the radiator pipe. Since electricity was expensive, I was not allowed to use the iron. Mrs Bishop looked at my sad face and must have seen the black and blue marks on my arms and, as she gently pulled up my skirt, the same on my thighs. She said nothing.

Shortly thereafter I was given a poem to learn. 'Learn this as soon as you can,' said Mrs Bishop. I had no idea why, but I learned the poem word perfect in two days. When I recited it in class Mrs Bishop crossed her arms and bowed her head as she leant over her desk. All was silent for a moment when I sat down. Some time later I was sent downtown with a dime from Mrs Bishop to go for an audition for the New York School of Performing Arts: a nickel there and a nickel to get home. I was introduced to the class by their teacher, Mrs Banks. Hypnotically I recited my poem. It seemed to me like this poem would never end. All were silent.

When I finally finished reciting, nothing was said until Mrs Banks came to me, led me to the window and said, 'You have something special.' I was accepted.

6 Cue Eartha Mae Kitt

As time went on I was given parts in the school plays, some of which involved song and dance, and soon I became the most popular girl in the school. I was one of the six black kids there – two girls, four boys.

Since the school was in two different buildings I had to walk a few blocks from one to the other. The black boys had formed a gang that would follow me at times along the way. I paid little attention to this since they did me no harm until one day I was caught on my own. A yellow-freckled red-haired boy was sent ahead to catch up with me. 'Bruno wants you to be his girl,' the boy said. I laughed, thinking this was all a joke. 'Bruno wants an answer: you wanna be his girl?' The faster I walked to get away, the faster the yellow-freckled-faced red-haired boy would walk. Catching me one day, he pushed me into the arch of the Knickerbocker building doorway, saying, 'Bruno is gonna get mad if you don't say yes.' Too frightened to say anything, I eased myself away from him and went nervously on to class.

I was kept after school by Miss Banks who continually tried to get information out of me, sensing I was a troubled child. I was on my own going to the subway this day when the gang came up behind me from nowhere. Their emissary ran ahead to catch me up. As he walked beside me he said, 'Bruno don't like you not giving him an answer.' I kept walking as the emissary fell back to group in with the gang. Standing on the subway platform waiting for my Lexington Avenue express train, I saw my friends Yvonne, Barbara and Louise-Audreala further along. As I ran to join them the express train was also running along. Faster and faster I ran, faster and faster the train came. I reached them just as the train was about halfway to us when suddenly I felt myself toppling onto the tracks. There was a yank on my coat tail and the three girls gathered round me, wide eyes staring. The train had just missed me, screaming to a stop.

'He pushed you,' one said.

'Yeah, that boy pushed you,' said the other.

Bruno had obviously sent his emissary to do his dirty work since I would not become his 'playmate'. Louise's quick thinking in grabbing my coat tail had saved my life. The next day all three, Louise-Audreala,

Barbara and Yvonne, reported this to the Principal, Dr Keller, who had every one of the gang drafted into the army within two weeks.

My aunt gave me a quarter each schoolday – fifteen cents for lunch and ten cents for the subway. These quarters gradually dwindled down to just a dime. Nothing for lunch. Lunchtime found me sitting alone wherever I could find a space, pretending to study with a growling stomach. Louise-Audreala, Yvonne and Barbara sometimes gave me a bit of their lunch, seeing I had none. Mrs Banks sometimes took me to lunch in the dining room, trying to get information from me about my family life. I suppose she guessed more than I verbally revealed for my aunt walked into class one day. She and Mrs Banks had a talk, keeping me in my seat until they bade each other goodbye and Aunt Mamie took me home. The twenty-five cents started again for a while, then it was back to a dime.

I decided to get an after-school job. 'Stationery Packers Wanted' said a sign between the subway station and the school. I could do that. I applied – five dollars a week, two hours a day, which meant I would be getting home about seven p.m. My aunt did not get home until about seven-thirty or eight so I could manage since the subway was only about thirty minutes. I did not tell my aunt I was working because I thought she would take it all, and I wanted to save enough to buy myself a dress. I hid the dress in the closet behind whatever else was hanging there, hoping she would never find it.

Aunt Mamie would cook a dish on Sunday that was supposed to last all week but often it lasted only until Wednesday, maybe Thursday. Friday, Saturday and part of Sunday I was scrambling for food. The family living on the top floor – whose little girl was a playmate of mine – would sometimes feed me if I helped peel the potatoes, though I was reprimanded if I peeled them too thick.

Aunt Mamie found the dress! Without any questions asked, the ironing cord came down on my behind as she assumed that the dress must have been stolen. Finally, when the beating was over, I confessed I had been working. Since I had no work permit, I was cheap child labour and I got another whack for lying. I never returned to the stationery packing.

Mrs Banks gave me a theatre ticket one day, telling me not to come to school the following day. It was a matinée with José Ferrer – *Cyrano de Bergerac*. Alone in the top of the theatre I sat; there weren't too many people in the vicinity so I felt fine. My first time in a real theatre – I was mesmerized. That's the feeling I wanted: the feeling of an audience loving you and telling you they love you. If I could only do that. The play was over, and when the curtain came down the applause deafened my ears. My body went numb and I cried with the joy I felt as people stood, applauding. How can I do that? In a state of hypnosis I walked the streets along Broadway, sensing people around me but not seeing them; not wanting to talk, not wanting anything but this feeling to stay, not wanting to lose it as I walked. Into Central Park from Forty-something Street, through the park to 1756 Madison Avenue, dreaming, wondering, thinking. How can I do that? How can I make people applaud for me like that?

I wanted that feeling to live in me for ever, with laughter, with tears, with all the emotions. I walked through the areas where I had spent many times alone, watching the birds and the blossoming trees in spring and the beautiful pictures the clouds made while the squirrels chased the birds for food. Now I saw none of it. At that moment I was in limbo, in a trance, holding onto the feeling of *Cyrano*. My first experience of theatre.

I played with the kids of the neighbourhood between Park Avenue and Madison Avenue, and 114th Street was our playground. On Friday and Saturday nights we would partner up for the Latin dance balls if we could get fifty cents for the girls and a dollar for the boys. These were great places for the young to socialize. All the famous Latin bands were there – Machito and Graciela, Tito Puente, Perez Prado – three or four bands in one night. Only soft drinks and, I think, beer were available. Bouncers who were more like truant officers were prominently placed in vigilance for anyone getting out of hand. All we wanted to do was dance, dance, dance.

There were a lot of Latins in this neighbourhood, especially Cubans who had fled Cuba, so it was almost essential to speak Spanish. There were also Italians, Jews, a few Haitians and American blacks, who all got along because the children did not care who was who. We were all rowing in the same boat of poverty. Playing and dancing with one another forced us to get acquainted through trying to learn the other's language.

I had run away from my aunt several times by now and was living with anyone who would take me in, working at little jobs here and there to pay my way. But I was still at the New York School of Performing Arts and I hoped in a way that my aunt would come looking for me. The mailbox at my aunt's apartment door said 'Charles', but I was ashamed for it to be known that we were living in the house of a man my aunt was not married to, so I changed my name to Kitty Charles so visitors would think I had a mother and father, giving me legitimacy. This was the name I was going by in the neighbourhood when I ran away. Also, Eartha Mae Kitt was a strangely different name and no one seemed to be able to remember it, so Kitty Charles was easier. It also made it more difficult for Aunt Mamie to find me. But since one of my jobs was only five blocks or so from 1756 Madison Avenue, she did find me. I was a seamstress on a sewing machine. Somehow I learned anything fast; no matter what it was, I had to be able to fend for myself.

Now and then I would break out into a popular Latin song which had something to do with the trembling latch, probably relating to what was happening in Cuba – Batista versus Castro, fighting little wars. The more blood I saw on the army uniforms we mended in this factory, the more I entertained the others. The uniforms had been laundered but the blood of war could never be erased. Young girls and older women worked there from five to eleven at night.

A hand came down on my shoulder just as I sat down from dancing and singing and playing around my machine. 'They want to see you,' the manageress said, looking towards her office. My heart leapt into my mouth. My aunt had found me. All eyes peered at me walking to the office where two plain-clothes men were standing in wait outside. Inside the office I was shown their badges of authority as they said, 'According to this photograph you are Eartha Mae Kitt who lives at 1756 Madison Avenue.' Not a very good likeness of me but enough to be recognizable: a photo of me as Snow White, taken in the school play. 'Your mother is looking for you.' I slumped my shoulders as I heard them say, 'We give you until midnight tonight to return home or we will have to put you in a home of detention.' Boy, that sounds crazy, I thought, returning to my machine.

I finished my work thinking, 'Gee, my aunt really wants me. She went to the trouble of finding me. When I get home she will hug me and kiss me saying how she missed me.' I couldn't wait to see her happy face. On my way along the few blocks I began to anticipate Aunt Mamie's relief on seeing my face. I imagined her saying, 'Oh you poor child, where have you been? I have been worried sick over you. Why did you run away?' as she pulled me into the apartment, looking me over to see if I was all right.

'Oh, there you are,' she said as she opened the door and went back to bed. I sat on the sofa looking at the upright piano someone had given her for me to practise on, remembering how many times the piano flaps had been slammed down on my fingers when I went into a boogie version of Beethoven's 'Für Elise'. Without thinking about it, I took a hot bath, washed my hair, changed my clothes, tied up my wet thick hair and walked out again. All I wanted you to do, Aunt Mamie, was hold me.

'Don't fool around with boys, you'll bring shame on me,' her words haunted my ears. 'Join the church, let the church know you're a child of God,' her words haunted me. I did so one time to please her. I had gone to church alone that Sunday. The preacher was preaching, the people

were moaning and groaning, shouting and crying, amening and hallelu-
jahing, panting and fainting. The preacher shouted and preached.
When he was finished with his shouting and preaching he asked those
who were not members to come down and kneel at the altar to be given a
piece of sweet biscuit and some kind of liquid to drink. I reluctantly did
as I was told, thinking this would please Aunt Mamie. After this little
ceremony we were led into a back room. I didn't realize you had to pay to
be a child of God so I left quickly.

I thought of all this as I walked through the wet snow in the streets,
with nowhere to go except the place in the Bronx where I had been
staying with a Cuban family. I had no money as Friday payday had not
arrived yet. Feeling a bit embarrassed about this, I hoped I would still be
received though it was the wee hours of the morning. Alex, the son of
the Cuban family, let me in. I stayed there for a few days feeling a bit
weak, but still going back to work in the sewing machine factory, until I
really came down with something.

One of the factory girls took me to her house at 115th Street, half a
block from my aunt, where I got sicker and sicker. I had to move again
some days later due to lack of space and I went to the apartment of a
couple who rented me a room, which I paid for with one month's salary
from the factory. I had become so ill by now that all I could do was sleep;
dragging myself to and from the kitchen when the house was empty,
looking for food, forcing myself to eat to try to gain strength, knowing I
had to take care of myself. The couple never knew how ill I was, since
they didn't see me except on the day I arrived there and the factory girl
didn't come back to visit.

When I finally returned to health I went back to 115th Street and the
factory girl found us another job in the Bronx: filling bobbin machines
that made embroidery material and emblems for uniforms. Here again I
amused the workers with my 'act', but my aunt found me when my
teacher told her I was not going to school.

When spring came I romanticized under the blossoming trees. The
birds in my imagination often carried me on their wings into another
world. The clouds were my horses, the wind my harpsichords, the sun
my hugs of warmth. I was in this little world of mine one day when I
decided to go to a movie. I had worked some days of that week at the
factory so I went there to ask for the money they owed me.

'Kitty, you're gonna be fired. They're not gonna keep someone who
comes in when she wants to,' one worker said.

'Oh, I don't care, I'm going to join the Katherine Dunham Company
and go around the world,' I heard myself saying.

Why did I say this? I had just seen the Dunham Company in a movie
called *Stormy Weather* and had read about the Company the day before.

'You're fired,' the manager said, handing me my pay envelope, which contained just enough for two tickets to a movie downtown and a dime over. I danced out of the factory singing 'Babalu', another Latin song, got my girlfriend Joyce from 115th Street, and we went to the movies: the Roxy on 44th Street at Broadway.

I immediately got fidgety when I saw all the people crowding into the movie house. My nerves go in a crowd. I started to change my mind when Joyce said, 'Let's see the stage show anyway.' Afraid of being stepped on I made myself as small as possible as I eased my way in between the ant-like people. I sat fidgety, watching Carmen Miranda coo-coo-coo-coo-coo-coo in a Brazilian number dressed like a fruit tree on platform shoes. I could not get out of there fast enough the moment she had finished. The crowd began to buzz like bees in a beehive, fraying my nerves to a frazzle.

I pulled Joyce out onto the street and we stood there deciding what to do with our leftover dime: take the subway home, or walk home and buy a bar of candy – a nickel each for the subway or a nickel each for a chocolate bar? During our moment of decision I saw a girl in search of something. She was my colour and about my size. I was fascinated by her.

'Can you tell me where this make-up shop is?' she asked, looking at me. She showed me a list detailing enough make-up for the cast of *Cyrano*.

'Why do you need so much make-up?' I asked.

'Oh no, it's not for me,' the little voice said. 'It's for Katherine Dunham.' The bulbs went off in my head like a bomb.

'Do you know Katherine Dunham?' I asked in great curiosity.

'I'm one of her dancers, she sent me for this make-up,' said the little voice.

'If you take us to meet Katherine Dunham, I'll show you where the shop is,' I said, surprising myself.

'Okay. As a matter of fact, Miss Dunham is looking for new dancers. She is having auditions today at her school. Maybe you can audition for her,' said the little voice, relieved to have our help.

'No, no, no. I'm not a dancer. Besides, my aunt would kill me,' I said.

When we got to the school Joyce and I sat in the studio waiting to meet Miss Dunham, who was never to be met. The auditions started and Joyce and I waited in great excitement. Suddenly the girl with the tiny voice came to me and said, 'Why don't you join the auditon class?'

'I don't know anything about dancing.'

'Go on, Kitt, you can dance all those dances at the Palladium, why not here?' said Joyce.

Another voice from the room said, 'Sure, go on, ya never know what you can do till you try it.'

'I dare you, I dare you,' said Joyce. All three voices were yelling 'I dare you' when someone threw me a rehearsal garment.

'I dare you back!' I laughed as I went off to the girls' room to change. I laughingly joined the class, followed the teacher, and joked my way up and down the dance floor to the rhythm of African drums. When the class stopped, I playfully returned to my place next to Joyce. We were both laughing like two hyenas when a tall, black-haired lady squatted in front of me.

With a very strong foreign accent she asked, 'Can you come back on Monday at ten a.m.?'

'What on earth for?' I asked, still kind of laughing.

'You have won a full scholarship.'

I looked at Joyce. 'What does that mean?'

'That means Miss Dunham will pay you ten dollars a week for you to learn her style of dancing,' the tall lady said.

'What does *that* mean?' I asked in bewilderment.

'You will have to take six hours of classes a day – ballet and Dunham technique in the morning and in the afternoon Dunham technique and styling. All from ten to five.'

I was too busy thinking to take it all in. How could I tell Aunt Mamie who wants me to be a concert pianist, even to the point of taking me to see Earl Garner at the Apollo Theatre? If I was to mention anything to her about dancing, especially with practically no clothes on as I saw in the movie, she'd kill me. I was thinking fast. Best thing to do is not to tell her. But how could I leave home at nine in the morning for classes at ten? I was thinking hard and fast . . . Best thing to do is not to go home.

'I have no place to stay,' I said to the girl who had thrown me the rehearsal garment.

'You can room with me,' she said.

And that is where Eartha Kitt came in.

7 Mexico to Hollywood

I was on ten dollars a week. I paid five for sharing a bedroom with Roxie (the dance garment girl) in her mother's apartment – three bedrooms, a large sitting room, two baths and a kitchen, very luxurious by my standards. On weekdays I would use my other five dollars to go by subway to the Dunham school. Fancy this, the same five dollars also bought lunch: a hotdog and a cup of coffee, maybe a hamburger. The greatest treat was a twenty-five-cent meal at the automat.

I must have been in the school about three months when I was placed in what was to become a second company, which was to be used in a broadway musical called *Blue Holiday* with Ethel Waters, Avon Lang, Willie Bryent and Josh White. We girls were supposed to be Hawaiian dancers. We were dressed in very scanty costumes, placed on a block and then told to wiggle wiggle our way across the stage. Here we were all doing our wiggles when a voice screamed in the harshest tones, 'Get those naked bitches off my stage!'

This was the start of my experience in the theatre world. Thank God, this was only a rehearsal. We all looked in the direction from which the voice came, to be met by the thunderous sound of footsteps coming towards us from the wings. Ethel Waters came on stage with lightning speed, shooing us away with arms flailing.

'I don't want those naked bitches on my stage. Get them damn things out of here!' she cried.

She and the producers and directors had a small conference on stage as we hovered in the wings trying to hear what was being said. Eventually we were called back to begin our routine again on the beach-like stage. We continued to wiggle wiggle along when suddenly, without warning, a tap dancer (who turned out to be Ethel Waters' lover) entered on stage in front of us tapping on the beach in a routine from the Apollo Theatre. We all stood stunned, wondering how a tap dancer could tap on sand, but that was the way Ethel Waters wanted it and that was the way it stayed. Needless to say the show did not last more than a few weeks, if that.

My first salary in a Broadway show was forty-five dollars a week, out of which I paid my union dues and bought a grey two-piece suit with two different blouses to match and a pair of high-heeled shoes. I was really dressed to kill, I thought, and well on my way to being independent. But when the show closed at short notice after all the nit-picking backstage among our highly respected artists, the kids were, so to speak, back on the streets again.

Classes still went on when the school moved to 43rd Street. The second floor at the back of one of the 42nd Street cinemas was then our home base. Sundays were for backers' auditions. People such as Doris Duke, Gloria Vanderbilt's family, the Rockefellers and so forth, would sit along the rehearsal hall wall to watch us go through different pieces of choreography. Miss Dunham sat in the centre like the queen of the beehive which she claimed to be: 'I am the queen of this beehive, and if I ever catch any of you with one of my men . . . .' The sentence was never finished.

Since I never heard anything more from my aunt, I felt safe at last. What better place to hide than in a travelling dance company? It seemed to me my aunt could never find me. Soon the company was to begin its tour across the States and into Mexico where we would be playing for about three months at the Bellas Artes Theatre. I don't remember if we needed passports for Mexico, but it seems not. Eight of us girls were to live in a small village house just outside of Mexico City called Villa Obregón, which I shall never forget because until this day it haunts me that the right hand of General Obregón (who was a Mexican hero) was supposedly encased in a block of marble in the village park. What bothers me even more is a conclusion that I reached after standing in front of this monument for God knows how long comparing my hands against his. It's not his right hand at all. It's his left hand.

We travelled to Mexico City by train, the full company of dancers, singers, musicians and drummers, with all of the instruments and costumes. At the border the train stopped, and we were at a standstill for hours without anyone telling us what was going on. Some hours later the train meandered on into the city itself and we were all driven to the theatre. We were assigned dressing rooms, and then came the time to collect our costumes and necessities for the show. No costumes, no drums and no scenery were to be found. The customs men decided to make a deal: 'You want to put on a show, you have to pay duty on everything.' There was obviously no money left over to pay on the spot, so arrangements had to be made to free everything.

Meanwhile, since the show must go on, Mr Pratt – Miss Dunham's husband and the costume designer – pulled down the theatre curtains and any materials he could get his hands on, telling us to start sewing as he cut. Instruments were begged, borrowed or stolen from various places and, with no scenery, the show went on at eleven p.m. and was a great success. I think the audience was probably so intoxicated from berry juice after five hours of waiting that they hardly noticed what happened on stage, especially since we also had very little lighting. But the drummers – four of the greatest of that time – made us dance like we were hypnotized in a frenzy. It was probably the truth, since Miss Dunham had studied voodoo in Haiti and we often felt she put her 'spell' on us at times.

Our little village cottage contained about four bedrooms, a sitting room with fireplace, a large enough kitchen, two baths, two patios front and back, for eight girls. The boys and the rest of the company stayed in town. Miss Dunham's success made her the queen of the moment in Mexico. All the dignitaries and important figures of the time were seen in the theatre; photographs of her with many of the VIPs were frequently in the newspapers.

When our three months' run in Mexico City and Guadalajara was at an end we were supposed to go on to Hollywood to make a film, but the plans fell through. Then we were stranded. Miss Dunham had spent much of the earnings on unnecessary luxuries and the money had run out. We had no engagements and nowhere to go. Miss Dunham managed to scrape up enough to allow twenty-five dollars a week for us eight girls to live on. Since the cottage was free, we had this to eat and amuse ourselves with. Lucille Ellis was the company's mother bee and she held the purse-strings. I have no idea how the boys of the company survived life in the city, but I can imagine.

Classes still went on. Ten o'clock each morning one class, two in the afternoon another class, sometimes with Miss Dunham present.

'You'll never become anything, Kitt, you have too much excess baggage,' Miss Dunham said to me one morning, meaning I was fully developed and had long hair, of which she had neither. To me she was so beautiful, with those long gorgeous legs that were often spoken of by the critics, that there was no need to pick on any of us. The girls especially were her targets: the prettier the victim, the worse the abuse, insults and sly remarks, which made the company laugh in Dunham's favour.

'If you thought that before, Miss Dunham, why did you put me in the company?' I heard myself asking.

As the whole company erupted in a roar of laughter, I rushed to my room in tears, ashamed not only because of the rude remark but also for having spoken back to an elder, something I would never in my life have done. But this was not the first time I had received a lashing from the tongue of the queen of the beehive. I lay on the bed with tears soaking my pillow, convinced I was going to be fired. What would I do if I was?

I was not only a dancer but also a singer, drummer, rehearsal pianist, seamstress and interpreter in Spanish (which I had learned on the

streets of New York in what we called 'Spictown Harlem'). As interpreter, one of my jobs was getting as much for our twenty-five dollars as
was possible from the marketplaces. We were paid on Friday after classes
and did the shopping on Saturday mornings. We had great meals usually
for about four days, sometimes inviting friends that we had met in the
city. They supplied the drinks, we supplied the food and entertainment.

If we wanted to go into the city for a movie, I would be the one to find
a car to take us there. I would stand on the side of the road thumbing a
ride while the others hid in the bushes alongside. When a car stopped
for me the others ran out, jumping into the car before the driver had a
chance to change his mind.

I met Pedro Armandariz, the actor, at this time. I don't remember
exactly where or how but it was probably at some cocktail party at the
Hotel Del Prado, since we had done a show there for about two weeks
trying to make ends meet and lessen the financial burden on Dunham.

I remember Johnny Weissmuller doing his Tarzan call from the
rooftop of his hotel one evening as we prepared for our show. We
thought someone was being killed and ran out to see what was
happening. Johnny Weissmuller had his arms around a very beautiful
woman in the 'Me Tarzan, you Jane' pose, yelling his Tarzan call which
was soon joined by police sirens. We all laughed as Johnny Weissmuller
and his Jane were escorted from the scene.

One of my solo numbers in this show was 'La Bamba' and it attracted
the attention of the Mexican critics, giving Miss Dunham more motive
to practise her sharp tongue on me. Since we were often put on display
for VIP gatherings we were able to meet and mingle, getting to know
people such as Pedro Armandariz, who took a fancy to me, inviting me
for lunch or dinner at times when I was most hungry. Our relationship
grew to a very warm friendship; he felt I was like a child needing
someone to care for her. Pedro took me to various places outside Mexico
City, to tiny villages where the 'real people' (as he described them)
were.

This was a lot of fun for me. I was like a schoolgirl listening to
a teacher as he told me stories from Mexican history and of his
relationship with his best friend, the film director. Pedro and his
director had a sixth sense about each other. Sometimes when Pedro was
miles away, he would suddenly sense that his friend was in trouble, and
he'd show up just in time to save him from being shot in some bar brawl
or other kind of danger – and vice versa. Pedro was a fascinating man to
me. I was in awe of his company, listening intently and hanging on his
every word. Sometimes we didn't talk at all but it seemed I could still
hear his thoughts.

We visited the studio one day to see his film *La Perla*, with Dolores

Del Rio. His director was there. I was like a child at a magic show as I watched these great personalities on the screen. I was shy but comfortable in my excitement. The story of the film was about a fisherman and his wife and child. The fisherman found a black pearl that could take them out of poverty into a world of riches, but when word got around about this pearl, the miser of the village wanted it more than life itself and made the fisherman's life impossible. The fisherman fled the village with his wife and child with the miser's gang of hoodlums in pursuit. The baby was shot and killed by the hoodlums. The fisherman returned to the village with his wife, and gave the pearl to the greedy miser who got intoxicated with the excitement of possessing it; he drank champagne with the pearl swilling around in his mouth as he wallowed over and over on a huge bed of silks and satins. This is one of the sexiest scenes I have ever seen on screen. Even this fat slob, the miser, became sexy. I don't remember how the film ended but this scene has always stuck in my mind.

After the screening we visited the director's house, a grand villa with a swimming pool that he and Pedro would dive into from the bedroom balcony when they got up in the mornings – a dangerous exercise, but that's how the two of them lived, always on the fringes of danger, or so their stories went.

Pedro gave me a gift, a black puppy which I named 'Babalu'. Since food was often scarce in our home, we had to find it by hook or by crook. I was sitting on the steps of the front patio one day, watching little Babalu play. The rain, as usual, had come and gone that afternoon, the daily four p.m. Mexican shower. Excess rain was flowing down into a drain and I noticed a small chicken coming along with it. 'Aha,' I quietly thought. 'This has possibilities – supper!' I carefully held Babalu close, watching the chicken move further and further into the yard, waiting for it to become a fixed target. When it was, I set Babalu onto it. With great pride, Babalu and I took the chicken into the house, showing it to our mother hen, Lucille, as the other girls ran down to see what all the squawking was about.

Our dinner was in hand. But when I looked round at all the girls gathered in one place it occurred to me that this little biddy of a chicken was never going to be enough to go around. It also occurred to me that where there is one chicken there is always another as they are so stupid that if one goes missing then another will follow in search. Babalu and I returned to our previous spot on the steps, waiting in silence. Not a squeak was made, as I had warned the girls to stand like soldiers waiting for an order. There it came, another poor little chicken to join its mate in the stomachs of the Katherine Dunham Company.

'I don't know anything about killing a chicken,' said Lucille. A murmur to the same effect went through the group, giving me another opportunity to demonstrate my canniness.

'I do,' I said. I took one of the chickens into the back yard and started wringing its neck. Round and round I twirled it as I had seen them do down South, only in my case the chicken would not die.

The girls ran back into the kitchen in horror as I insisted on fulfilling my aim, feeling more and more sorry for the chicken. As I twirled and twirled the chicken became more and more alive and noisy. In my embarrassment I became more and more determined to bring this cackling chicken to its death as soon as possible. How in the hell did they do that down South? They swing it around in the air several times, throw it to the ground, and the life goes out of it. That's all they do, I remembered.

My attempt probably brought more sorrow and suffering to me than the poor chicken. In disgust, I took the chicken into the kitchen, picked up the butcher's knife, laid the chicken on the chopping block and whack! Off went the head. But still it did not die. Headless, it leapt to the floor with blood spurting everywhere and wandered out the door into the yard as the girls squirmed in horror and nervous laughter. Finally the last breath was exhaled and a stillness fell over all of us. Now the other chicken, that had had its feet tied so it couldn't roam away, had to have the same treatment. I did not let the others know how painful this job was for me. Since none of them would take any of the guilty blood from my hands, no matter how hungry they were, I took on the job now like an expert. The second time round it was faster and cleaner.

'Now, what do we do?' asked Othella. I said nothing. I boiled some water in our biggest pan with which to scald the chickens and then plucked the feathers until they were all softly ripped from the corpse. I got a little help with this, then when it came to the dissecting bit little old me, like a butcher of full experience, came to the fore. Oil was found somewhere in the back of the food cabinet, flour came out of nowhere; salt and pepper was always on hand, but we had no vegetables. We ransacked every garden adjacent to our little villa that had anything edible, poking our hands through the fences and darting to and fro grabbing whatever we could until we had enough for all. A hilarious evening of jokes and laughter followed and I revelled in the glory of having come to the rescue of a starving army of ballet dancers.

Out walking one day, I stopped to look at a hut where a Mexican family lived. One of the girls of the family was about my age. When I said hello to her, she invited me in to meet her mother, father, sisters and brothers. There were about six of them living there, in a small hut made of shingles of different sizes and shapes. There was a dirt floor and piles of anything that could be slept on were arranged along the walls. In the centre was the cooking area put together in an ad hoc manner: baskets containing this and that hung from poles which also supported the walls and roof. A place for worship containing an image of the Virgin Mary and a statue of Christ was in one corner.

I went back to this hut often as the young girl and I became close friends. Once I saw the father praying in the worshipping corner; I saw him put a *peso* in a can beside the statue of Christ, obviously to be given to the Church at a later date. I wondered why Christ would need money? Why would Christ ask for money when he can see this family is practically starving? How can a religion and the Church be so selfish? How can the father be so stupid as to feed a statue or a philosophy before he feeds his children, especially when he probably only gets a *peso* a day for work? Questions, questions, that I could never find an answer to.

The company was stranded in Mexico for about six months before the Hollywood contract finally came through. We were to make *Casbah*, a musical version of the Humphrey Bogart/Ingrid Bergman film *Casablanca*, this time with Tony Martin, Peter Lorre, Thomas Gomez, Yvonne de Carlo and the Dunham Company. Hollywood! The thought of it made our mouths water. We couldn't wait to get there. Movie stars! We could see them in our imaginations. 'I will meet Shirley Temple and Bill Robinson,' I dreamed. 'Hollywood, here we come!' was the cry of the whole company.

On our arrival in Hollywood we were assigned places to live: the black area only. Some roomed in a house here, others in a house there. Miss Dunham had a beautiful villa in Beverly Hills, donated by a friend or so we heard. Once we got settled in, a company meeting was called at this beautiful Beverly Hills villa. It was wonderful – marble floors and walls in most of the rooms, a garden and pool area with flowers climbing the walls; the same kind of flowers and plants we saw in Mexico, but this house also had orange trees growing in the back yard. I had never seen an orange tree and I had only seen personal swimming pools in the movies. I wondered where Shirley Temple and Bill Robinson were?

Being used to the idea from my upbringing that blacks could only live in areas designated for blacks because the whole world belonged to whites, I had little desire to move into a white area. I was just amazed in a child-like way at how beautiful Beverly Hills was and how rich you would have to be to live there. I did feel a twinge of jealousy as I gazed at the luxurious path around the house and yards. We were not allowed upstairs, and I felt odd to be in a strange house, especially a white man's house. When the meeting telling us our calls and how to get to and from the studio was over, we walked outside, stood on the sidewalk and waited for transportation to return us to our destinations. At that time it was inadvisable to be caught walking in Beverly Hills, especially if you were black, unless you could identify an address in that area. If picked up by the police, you would have had a hard time explaining your way out. I can imagine the interest of the neighbours seeing what must have looked like a tribe from another planet invading the neighbourhood as we stood nervously waiting in this white man's world. An electric tram finally took us over the hills into the valley to Universal Studios, where the film was being shot.

It was a fantastic experience and a fantastic fiasco. Mata Taren was the female lead who blinked and winked as Tony Martin sang his way into her Scandinavian arms. Our job as dancers was to leap around and creep up the walls of the Casbah to keep things exciting. I still don't know what Dunham did in this film but she was there somewhere, as was I. When the camera panned in on me I was to say, 'Come on, Pepe' – but the line was never heard.

I designed a pair of sandals to stop my feet being cut and bruised on the cobblestone set. I stayed up all night designing them and making them. With a heated ice pick I burned holes for leather thongs which I threaded through to hold them on. The demand for these special sandals quickly spread through the whole company, so I sat up all night making them and handed them in at the studios the next day. They were accepted by Miss Dunham and the *Casbah* representatives, but not by the union. Everyone argued in my favour because the sandals were unique and well-made with no buckles or ties, and they were also very comfortable and ideal for dancing in. But I was not a member of the shoe-making union so my sandals were thrown out.

The salary for this film was the most we had ever earned. I started a savings account at the Bank of America thinking of rainy days that might come in the future. Finding ourselves surrounded by movie stars made some of us go a bit round the bend. Dolores fell in love with Burt Lancaster, whose mobile dressing room she could not stay out of. He was the macho acrobatic do-it-yourself stunt actor and one of our favourites. Errol Flynn was another favourite, but we never met him. Othella fell in love with Peter Lorre whom, she said, she dreamed of nightly. We teased Othella a lot about her taste in men, remembering the night in the Villa Obregón when she returned from a date with one ear dripping with blood because her date got over-excited while trying to make love to her and ripped the earring from her pierced ear.

Hollywood was a strange kind of fun – like a village that never ends, with orange groves for miles and miles, and date groves which made one think of Egyptian movie scenes. It was not a place one thought of living in but it was a great place to play in. When *Casbah* wind-up day was over, we bade Hollywood goodbye to tour across the States to New York. Whispers went through the company along the way that we had been approached to tour Europe.

8 First Stop: London

Europe: that was only a name on the map, stories from history books and scenes in the war newsreels. London: Sherlock Holmes and Laurence Olivier. Paris: the Eiffel Tower and French perfume. The closer the tour got to New York, the more serious we became about going to Europe. We had to get special papers; a passport with proper identification must be obtained with the consent of one's parents. How in the world was I going to get that?

I had last seen my aunt at the Ziegfeld Theatre in New York while I was rehearsing with the company there. One day she just walked down the aisle and tapped me on the shoulder as I sat watching the others rehearse for a new show, *Caribe Song*, that Katherine Dunham was making with Avon Long. In it, she mixed the first company with the second. The story was something about a young girl who was supposed to marry a successful fisherman but who fell in love with an undesirable character instead, thus causing turmoil for everyone in the village in Jamaica or Haiti or wherever it was. All I remember is a wake for the dead mother or aunt at which we had a lot of fun eating, drinking and dancing voodoo rituals as Miss Dunham tried to act whilst Avon Long danced and sang his way across a fishing pond.

When my aunt scared me to death, putting her hands on my shoulders, I almost fell through the floor. 'So there you are,' she said, taking me to the back of the theatre. When she asked me to come home I told her I wanted to stay with the company and she finally gave up when she knew what I was doing and where I could be found. Aunt Mamie said very little at this meeting. She left the theatre and I did not hear from her again until a long time later, after she read about me in one of the critics' columns.

My contacts with her since leaving home had been few and far between. Before I got into the Dunham school, one summer I had read a brochure posted all over New York asking for young girls to join the Farmerettes, one of several organizations President Roosevelt had formed to get kids off the streets. Since most of the men and boys had been drafted into the war, girls were needed to work on the farms. I had joined the Farmerettes once after running away from Aunt Mamie. Since help was so badly needed the officers were not too particular about your details – anything that looked legitimate would do, and anything you said was accepted without question. The only rule was that you had to earn ten dollars a week to pay for your room and board.

To me, working on a farm was a breeze – hoeing the weeds, picking potatoes, berries or whatever. But because I was earning sixty to seventy dollars a week and was their best worker plus the Saturday night entertainer, the camp decided to use me as an example to all the other camps. There my name was, big as day, alongside the photograph that I had not wanted taken. I was too shy to argue so I let it go, hoping it would not reach my aunt. But it did, and she found me. I received a note from her asking me to come home at the end of harvest time. I ignored the letter and did not go home. The next time I had seen her was at the Ziegfeld Theatre and again I had refused to go home with her.

But this time was different – now I needed her help. Europe, London, Paris, identification, parents' consent. How am I going to do that? How can I get my aunt to help me obtain a passport? I have no birth certificate. I could try the thing I did once before to get a work permit: get two adults old enough to swear they were at my birth. No, I can't do that, this is much more serious. This is going overseas, a long, long way. Completely away from America. I'd have to get up enough nerve to ask her to help me or tell Miss Dunham I couldn't go.

An announcement was made on stage one night: 'We will arrive in New York at the weekend, then we have ten days to prepare to leave for Europe by boat. Everyone has to go to the American Consulate with ten dollars and all the necessary information. A list will be placed on the stage door bulletin board.'

You have to do something, Eartha, so you might as well make up your mind. I wrote to my aunt, explaining all with my heart in my hand. The days I waited for her reply were the hardest I had ever spent. Not to go to Europe, London and Paris – I didn't want to think about it. Finally my aunt replied, 'When you get to New York I will pick you up.' The next few days were the happiest of my life up to that point. My aunt met me at the station and took me to 1756 Madison Avenue where she became the kindest person I had ever known. She not only helped me to get my passport but she also bought me a set of luggage and a complete wardrobe. She was soft-spoken, and her eyes were warm and gentle when she looked at me. Aunt Mamie and I, we were having fun, we were fun for each other. She touched me, she combed my hair and braided it, we ate together, we walked side by side, she held my hand. She smiled as she handed me my passport when it arrived in the mail. My aunt was kind to me.

'This might be the last time I see you,' she said, standing on the deck of the boat. Everyone was yelling and laughing through tears of goodbye, getting on and off the SS *George Washington*. My aunt's majestic figure shrouded over me with her hands on my shoulders, tears dampening her eyes: 'I may never see you again,' she said softly and turned away as I stood in wonder watching her back as she slowly walked down the ramp, through the crowd and was gone, never looking back.

We settled in for the long journey. The girls were put in a bunk-bed cabin for eight (the boat must have been converted from a war carrier). We never managed to get comfortable. The food was worse than army food, recreation was nil – except to walk the plank. Classes were tried but then stopped. The sea was rough so we were sick for the first few days and the ship was slow to England. There was some dance music which gave us a chance to exercise our muscles a bit and at least kept us amused for a few hours a day until the ship's priest or pastor or whatever gave all young people on the ship a curfew – none of us were to be seen after eleven p.m. We were already so miserable after days of rotten food, cramped quarters and no recreational facilities that this made the company argumentative and fidgety to the point of mutiny.

Lenwood Morris and Lucille Ellis had been put in charge of the cases of alcohol and fancy foods Miss Dunham was sending to London for friends. I only heard rumours about the alcohol being consumed since we younger ones obeyed the curfew rules and were in bed as requested by eleven p.m., but we did notice the older boys looking very happy. We also heard rumours that the priest and the boys had a lot of fun in his suite after midnight.

We arrived in England after passing the cliffs of Dover, which gave us a real feeling of going into a very strange and completely different world. I began to think of films I had seen and books I had read about the old world. I had taken a book of French lessons on board so I was always busy studying, anxious to learn the language, making the company more and more convinced that I was not very sociable.

Back in Las Vegas, when we had worked at El Rancho, one of the two hotels on the strip at the time, I had been accused of being antisocial. Here too we had to live on the other side of the railroad tracks, in humble abodes in the black area. At El Rancho none of us were allowed through the front doors: through the kitchen to our dressing rooms was the path, and no mingling. Immediately after our show we had to return to our quarters in the black area. Parties were given in the house where most of the girls lived. My room, shared with one of the other girls, was across the hall from the sitting room where the parties took place.

'Where is Kitt?' a male voice asked.

'You don't want to be bothered with her,' I heard a female voice say.

'She's in her room, probably with her head in some book. She's not much fun,' another voice continued. They all laughed.

I walked out of the bedroom, took the first bottle of liquor I saw and glug-a-lugged it down to about halfway, not liking the taste at all. To me it looked like water. Never having experienced alcohol before, I had no idea how sick one could get, except for what I had seen of Mama Rosa's husband who just vomited and went to sleep. I started to feel a bit ill as I listened to the stunned laughter from the company and guests. I walked slowly out onto the porch of the house and was sick as a dog for the next three days or so, but still managed to dance my head off though I was somewhat, shall we say, out of it. That was the beginning and end of that.

Arriving in England was a very exciting experience, with photographers meeting the boat, our getting on a train, arriving in London and finding a place to live. Julie Robinson (now Mrs Harry Belafonte) and I went to a Jewish restaurant in Soho with our bags. She obviously had instructions from her parents as to what to do. We were given an apartment at 10 Manchester Square, where we paid about ten pounds a week rent: two bedrooms, a good-sized kitchen, a nice bathroom and a large sitting room, all very comfortable. Julie and I stayed there the whole time in London.

The Prince of Wales Theatre was to be our theatre home for the next six months. On opening night, after a long day of rehearsing and being photographed, we were more excited than ever to hear that the King and Queen were coming. A buzz went through the company that one of the dancers had to greet the King and Queen in a dance number as they came through the lobby. I was more scared than elated when I was the one chosen. I don't remember what happened, except that I was very scantily dressed and wriggled to the sound of four Cuban drummers as the ceremony passed through the lobby of the theatre. I was numb with shyness.

The show was a great success and was the talk of England and Europe. We were given a police card and food stamps since England was still on rationing. Meat, butter, sugar and chocolate were the hardest things to get. Most of my chocolate and meat coupons were given to the ushers of the theatre who had older members of their families to look after. I felt so guilty about these coupons that I shared them with the Londoners who worked in the theatre and friends we met. Meat was extremely rare: while steaks of horse meat were usually all that could be found in restaurants, there was a Greek restaurant near the stage door serving moussaka on Thursdays with real meat between layers of vegetables and cheese. Those who could afford it had this treat once a week.

I was trying to save a few pence for a rainy day, opening a bank account and sending money to Los Angeles. I was now earning about ninety-five dollars a week (though I had to pay taxes on this) since I had become a solo personality and was singing as well as dancing. The critics kept picking me out, forcing Miss Dunham to give me a solo spot.

'Quirino con su tres', I sang, moving across the stage in a rumba-style costume with Jesse Hawkins trailing behind pretending to strum a guitar. My costume had frills that trailed the floor and a bandana had to be worn over my long hair: this was a rule. Since I wanted to show my long curly hair, I put the bandana as far back on my head as was possible with two or three bobby pins to hold it.

'Five dollar fine, Kitty,' Miss Dunham would say each time she caught me as I came offstage. 'Black people don't have long hair,' she would say.

At times I would stand in the wings watching this beautiful woman extend her fantastic legs into the air with Vanoy Aikens holding her, moving her, lifting her – the most fantastic thing I had ever seen. I was proud to be in the Katherine Dunham Company. I was learning through watching and observing.

'Five dollar fine, Kitty,' she would say leaving the stage. 'I don't want you watching me. Your eyes penetrate my soul.' There were weeks when my pay envelope was practically nil from five-dollar fines.

Our six months in London was to me a great learning process: museums, British movies and exploring the sights were my pastimes. Walking the streets of London and riding the double-decker buses to areas that had been bombed and not cleared or rebuilt yet made me feel so angry. The movie newsreel scenes were nothing compared with the reality. To see a church half blown away, whole areas bombed and left in memory of man's inhumanity to man, would leave me standing in awe and rage.

The images from the newsreels began to focus in my mind – the blond-haired blue-eyed Germans we were taught to hate; how Hitler killed so many Jews in search of a perfect race; how Jesse Owens, the fastest man in the world, was called a monkey when he won the gold medal for America in the Olympics and how he did not even get a handshake from President Roosevelt on his return. Confusion and more confusion. Germany against the Jews – no place for them to rest their heads, no place for blacks to rest their heads. Is the whole world only for whites? And what about those of us who are in between, neither white nor black? My childhood experiences flowed through me. The more I saw of blitzed London, the more curious and confused I became. Where and to whom do I belong? Here? There? Everywhere? Nowhere?

9 Paris: The Next Dare

Paris: Maurice Chevalier, Charles Boyer, the Eiffel Tower, Sacré Coeur, Montmartre, Montparnasse, the Quartier Latin and Josephine Baker. On the night of our arrival, Julie and I dropped our belongings in our inkey-dinkey hotel room and fled to see Josephine Baker. I did not know much about Josephine Baker, but once seen never forgotten. She was beautiful and elegant and had suave chicness. 'J'ai deux pays' she sang in a slight French-American accent. Julie and I were thrilled to have had the luck to see her and we talked about her for days and days.

Our success was huge. Here again we became the talk of the town. Three hundred and fifty francs to one US dollar, so we thought ourselves rich on pay day after converting dollars into francs. I was still saving money for a rainy day, sending fifty dollars a week most of the time to my Bank of America account in Los Angeles, and some to a bank in London. I had so much in my Los Angeles account and so much in my London account, but then, to my horror, the US government changed the rate of exchange overnight and flooded the market with script money without warning, leaving me with half the value of my money in the London banks and a bad taste in my mouth for banks and savings accounts.

There were a lot of jazz musicians and American artists in Paris at this time. Since Josephine Baker had become so famous here I think many American artists thought this was the place to be. The Mars Bar was one of our hangouts. Here you could get a great American hamburger, served by an American who was married to a French lady. There was always an American pianist and people like Oscar Peterson appeared as guests on occasion. Sidney Bechet also visited at times. I was often asked to sing a song or two for a free hamburger, completely unaware that it was being recorded. (I was to find out years later when a record came on the market featuring me and some jazz artists.)

I met Bayeux Baker in Paris, an extremely handsome American who was a student at the Sorbonne. I was introduced to him at Chez Inez, a place we also frequented. Here you could have Southern fried chicken, collard greens, blackeye peas, sweet potato pie and the likes – home soul food. Chez Inez was where the black and white folks met. 'You two look like brother and sister,' Inez said. 'You should know each other.' We did get to know each other, only for him to leave town just as we were getting too close for comfort. Bayeux disappeared without an explanation or a call.

The show went on with more and more important personalities coming backstage to meet Miss Dunham, one of them being Rubirosa. All the girls snickered and peeked around the theatre walls and curtains when we heard he was there. Handsome? God, was he handsome! The newspapers in Paris were full of news about Rubirosa and Barbara Hutton at this time. Some revealed all about this handsome ambassador from Colombia being divorced, with a million-dollar settlement and a house in the Quartier Latin.

'I am the queen of this beehive . . .' The memory of Miss Dunham's warning mingled through the company. Each one of us, though afraid of being fired, secretly desired a date on the town with Rubirosa. I was standing by the side of the stage one night when he was being ushered to Miss Dunham's dressing-room suite. There were several men with him. I squeezed myself against the wall, giving him and his group more room to pass. He looked at me with a slight smile, making me cringe in embarrassment.

I never had the slightest idea he would actually take me out on the town until a note came to my dressing room some days later saying, 'I will pick you up tomorrow night after the show for dinner at Maxim's,' signed 'Rubirosa'. Jackie Wollcott, who was my dressing-room mate, giggled at this the whole night.

'Kitty, you have a date with Rubirosa,' she giggled. 'What are you going to do? If Miss Dunham finds out you'll probably be fired.' I said nothing, thinking hard. 'Well, you gonna go?' Jackie asked.

'I can't go out with anyone like that,' I said, wanting desperately to go. 'I haven't got anything to wear. Besides, he and Maxim's are too fancy for me.' At the same time, I thought, this might all be a joke. Why me?

I slept very uneasily that night, half hoping that it was not a joke and half hoping it was. The phone rang the next morning: 'I am calling on behalf of Mr Rubirosa,' the male voice said. 'He is confirming his request for dinner at Maxim's tonight. Will that be all right?'

My brain went like a computing machine. How can this be? How did he get my phone number? How did he know what hotel? My mind ran faster and faster.

As though my thoughts were being transmitted to the other end of the phone, the voice said, 'We got your whereabouts from the stage manager.'

'Oh . . . uh . . . I have nothing to wear,' I called out. 'No matter, Mr Rubirosa has given me instructions to take you wherever you want to go shopping for anything you want – at his expense of course.'

The only time anyone had done something like this for me before was when I was in *Blue Holiday*. Josh White, who had taken a fancy to me, had bought me two cocktail dresses and a pair of shoes with a handbag to match for him and his friends to escort me around New York. This afternoon in Paris I was taken to Pierre Balmain. I chose a very simple black silk dress with shoes to match and a small black silk handbag. Saying nothing to Jackie about this the whole night in the theatre, I calmly got dressed in my finery after the show while Jackie stared at me in surprise with her mouth open. Not being in the habit of talking a lot, Jackie left me in silence with just a murmur of, 'Kitty, you're gonna get fired. . .'

I pushed my long thick hair into place a thousand times, and looked at myself in the mirror equally as much. I calmly walked downstairs, almost in a trance, where I found the most glamorous car with a chauffeur waiting and Rubirosa standing with his hand held out to beckon me to him. Suddenly four men were around us (they turned out to be his bodyguards) and off we went to Maxim's.

On our entrance into Maxim's, the violin quartet violined us to a table with orchids, Dom Pérignon champagne and Beluga caviar displayed on ice. To me this was all a dream, a Hollywood I had missed when in Hollywood. Rubirosa was Cary Grant, Errol Flynn, Charles Boyer, Burt Lancaster and Tyrone Power all in one, and I was out on the town with all of them. Of course, I feared the fangs of Miss Dunham, but I was Cinderella, I would worry about that later.

A box wrapped in blue paper tied with a blue ribbon with a silk rose attached was on the silver plate in front of where I was beckoned to sit. Rubirosa held the chair back as I placed myself very lady-like in place, nervous as a mouse. The bodyguards took their places around the table after Rubirosa took his place next to me. The chair at the head of the table was not taken, making me think a lady was expected; but when the waiter took the chair and place-setting away I realized I was the only lady for the rest of the evening. I better start thinking: how do I get out of paying for my dinner? I remembered other cases in the past when men had taken me out. Here I go again, killing the plants with alcohol, making the men think I have consumed it. I had played this game so often it was now an automatic reaction to an invitation to dinner. Men to me were very funny creatures. In America the boys invited you for a meal but tried to fill you with alcohol, hoping to weaken you for the attack after. But, as the saying goes, there's no such thing as a free meal. All sorts of 'get out' tricks came to mind. Plans, plans, plans – my head was crazy with plans.

'Aren't you going to open your present?' asked Rubirosa. My unmanicured fingernails scratched at the wrapping paper which finally gave way in my nervousness. When I got the box open with the eyes of all staring at me, the most beautiful string of pearls appeared before me. Simple, chic luxury. My first string of real pearls. I giggled, putting my hands over my mouth to calm my joy. Rubirosa bent over to fasten the catch. The waiters served the champagne that I was not accustomed to, though I soon got used to it as the evening lingered into deep night. I had no problem with the caviar and the etceteras for I was now too hungry and fascinated by this world of luxury. The evening was so romantic I felt like the heroine of a romantic novel. The music was continental, mostly Latin. At times the violins surrounded our table playing old favourites. Rubirosa must have been tipping well because they played to us more than the others. The evening was so grand I never wanted it to end.

When it finally came to the end my head started its plans again, for now came the pay-off I thought. No such thing. I was driven to my hotel and bade goodnight at the door as the concierge took custody. I stood there in a glorious warming light as Rubirosa and his bodyguards drove off into the dawn. I did not sleep until the sun was shining heavily through my window. 'Will he ever come back?' I wondered, staring at the ceiling. For the next two or three weeks he was at the stage door every night, waiting to enjoy the same kind of evening. Each morning I was called by one of his representatives asking if I needed anything, and again I would be taken to Pierre Balmain for an outfit for the evening. I don't know if Miss Dunham ever knew about this but nothing was ever said.

Rubirosa left town after a while, sending word that he would return soon. I went back to my usual style of living, my beautiful Balmains hanging in my hotel closet with nowhere to go. Some months had passed, and the plan now was for the company to go elsewhere. A tour of Europe was talked about. Hugh Shannon, the regular pianist at the Mars Bar – who accompanied me on the occasions when I had the nerve to sing for a hamburger – came to see me one evening after the show. 'They need someone to take the place of the Cuban singer at Carroll's,' he told me. I paid little attention to this as I was not interested, and did not think I was the someone he might be referring to. The subject was dropped.

A few days later Hugh Shannon brought a couple in to see the show and then to my dressing room afterwards. 'This is Fred and her brother,' he said by way of introduction. The most beautiful manly-looking lady in the world stood in front of me. Greenish eyes, short cropped hair, wearing a black tuxedo but with a skirt, a white frilly shirt and bow tie; no make-up. She looked at me strangely as I looked at her strangely.

Nothing was said more than the niceties but I learned that they were the owners of Carroll's.

As I continued to visit the Mars Bar, Hugh came to the point of asking, 'Would you like to do a stint at Carroll's, Kitt?' I pretended not to know what he was talking about and turned it all into a joke.

'Why would I want to replace a Cuban? I'm not Cuban,' I said, with sense enough to realize I did not have enough of a Spanish-Cuban repertoire to make up an hour's show.

Hugh said, 'They don't really want a Cuban singer, they just want someone to take the Cuban singer's place.'

Even though I had never heard of this Cuban singer, my instincts told me she was very important. I let it go with no reply except to pull a slight joking mimic smile. I was cajoled into singing for my American hamburger before the night was over, only to discover Fred and her brother greeting me from a corner as I left the microphone, much to my surprise.

Nothing more was said about the Cuban singer's replacement at Carroll's. I still saw Hugh Shannon frequently at the Mars Bar, which was our nightly haunt. On Sundays we would sometimes all meet at the apartment of the male partner of the Mars Bar. We used to ride up and down the Champs Elysées in an old convertible Rolls Royce owned by Jacques Bernape – often with just enough gas to get us to the Arc de Triomphe from Place de la Concorde and pushed back. Sometimes the Rolls would take us as far as the beautiful apartment of the female Mars Bar partner, though often she was away and the mice would play. I was too innocent to realize what was going on in that flat at the time; while some sat around telling stories, others would disappear to the other rooms, saying that they were going to look at different views of Paris from this or that area of the apartment or its balconies.

I was suspicious, without really wanting the reality of this suspicion to surface. Being the only real female among all these macho women, I was comfortable without analyzing anything too deeply. I had no worries or 'How am I going to get out of this?' feelings. In their company I was at ease, treated with respect and all the courtesies of good upbringing, having fun in clean, gentle ways. Sunday fun in the Bois de Boulogne – picnics, wine, cheese, French bread, pâtés of all sorts, salads, all served on real Dresden plates and with silver cutlery. We had wine in crystal or silver goblets, and even cut flowers in a vase on the picnic blanket. It was fine, with jokes and laughter and no strings attached. The Bois de Boulogne to me was like a Cézanne painting, with families and children running and playing out a scene of a painting I had seen at the Louvre or one of the other museums I spent so much time in. Since I was a hopeless romantic dreamer I could see pictures being replayed of scenes in a film or a painting even though my ears were filled with great hoots of laughter or the hoink-hoinks of taxis or the clop-clop of the horse buggies. I could hear a thousand sounds and still decipher the conversation going on.

My great, great love was and is conversation. Some of us belonging to our little group would meet day after day at Deux Magots, St Germain des Prés, Café des Fleurs and other bars to talk about things. Someone had read the great classics, someone else had visited a museum, another had visited an historical site. We would share our experiences over a grog of hot wine and lemon consumed with a plate of chocolate or whatever we could afford. We were joined in these conversations by people like James Baldwin, Richard Wright, Jean Paul Sartre, Brigitte Bardot and Jean Gabin. There were many stimulating arguments and intellectual challenges, and life was totally fascinating. Sleep seemed like such a waste of time – I wanted to be awake, alive, learning and experiencing life to the full. We had to define everything, physically and intellectually, and we wanted our tomorrows to come fast so we could analyze what we did with our yesterdays.

Paris was pulling herself back into focus just as London was pulling herself together, and we were all like sponges soaking it up; enjoying the now, analyzing the past and forming our hopes for the future. We had no idea where we were going or what the future had in store, but we were prepared psychologically for whatever came. Prepare for tomorrow today.

'Don't you think Kitty should take that Cuban singer's place?' Hugh was saying as my mind surfaced.

'What Cuban singer?' someone else asked.

'Hugh, leave it alone,' I said.

Even though I told Hugh to leave it alone, the thought stayed in my mind. 'Forget it, Kitty,' I told myself. 'You don't have an act anyway.' Some days later Hugh met me at the theatre after a Friday night show.

'Fred wants to know if you are interested in taking the Cuban singer's place,' he said.

'Will I never hear the end of this Cuban singer?' I asked.

Hugh took me to the club almost forcibly that night. The Cuban singer was great, everyone loved her. I could never do that, I thought to myself. Fred came over to our table; she said nothing, but just looked at me and Hugh. Her brother came over, took care of our bill, said nothing beyond a polite greeting, and left.

It's the Cuban singer's last night tomorrow,' Hugh said. 'They have a week to find someone to replace her,' he continued. We finished the Dom Pérignon champagne and Hugh took me home in a cab. 'You can do both, you know. Your curtain comes down about eleven p.m., you don't have to be at Carroll's until midnight,' he said, knowing this would keep me up all night planning how I could or if I should – which I did.

Next day, a Saturday, I was about to pass Miss Dunham's dressing-room door when, without giving it a second thought, I knocked. Annie, Miss Dunham's dresser, opened the door.

'I'd like to speak with Miss Dunham please for a moment, Annie,' I said meekly.

'Come on in, Kitty,' she said loudly.

Miss Dunham had heard me. She was at her make-up table, playing with her face. She kinda sorta looked at me in the mirror as I stood behind her. The front part of her hair was braided in tiny corn-rows; a twisted French bun was placed at the back, held on with hair pins and bobbies; her eyelashes were yet to be placed but most of her make-up was on.

I had nothing planned to say so I blurted out: 'I have been asked to replace a Cuban singer but it will be after our last curtain so it will not interfere and I would like to try it out to see what I can do on my own.' I was glad to get it all out without stumbling on my words.

Miss Dunham laughed cagily as she reached for something on her lap. This movement took her eyes away from the mirror, giving me a moment to catch my breath, easing my beating heart. Her head came up, putting her eye focus back to the mirror and onto me: 'Kitty, I think it's wonderful that you want to try yourself out on your own but I don't think Tavel and Marouani would allow that. You see, if we let you do that, then we'd have to allow everyone else the same. Next thing you know I won't have a company.'

I watched her in the mirror – her face became more and more beautiful as she applied make-up, powder puffs and then the eyelashes while she continued explaining why I should not replace the Cuban singer, with a little giggle in between sentences. 'But I will ask Tavel and Marouani and we'll see what they say, okay Kitty?'

I went to my dressing room feeling perhaps it was possible. I could do both. If I was not successful at Carroll's, at least I still had my place in the company. If I was successful, at least I would have an idea of my capabilities. I had not said anything to Jackie, my roommate. Before the curtain went up for the second act I was summoned to see Mr Marouani in Miss Dunham's ante-room. He was a very handsome man and usually his face was pleasant to look at, but not on this occasion. I stood uneasily facing him as he sat on the side of the table.

'Miss Dunham said you would like to have a try on your own,' he said gently. 'I think it's wonderful to have such ideas. I am sure you would be fine.'

I was about 12 when this photo was taken by a boy who worked at a news-stand. I am wearing one of my relief dresses, a jacket someone gave me and the only pair of shoes I possessed.

With one of the Dunham
Company dancers, Tommy
Gomez, in 1948. We had a
crush on each other but it
never came to anything.

With the Dunham Company
at the Shubert Theatre in
1949 after our production of
Carib Song. Katherine
Dunham is signing an
autograph and I am standing
beside her, to the right.

Rubirosa, the first real gentleman I ever met and my first contact with the 'High Life'. He introduced me to champagne, caviar, jewels and designer dresses. *(Associated Press)*

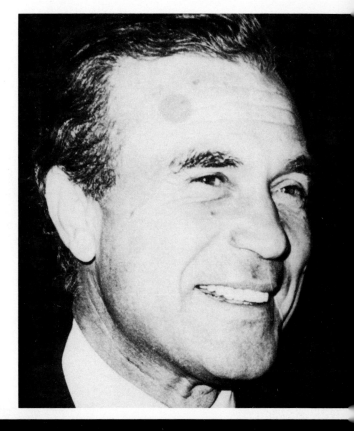

With Orson Welles, rehearsing 'Faustus' (or *The Blessed and the Damned,* as his production was called) at the Edward VII theatre in Paris, 1950. *(Associated Press)*

A James Kriegsmann photograph taken in 1953. The diamond ring I am wearing was a gift from John Barry Ryan.

Working at the Copacabana in New York – this is a Don Loper dress.

An early publicity shot for
'New Faces'.

Singing 'Santa Baby' on 'New
Faces' in 1954. Note the 'strap'
across my shoulder – this was
actually drawn in by prudish
executives who thought the dress
was too risqué otherwise.

Arthur Loew Jr, a quiet sensitive man with whom I felt an instant empathy and a deep love. *(Associated Press)*

Coming out of a Hollywood nightclub with Loew.

Working out with Jamie Dean at Katherine Dunham's dance class in New York, 1955
(Magnum Photos Inc; Photographer – Dennis Stock)

With Patricia Neal and Leo Genn in *Salomé,* 1954.

I began to feel okay with the thought of it all. He's going to let me do it, I thought.

'We've lost one of our best dancers, Tammy Gorney,' he continued. He took a breath before he came back with, 'I dare you to take a position outside of this company. I brought you over here, I got you work permits, I paid your way here. I dare you! If you do it, I will see to it that you never work anywhere in Paris again, or in Europe.' He waved his finger in my face at the words, 'I dare you, I dare you!'

Like a zombie, I left the room and walked upstairs to my dressing room. 'What are you doing?' asked Jackie. I said nothing.

In my zombie, hypnotized state I knocked on Miss Dunham's door, which was again opened by Annie. I handed her my two weeks' notice and returned to my dressing room, still in a trance. I was now completely boggled, but I knew I had two weeks to get myself together: two weeks' salary to buy a costume, get an act together, do all I had to do to make this new step. Hugh would help me. Two weeks should be plenty of time, I was trying to convince myself all through the second act.

But Miss Dunham won't let me go, I know she won't. They need me. I don't really want to leave this company. I am sure Miss Dunham will ask me to stay. She will probably give me a raise too. But I don't want to leave the company, I just want to test myself on my own. Miss Dunham must see that. I talked to myself all through the second act. The last curtain went down to tremendous applause, and Miss Dunham called the company on stage. I lingered in the background with my heart hanging on very fragile strings.

'Kitty has given me two weeks' notice,' Miss Dunham said, 'and I'm afraid we will have to accept it.' She looked slightly in my direction. Members of the company bowed their heads, some looked around to see where I was. I had almost wrapped the curtains around me, trying to hide as Miss Dunham continued, 'Rosalee, have Kitty replaced on Monday. Kitty will not be requested in the future.'

The fragile strings gave way. My heart choked me with the surprise that Miss Dunham would not even allow me to work out my two weeks as union rules stated. God, what do I do now? I still have the two weeks' pay, I thought. No such thing. Word was sent to me in unequivocal language: no job, no pay. We all went to our dressing rooms in silence.

'What are you going to do, Kitty?' asked Jackie.

'I'll think of something,' I said – my usual reply.

'What'll I do without you, Kitty?' Jackie hugged me.

'You'll think of something,' I comforted her, as we both laughed tearfully.

10 Happening in Paris

I went to the Mars Bar to get Hugh Shannon to go with me to Carroll's.
'May I have twenty-five thousand francs, please?' I asked Fred and she
referred to her brother, who gave it to me. No questions were asked as I
left Carroll's. I was thinking hard.

'They want you to open on Tuesday,' Hugh said.

'What time is the rehearsal?' I asked.

'Any time you want, but the lead will be there from noon on,
rehearsing another act and the comedian.'

I said nothing. I was thinking hard. All through Sunday I was fidgety,
thinking hard but with nothing coming to mind. I remembered Miss
Dunham calling me to her dressing room some time before: 'They want
you to do a film, Kitty, the lead,' she had said to me. 'They have sent me
the script. It's a very good script but I want to direct it. This is what we
are negotiating now. Since you are so young and would not know how to
deal with these things, as your manageress I will take care of everything.
You are in my charge!' To me this was wonderful. I would be well
protected. But I learned later that not only did Miss Dunham want to
direct the film I was offered but she was also to get whatever the fee was
for both of us, giving me only my usual weekly salary.

I was getting a bit sickly thinking of all this; memories spread like the
cobwebs on my hotel room ceiling. Miss Dunham's request to direct was
rejected and so, therefore, was I. I had no love in my heart for Miss
Dunham, though I admired her for what she did and represented. As far
as we knew, no other black ballet company existed. She gave us a sense
of pride and dignity and we were respected and revered for our
sophistication. I could never understand why she cut us down in what
seemed to be jealousy and selfishness. 'I am the queen of this beehive.
You will never be anything without me.' The words haunt me to this
day, and to this day not one of Miss Dunham's company has become
anything much – except Carmen de Lavelad who is now a university
teacher and was the first coloured ballet dancer at the Metropolitan
Opera in New York, under the direction of Katherine Dunham. And
there's Arthur Mitchell, who now runs the Ballet of Harlem. He took
the Dunham technique and carried it into a stronger primitive/

classical ballet company of which we are all very proud. But Dunham was the first, the pioneer.

I bought a piece of white silk material on the Monday, together with a pair of white silk high-heeled shoes, a pale pink rose, needle and thread and a pair of scissors, and I stayed up all night to make my dress – a very simple sarong, a Dorothy Lamour native-island look. It was dragged up on the left side into a fold at the top of the hipline, showing the leg and thigh to their fullest. My Balmain rose was placed in the folds. I went to the rehearsal at about two in the afternoon with nothing more than this costume.

'Where is your music?' asked the conductor.

'I don't have any,' I replied.

'What are you going to do?' he asked in disgusted surprise.

I had been in the club with Hugh Shannon and watched the social dance nights as well as Juliette Greco's show. This had given me an idea of what an evening at Carroll's was like. I knew most of the dance music and the songs were familiar to me.

'I'll tell you what,' I began, 'you show me your regular repertoire for dancing, I tell you the songs I know. You delete those from your dance repertoire, and that will be my act.'

The conductor threw his hands into the air and reluctantly did as I requested. We rehearsed the songs along with a few blues numbers they knew, and ad-libbed songs like 'St Louis Blues' and 'I Can't Give You Anything But Love'.

Time came, the moment of truth. I was in the dressing room making up my face a dozen times, over and over and over. I had curled my bushy hair with bobby pins the night before. Now the curls would not comb out like I wanted them to. Since I had no idea as to how I wanted to look, I decided the hair would be up on top of my head, held up with pin after pin and fluffed out to wherever it wanted to go. Thin long earrings hung to my shoulders. Nothing went right. I cleaned my face again and again, remaking it over and over. Finally the moment came.

'You're on in about ten minutes,' the Maitre d' told me.

I stiffened. 'I'm not ready, I'm not ready!' I cried, tears coming down like rain drops.

'It's midnight, you're on,' was his reply.

I was helped into my strapless sarong-type dress by one of the waitresses. All the waitresses wore black skirts with a tuxedo jacket, and white frilly blouses with bow ties. This made me a little uncomfortable but I thought little or nothing of it. Fred came in and saw the girl helping me into the dress. 'Are you all right?' she asked.

I said nothing, putting on my lipstick. Fred gently pulled me to the stage entrance. As she did so I heard her say to a couple of waitresses who had come in, 'This one is not to be touched,' but I paid no attention, not knowing what she meant. I stood in panic in front of a curtain with Fred and one of the waitresses standing by me. I became numb as the music to my introduction started. A push in the back forced me into the public view. A spotlight was thrown on me. Instead of walking normally to the front of the stage I walked sideways, shying away from letting the audience see my thighs. I had been told by the stage manager, as he ripped a huge slit in the side of the dress, that I looked like a nun. Now I tried to hold the skirt folds together, and since the whole thing was mainly tied at the waist with no straps to hold it up, I walked in fear that it might fall off, revealing only flesh-tone French panties – almost a G-string, in fact, that I had flesh-toned with my breakfast coffee.

There I stood at the microphone. The music went on and on. The conductor, standing slightly to my side, looked at me and waited for something to come from my mouth. The music vamped and vamped, the knives and forks rattled on the diners' plates, and the audience talked and talked. I stood in the spotlight like an insect trying to camouflage itself. As frightened as I was of the noisy audience, I became even more frightened when suddenly all became quiet. Now you could hear a pin drop. Now I must do something. So afraid of my voice trembling as my knees were, I stood even more still, just staring at the audience. Not a sound was heard except the music that vamped until I softly began to talk the words of the song; as I gradually found confidence the singing began. I moved from table to table. I must have been under the direction of God because the applause at the end of whatever I did was great enough for the critics to say in the next day's papers that I was 'The most exciting thing that has happened to Paris in twenty-five years.' I can't remember how it went on. Something about the 'beautiful café-au-lait creature that happened upon the scene . . .'

My engagement was a try-out for two weeks initially. Three months later I was still there, extended and extended, with no act, but still the 'happening of Paris'. There was no contract with anyone. An envelope containing thirty-five thousand francs was given to me each night when I came off stage. Hugh Shannon negotiated for me with no percentages to anyone. The club paid the taxes as well as getting me a permit for the engagement. I was still sending money to my account in Los Angeles for that rainy day, and having a good time with the remainder. Now I could feed my existentialist friends and pay my hotel bills on time. Now I was not so shy in our meetings at the Deux Magots, St Germain des Prés and the Café des Fleurs.

Jacques Fath, Pierre Balmain, Madame Schiaparelli and several other designers gave me anything that was left over from their seasonal fashion shows. I was the best dressed pauper in Paris. I collected an extensive wardrobe from the best of the Paris couturiers, who would call me and say, 'Erza, there is somesing here I am sure would be good for you, somesing left over from the fashion show that Mr Fath would like you to have.' Since there is no 'th' in French pronunciation, 'Eartha' was difficult for them to say. Fred had it spelt 'Erza' in the offices around Paris until an American called me 'Ezrah' one day and I had the spelling changed back to 'Eartha'.

Fred and her brother were very good to me, keeping me well protected and introducing me only to those whom they knew would have respect for a young woman. My life was heaven, but I still did not know what I was going to do with myself. Carroll's had a clairvoyant who roamed through the audience on certain nights of the week. She read cards, hands, faces, and anything else she could that might reveal one's destiny. I had no belief in this, but having been born in a world of superstition I did not dismiss it either. I was sitting at a table of friends one night when the clairvoyant asked if she could read my horoscope. What day? What year? What area of birth? she wanted to know. Since I could only tell her the date and area, and not the year, she looked at my hands instead.

'You are doing exactly as you are meant to do but you are going across a long body of water, and there a lot of money is waiting. If you are not careful, this money will be taken from you by a dark man and a fair-haired lady. You will not be happy there. You have the possibility of becoming very successful there, but you will not be happy. You will then cross another large body of water where you will become successful. You will stand on a plateau of success there for a while. Then you will have problems with your health, you must be careful about this. You will travel over a body of water again where nothing can stop your star from rising. Then you will lie dormant in this success at that level before your star rises again. Then there will be no stopping.'

The clairvoyant did not ask to be paid. She just slowly smiled and walked away. We all looked at each other, laughed, shrugged our shoulders, and returned to our Dom Pérignon champagne.

Fred and her brother called me to their offices one night after the show. 'You have become very popular in Paris,' Fred's brother (whose English was much more advanced than his sister's) said. 'We want you to take a rest.' My heart jumped a beat. 'We are building another club. It is to be called "Le Perroquet". It is being built especially for you so it means we would not like you to work in any clubs in Paris until Le Perroquet opens. We want to save you especially for that.' This sounded great, but I did not have any idea how long it would take for the French to build a club almost from scratch.

My last night at Carroll's was soon after this conversation. I was verbally contracted to hang around Paris with no 'hold on' pay as a retainer. It never occurred to me to ask for it. So there I was, having spent all my money (except for that in my Los Angeles account) on a good time. I did not send anything back to my London account as I had watched my pounds cut to half their value when the American soldiers' script money flooded the market in the late 1940s. No more banks, I promised myself; under the mattress from now on or spend it. I still question how a bank can take half your money away.

Anyway, here I now was, with no money on hand, no job and no immediate prospects of one – but with a great wardrobe. I was sitting with some friends in the Mars Bar when Eddy Marouani came in.

'May I speak with you a moment alone, Eartha?' he asked. 'You must call home right away. A Miss Wayde has been trying to contact you,' Eddy said when I joined him, away from the others.

A Miss Wayde, I thought? I had not heard from them for years. Why would they want me now? For what reason? My mind ran away with questions.

Eddy gave me the number to call in New York as he said, 'It's something about your aunt being ill.' The aunt everyone thought was my mother. Here began the fulfilling of the clairvoyant's reading.

It took some days for me to get through on the phone finally to hear my aunt had died some days before. She had said she would never see me again. The memory of our last ten days came keenly to my mind. Those last ten days, which had been more positive and wonderful than all the other times we had had put together. I gave Bernice Wayde the Mars Bar number to call me as soon as the ticket was obtained from Aunt Mamie's insurance company. The ticket came through some days later at Tavel and Marouani's office.

Bayeux Baker had returned to the scene. I called to tell him I was going back to America and he came and watched me pack for the journey. He had arranged a farewell party for me with some friends and we all ate a hearty breakfast. Bayeux (a famous Paris playboy) decided to try to snap me out of my misery and bought a bottle of Dom Pérignon, teasing me with my newly acquired taste. We had mimosas, champagne with freshly squeezed orange juice, and soft omelettes wrapped over herbs. Cognac and different kinds of aperitifs were also consumed, leaving me in a giggly state which gradually became a numbness as the fresh air hit my lungs when we were driving to the airport.

I'll never know how I got on the plane, but when I came to my senses I was crying chokingly, 'My mother is dead! My mother is dead!' The purser came to quieten me down with a blanket and another drink, which made me go back to sleep until we reached New York and La Guardia airport.

11 Back to the South

Bernice Wayde and her brother, Buddy, met me. After greetings of sorts
we got my bags and went to the same apartment my aunt had brought
me to when I first came up from the South. I was put in the same room
we had lived in. Since the closet was too small for all my fancy Parisian
wardrobe, my gowns were hung on every door I could find from one end
of the apartment to the other. Preparations for Aunt Mamie's funeral
were being arranged by my aunt's so-called 'cousins' and relations. Some
I remembered from the Christmas when Aunt Mamie had taken me to
Philadelphia for a family reunion. She had been very upset at my
behaviour on this occasion, but each person who came through the door
of the cousin's house reminded me of how I had been treated down
South. It was they who had refused us shelter and made us sleep in the
barn. I remembered each face and every name and every rejection.
When my aunt accused me of having been rude, I said nothing. I just sat
and waited for a smack from her majestic hand to cross my face.

When I went to the funeral parlour, the undertaker told me he had
not been paid for the embalming and preparation of my aunt's body,
which had had to be kept well preserved until I was found. Some legal
razzmatazz or other said the body could not be buried until the next of
kin was on the scene. The 'cousins' who suddenly came out of nowhere
had already received sums of money from the insurance company that
could not now be accounted for. This was explained to me by Bernice.
She and her brother had had a difficult time getting the insurance to pay
for my aeroplane ticket, and in the process they had uncovered
information about what the so-called 'cousins' were doing. They tried to
get everything my aunt left. Even the apartment at 1756 Madison
Avenue had been stripped of all her possessions, leaving only those
which belonged to Mr Charles. Even her clothes were gone. But the
insurance company had only given them enough to keep them quiet
until I was found. Since no one knew if Aunt Mamie had anything
much as far as money went, they were continually conniving to find out.

When I saw Aunt Mamie's coffin, I did not want to look at her face.
There was a lavender veil over the opened coffin. I sat in a front-row
chair and just stared. Aunt Mamie had left instructions before she went
to the hospital in case she did not come out. The saying goes that if you

go to hospital with a packed suitcase you do not expect to return, and she went with a packed suitcase. There was talk among the Waydes and the cousins that Aunt Mamie should not have died, of some carelessness in the hospital. She only had an ulcer, they said. That's all they were supposed to have operated on her for, they said. But, they said, the hospital did not examine her to see if her heart was strong enough to take the operation and she died on the operating table. I often wondered why Aunt Mamie ate white starch all the time, or so much heavy cream. The starch especially I could not understand. I thought perhaps it gave her the same feeling of excitement I had as a child when eating red and yellow clay.

Aunt Mamie's instructions were that she wanted to be buried at St Peter's Church down South. All was arranged with the help of the Waydes. I was all in black when I got on the train in the first-class coach. My Parisian outfit made me look like a model from *Vogue* – my hair was done to the hilt with a small black hat and gloves to match, and a handbag large enough to carry make-up and my extras for overnight.

'You don't belong in this coach,' the train conductor said as he punched my ticket. I said nothing, as though I did not hear him, not looking at his eyes. 'You should not be in this coach,' he repeated, handing my punched ticket back. I still said nothing, returning the ticket to my bag. The train conductor walked away taking other tickets as he passed all the white passengers. There were not many stops, but after each new ontake of passengers he would say, 'Shouldn't be in this compartment,' as he passed me. I still said nothing. I pretended not to hear. I sat firmly in my seat among the white passengers who pretended not to see me. I arrived at the station in what must have been Orangeburg or Columbia, where the relatives met me.

Seems like the whole town turned out for the 'movie star', as they thought I then was. 'That's Mamie's niece. She sure is pretty,' I could hear in the fussing crowd. 'She's famous . . .' I did not recognize any of the faces but the one who took me in her charge said she was another of my mother's sisters. I watched the coffin being taken from the train a few coaches along the way. It was put in a hearse. The crowd quietened down with a mumble here and there. There were white folks and black folks standing around watching the 'famous' cousin get into what looked like the same inkey-dinkey automobile that took me to the station for New York all those years before.

Nothing had changed: the people were the same, the cotton fields and the dirt roads that led to nowhere were the same. My mother's sister sat next to me in the dilapidated automobile talking about something I could hardly understand – my ear had lost the Southern accent. I listened hard, trying to capture some meaning from this yapping of hers, but without success. Two of her children sat quietly in front with whomever was driving, and a third sat next to her in the back. I looked out of the car window at the world that did not seem to have progressed beyond the memory of my years here. It all flowed through my eyelids like it was a thousand years ago.

We arrived at my mother's sister's house – a shack off Tobacco Road. The hearse had taken my aunt's coffin to the funeral parlour to wait for tomorrow's funeral. There must have been at least six children standing around to greet us, some in the yard, some in the shack. The style of life was the same as it was when I was a child: the boys in ragged overalls, the girls in ragged semi-clean dresses, dirty feet, and dirty whatever else. A big wood-burning stove was in a corner with pots of something cooking. I was given a section of a room with a curtain around it to sleep in on a slab of board nailed onto four wooden stumps. A basin of water was on the floor together with a bed pan in case I needed it through the night. I washed, brushed my teeth and waited for the morning sun to please rise. I was not comfortable, wondering where all the children and the parents were sleeping. This shack was not big enough for four (let alone six or more) children, two grown-ups, and now me.

When morning came, I asked one of the boys (who had been up seemingly all night) for a pair of overalls and a shirt. He gave them to me. I dressed, went into the yard just as I did as a child, and kindled wood with the boy watching in surprise. 'You can't break that over your knee – it's too big,' he yelled. When the stick broke in half over my knee he looked even more surprised. I noticed the axe that had been left stuck in a log and I proceeded to chop all the wood to the correct size for the stove. The sound of chopping must have woken the other children who sleepily came out of the shack to watch.

We began to converse with one another, and I found myself falling back into the years. I could now understand what they were saying and when I imitated them I felt a warmth growing between us. Sometimes when they could not understand what I was saying I had to revert back to Southernisms. I built a fire in the stove, took whatever was to be had, prepared breakfast for them all, cleaned up after, then got washed and dressed for my aunt's funeral. We all filed into jalopies that came to pick us up and on we went to St Peter's Church.

Josh White had told me he would meet me at the church. I had given him directions so I was on the look-out for him. Josh wanted to do a song or two. There he was driving up almost at the same time as us. The church was crowded with faces I did not remember, and the ceremony went on forever. The old piano honky-tonked through the spirituals, the preacher preached in grandeur, and I remembered the time the congregation shouted so hard the church floor gave way and Aunt Mamie paid for it to be as good as new.

Aunt Mamie used to disappear for days at a time in the past, when I wouldn't know where she was. She must have been down here praying for something or other because her praises were many this day. Then Josh got up to sing his praise. The church suddenly went so quiet you could hear a church mouse breathe. As Josh walked to the pulpit he pulled a chair to him, put one foot on the chair, and began to pluck the guitar that rested on his knee. The whole congregation bowed their heads – a guitar to them was an instrument of the devil, something never to be brought into the church. Josh had not thought of this, and I did not realize myself until I saw the congregation's behaviour. Nothing could be said or done now – it was too late. When Josh finished, so did the ceremony. Everyone went to pass their last wishes over Aunt Mamie in utter silence. The coffin was rolled out of the church into the graveyard where the grave was already dug, next to Moma's.

I was at ease as I stood alongside the grave. My feelings were not sharpened by sadness or anything until the preacher took a handful of dirt, scattered it over the coffin and said, 'Dust thou art and unto dust thou shalt return.' Then I suddenly realized, with swelling soul, that this was my only family, this was my only connection with a blood kin. Now I am completely alone. Now there is no one. 'Moma, Moma, Moma,' I cried inside. There were no tears. I envisioned the same picture I had seen at my mother's funeral, the sun rays coming through the trees. I remembered the dog at Aunt Rosa's house lying there as I swept the yard near the arch of roses, and a vision I once had of my mother's spirit walking with Pearl in her arms and me by the hand and returning to heaven with us. I felt the body of people around me, but I was with the spirit of my mother. 'Moma, Moma, how many times are you going to give me away?' my soul cried.

I did not know what had happened to Pearl. I did not know if Aunt Rosa was still alive. I did not know the whereabouts of Gracie and Willie. But the sight of them in my mind brought back the pain of every peach tree switch lash I had taken from them; the tying up in the crocker sack to my waist, the tying to a tree; the dare not to tell; my eating red and yellow clay I found on the roadside because I was so hungry; their finding out, having another reason to exercise their joy in whipping me. All these empty faces brought back the pain of rejection and abuse. Though some of them may not have been personally involved, this whole world to me had become a prison of rejection and abuse. Loving and living in church on Sundays, but practising something quite different at home – hypocrisy. Like Ethel Waters, who cussed us 'naked bitches' with her sailor's tongue and then went immediately into the wings to wash her mouth out with readings from her bible.

The morning we left my mother's sister's house, I went to a department store with her and bought school clothes, books, and all the etceteras, a couple of dresses for her and several cartons of groceries; I also left money for the bill for Aunt Mamie's funeral, including the preacher's fee. Just as Josh put me into the car and was about to drive off back to New York, I heard a voice say, 'Aren't you going to pay us?' I looked at my mother's sister for an explanation. She said nothing. 'She will take care of it all,' Josh chimed in, pointing to 'she' – who was me. Before a week had passed I received a bill stating I had not left any provisions for Aunt Mamie's funeral. Needless to say I had to pay it all over again. When I got back to the Waydes I was then hassled by Moma Wayde who said she was entitled to part of Aunt Mamie's insurance money because she had been her best friend. The insurance man, who called me to a meeting in his office, said he wanted to invest what was left, about ten thousand dollars or so after bills.

'You are a very young girl, Eartha, and there are those who know something has been left. They may try to get if from you if you are not careful,' he warned me.

There was a policy left with this insurance company in the form of an account left at a bank on 116th Street, and a policy at the New Yorker Hotel, where Aunt Mamie had worked as a maid. The lawyer made it possible for me to obtain the policy, and gave me a book of cheques. When he reluctantly handed me the cheque book with the amount written on it, he said, 'What are you going to do with it? Why don't you let me invest it for you?' My idea was to get a job in New York, the kind of job I had in Paris, or even to return there. Now I had enough money to do what I wanted, and Josh White to help me.

Moma Wayde harped on at me daily about bills she had to pay and how she was entitled to part of all I received from Aunt Mamie's insurance policies; so I gave her a cheque for twenty-five hundred dollars plus money for rent and food. Feeling I was in the way with the Waydes, I moved out and went to live with Moma Foster, the mother of the rehearsal garment girl from the days of the Dunham Company auditions. Mary Chase, Josh's manager, found out where I was and phoned me. She asked me to meet her at her apartment on Fifth Avenue. When I got there, Mary told me Josh had got into trouble with the Un-American Activities Committee. The one man who gave black artists work in his club was accused of being a communist. For what reason? No one knows. Mary Chase had advised Josh to say that Barnaby Conrad, the club owner, was a communist by association. Josh was called to Washington to be questioned by the McCarthy

Committee. When he said what Mary had told him to say, Josh was ostracized by everyone in showbusiness thereafter. Unable to get work in America, Josh had nothing but bills, bills, bills. His family was about to be evicted from their apartment, his children were having problems in school, and now Mary too had lost her source of income.

Only now do I realize how everything that happened fitted in with the pattern read by that clairvoyant in Paris. It was all about to come true. Remembering how good Josh had been to me when we were doing *Blue Holiday*, I handed Mary a cheque for the amount she asked for. As Mary told me more and more about Josh's problems, I felt more and more guilty about having anything and not using it to come to the rescue. I told her I also had money in a bank account in Los Angeles. She rubbed her hands and said, 'You must get on a plane right away and go get it.' Mary was the fair-haired woman the clairvoyant had warned me of.

The next day a ticket for an aeroplane that must have been refurbished after the war was put into my hands. Josh took me to the airport. This must have been the most horrendous flight in history. I was certain it was going to be my end; it was worse than the boat trip to England. Everyone was sick, and on top of that it took forever. This was my second time on an aeroplane, and I wished it were my last, but since I had been asked by Mary Chase to return to New York right away, I went to the bank, drew out every penny, closed the account, got on the next plane and flew back to New York again to be met by Josh.

I don't remember exactly how much I gave to Mary and Josh – the dark man and the fair-haired lady – but I had only enough left to buy a ticket back to Paris. Since the plane fare and the boat fare would be about the same, I decided to take the boat. 'You can take the *Queen Elizabeth* first class and have a great time. It only takes about a week,' Mary said. She also said she would arrange everything. I wanted to return to Paris where I knew I could always find work. Perhaps Le Perroquet was finished by now? I added up my last few pennies to pay my expenses at Moma Foster's. I had a ticket for the *Queen Elizabeth* and about five hundred dollars, until that was given to one of Josh's girlfriends at the Café Society who claimed she was pregnant with his child. With just enough to pay porters, cabs and the like, I boarded the *Queen Elizabeth* for France.

On entering my suite I found Mary Chase unpacking her things. 'I decided at the last minute to go with you,' she said. 'I hate to see such a young girl travelling around the world alone.'

I thought this suspicious but since it was already done it would have been foolish to argue. Since it was a double room I let it go. I don't know if Mary took enough money from me to pay for her ticket as well as mine.

Here I was again, the best-dressed pauper around. My days were spent in exercises and books, but the evenings were spent night-clubbing and dancing. People were very friendly, and mingled at each others' tables. Mary coaxed me into singing a song or two with the band at times. I did so reluctantly, but was very well received. Maybe Mary had used this as a way of getting a free ticket, since I was persuaded to perform at least three times. It was fun though, so I did not mind too much.

On our arrival in Paris, Mary said to the cab driver, 'Plaza Athenée'. I knew that the Plaza Athenée was one of the most expensive hotels in Paris, but I said nothing and went along. Everything had been arranged beforehand by Mary. We were taken to one of the largest suites in the hotel – a huge sitting room with a bedroom on each side. I was feeling very uncomfortable about all this, but relaxed a bit at the thought that I was back in Paris, and could be working at any time. I went to sleep with plans for my tomorrow: get in touch with my friends, find Hugh Shannon, call Fred at Carroll's and start where I left off.

I was awoken next morning by the phone ringing. 'Kitty, where have you been? We have been looking everywhere for you.'

12   Orson Welles

It was Jesse Hawkins on the phone, one of the Katherine Dunham singers who had decided to stay in Paris when the company left. I explained to him what had happened and that I had just returned the night before.

'You crazy girl,' said Jesse, 'Orson Welles has been looking for you.'

'Jesse, you're very funny. Why would Orson Welles be looking for me? He doesn't even know me,' I laughed, thinking it was all a joke.

'If you don't believe me, I'll pick you up in an hour and take you to the theatre where he is rehearsing.'

Jesse and I took a cab to the Edward VII Theatre. We were thrown out by the stage manager who said, 'No more casting! No more casting!'

'But Mr Welles wants to see her,' said Jesse. 'This is the girl he was looking for.'

'I don't care who he was looking for, no more casting,' the stage manager argued back.

Shame-faced I almost crawled out of the theatre in embarrassment, hearing the door slam behind me. Jesse found me standing on the sidewalk alone in front of the theatre. I had noticed a very swanky car with a man sitting in front. He had a black derby hat on and I think his hand was leaning on a walking stick or an umbrella. Jesse took me by the arm in silence as we walked away. Our rejected, slumped shoulders would have made even a bum feel sorry.

'Hey miss! Hey miss!' a voice was yelling, accompanied by the sound of running footsteps. 'Hey miss!' the voice kept yelling as the running footsteps came closer. Jesse and I turned around to see the derby-hatted man with the cane umbrella staring me in the face. 'I know the part of Helen of Troy has been cast, but your face is so beautifully interesting, I think Mr Welles would like to see you anyway,' the derby-hatted man said. He turned out to be Hilton Edwards. I had no idea who this was, but he certainly looked swank enough to be kosher. 'Mr Welles will be back in the theatre about three o'clock. Will you come back then?' the man asked.

Now I was scared, scared of being thrown out again; but with Jesse's encouragement we said yes and returned at about three p.m. after popping back to the hotel. When we told Mary Chase what had happened she decided to come along. Now I was really scared as I stood in front of what to me was the greatest giant-artist in the world – he was not only physically humungous but his personality was equal to his size. I felt as small as an ant about to be crushed in one move. Mr Edwards said, 'This is the little girl you were looking for, Orson. We found her.'

Orson took us to a small room at the top of the theatre where he sat me in the centre. He turned his back to me after handing me a script, which he had opened at a certain page. 'Read this,' he said. I read without even taking the time to look it over. I just read to his back, not knowing or asking why. I just read.

'I don't know what I am going to do,' said Orson as he turned around to look at me, 'I have given the part to Susan Clautier. But take the script and learn it. We open on Thursday.' He and Mr Edwards left the room.

Thursday! This was Monday already. My blood was steaming with excitement as I left the theatre with script in hand. Mary said nothing. As a matter of fact, even though she was there, I did not see her; I just felt her presence. Jesse took us back to the hotel. I was numb when I heard him say, 'The stage manager said to be at rehearsal tomorrow morning at ten.' I stayed up all night, learned the script, and went to rehearsal at ten a.m. the next day.

The cast was rehearsing a one-act piece written by Orson Welles, *The Unthinking Lobster*. It was a satire on the non-thinkers of Hollywood with Susan Clautier and Orson in the lead roles. Needless to say it was not complimentary in any form or fashion. Orson had no love for Hollywood and this was his way of saying so. I did not understand much of it since I had no knowledge of what Hollywood was really like, having only done *Casbah* in the chorus of the Dunham Company. Nor did I have any knowledge of Orson's problems in Hollywood after he made *Citizen Kane*, or of his Mercury Theatre episode when he scared America half to death with his radio show by telling the country it was being invaded by Martians; or of his filming of the poor living conditions for blacks in South America where he had been sent to film a loving diplomatic picture of how happy and good the situation was. Hollywood obviously wanted to hear no evil, see no evil, speak no evil, especially if they were paying for it. Hollywood thought Orson Welles was a difficult genius they could not put reins on. Since this was the case, life in Hollywood for Orson became very difficult, especially since he was not enamoured of hypocrisy. He was more in love with reality, though he used make-believe to show the unfairness of those in power, who had enslaved people to obtain and maintain that power.

As I sat in the theatre watching the rehearsal of *The Unthinking*

Lobster, I saw Susan Clautier going through the poses and watched Orson's direction. Susan Clautier was a beautiful, blonde-haired, blue-eyed French Canadian. How in the world could Orson take the part of Helen of Troy away from her? The rehearsal for *The Unthinking Lobster* finished and we went into *Faust*. The stage was being re-set when Susan Clautier came up to me. Oh God help me, I said to myself. I felt so embarrassed when I saw her coming. I didn't even know for sure if I had the part yet. They had been rehearsing for weeks now, she must know the part backwards.

It is not the most comfortable feeling in the world when a part has been taken from one and given to another. I remember when Josephine Premice arrived at the theatre too late when we were doing *Blue Holiday* and I was given her song since I was the overall replacement for the whole cast (except for the male parts). 'Kitty can do it,' was the theme in the company since I learned anything and everything by imitating people. I had felt so ashamed when Josephine walked in at the last minute to hear me rehearsing her 'Yellow Bird' in patois French, particularly as Josephine's family was from Haiti.

Here I sat with the same feeling running through me as Susan approached. 'I am so happy Orson gave you that part,' she said. 'I did not know what to do with it.' My heart was relieved. I don't know why she thought I would know what to do with it either, but my relief calmed me down. At that moment we were called on stage to start our part of the programme. A group of us (mostly teenagers) was directed to come through the audience on to the stage where a museum scene was depicted. Orson Welles, playing the part of Faust, and Hilton Edwards, playing the part of Mephistopheles, were to be found standing as statues in the museum while we students of history passed through. I played one of the students, a romantic who always fell in love with the heroes of history. I had to stop at the statue of Mephistopheles, become transfixed by his presence, walk to the side of the stage and sit down on an elevated position where a dim spotlight was to hit me. As the student goes into her romanticizing, dream-like state, a spotlight falls upon Orson and Hilton Edwards, who come to life as Faust and Mephistopheles and then walk downstage debating who is the most exciting woman in the world. And the play begins.

I asked Orson at one point in the rehearsal who this character was. What kind of woman is she? How old is she? 'Don't ask stupid questions, you stupid child,' Orson told me. 'I chose you to play this part because you are the most exciting woman in the world. You represent all women of all ages. You have no place or time.' This confused me more than ever so I just played myself. The rehearsal went without problems. Since I knew each and every line and cue, Orson and Mr Edwards were extremely satisfied by my quickness and rewarded me with dinner at Calabados, one of Orson's favourite restaurants.

We were met there by Michael McLiammoir. I sat like a leaf on a tree, surrounded by three of the world's most fascinating men – all great conversationalists, so I kept my mouth shut for the rest of the evening. This was usual for me since I was still not a great talker, realizing more and more that silence is really golden; one can very often learn so much with a closed mouth and open ears. In company such as this if you have something to say and you don't know how to say it, it's best not to, leaving them to feel that you are either intelligent because you didn't make an ass of yourself, or you are stupid because you didn't have anything to say. Leave them guessing as to which you are; it doesn't matter, because you will have learned so much, often more than was intended.

Orson ordered everything from soup to nuts, starting with an aperitif for everyone. Since I recognized my ignorance in this area I let them do all the ordering, come what may. The dinner started about seven p.m. and ended at about eleven. It was like having dinner with Henry the Eighth. I can say for sure that Orson enjoyed good living. He not only ate what was on his plate but took some of what was on everyone else's too. There must have been at least six courses, all of which were consumed while the men recited great speeches from the classics and stories of themselves at different points in their lives.

One of the stories was of how they met. It seems Orson went to Ireland at the age of nineteen or twenty. His love for the theatre took him to the Gaiety Theatre in Dublin, where he found the owners Michael McLiammoir and Hilton Edwards. Orson convinced them that he was a great American actor, with a great American name, and that they should hire him – which they did. It turned out to be good for all concerned, so they remained friends forever.

I was supremely happy, listening to them and watching them enjoy themselves through their past experiences. Each would take a speech from Shakespeare, Marlowe, Goethe or some other classic, and sometimes a whole act was performed with the three of them taking on all the characters. The evening ended with brandy and a cigar before they took me home. The next few days we were in the theatre all day and part of the night, sometimes with just Orson and me staying on to paint the scenery. Very often Orson directed the others through the assistant director, saying, 'That person is too stupid for me to talk to. Will you please tell her . . .' Usually it was Janet Wolfe, whom I used to laugh with till my sides burst because she was so naturally funny, but Orson was not amused.

These few days of rehearsals brought an extremely warm relationship between Orson and myself, sharing dinner, maybe lunch, at Calabados with Hilton or sometimes with a few members of the cast, or just the four of us – Hilton, Michael, Orson and me. Then all three of them would walk me home along the Champs Elysées. We opened to a star-studded audience of French, American and British artists and were a great success. I was now known in Paris not only as a singer and dancer but also as an actress. I was nominated the best foreign actress in Paris that year (1950, I think).

This was a limited engagement of six weeks. Hilton Edwards did four weeks and returned to Ireland, leaving Michael McLiammoir to take the part of Mephistopheles. I had become so popular in Paris now that no one wanted to approach me for other engagements for fear that I would be too expensive. I did not think of this. I still had no idea what I really wanted to do with myself or where I wanted to go. I was having fun becoming a someone and was earning good money (though I was only paid three hundred dollars a week with Orson, half of what Carroll's paid me. But since there were three hundred and fifty francs to one dollar, I was still okay.)

The joy of having such success and being wined and dined by Orson Welles was rich enough for me; the thrill of Orson walking me to the Plaza Athenée along the Champs Elysées after dining nightly at the Calabados, often in the haunting spell of a rising sun when Paris was really in her glory of beauty – her silent awakening when she was most romantic. I could feel her, I could sense her wooing, her desire to be loved, her beckoning to make love, but don't stay too long. Paris may be a lady of the night, but she is most soft and gentle at dawn when she pulls the covers of night away after making love, caressing you gently at first then shooing you away to prepare herself to fight the long day of hustling for survival. Then the subtle sun sets over her beauty, beckoning to another lover. Paris always gave me the feeling of wanting to take everything you have: she will tease you into making love with her, but won't let you stay too long; she gets irritated very easily if you don't empty your pockets and leave. Though I enjoyed Paris and her help in moulding me in so many ways to become Eartha Kitt, I was always a bit uneasy, waiting for the day when I felt it was time to leave.

I was not seeing much of Mary Chase, but she was still there when Josh White suddenly turned up. Mary then tried to talk me into getting Fred, the owner of Carroll's, to give Josh an engagement there. I myself was still on reserve for Le Perroquet and was not allowed by Fred, with whom I had made a verbal agreement, to take an engagement in any other Parisian club. Le Perroquet was still being built. One night during the performance of *Faust*, Josh was seen sitting in the front row with Mary.

In my character as the history student I sat in my dimmed spotlight, just enough for me to be seen but not enough to distract from the scene being played by Orson and Hilton. The light came up on me as Faust said, 'Is this the face that launched a thousand ships?' The student then walks to Faust who takes her in his arms saying, 'Helen, make me immortal with a kiss.' He kisses her. On this occasion he was holding me so tight I could hardly breathe. My back was to the audience when the kiss turned into a crunch as Orson drew blood like a vampire from my bottom lip.

Orson Welles was not too happy with the response I constantly received from the audience at curtain calls, or from the critics. Though it surprised me, I also thought that when Orson had seen Josh White in the front row, he became annoyed at the thought that we might be lovers, and bit me in anger. I was no more a lover of Josh White's than I was of Orson's. There was a love affair going on between Orson and me, a bit like that which I had shared with Rubirosa, but it was not sexual. The most exciting men in my life have been the men who have never taken me to bed. One can lose a great friend by going to bed with them. Perhaps this is very often why we marry the wrong person – maybe we had sex with our best friend and not the lover; or we married the lover and not the best friend. At any rate, one can screw up one's life through having sex, and the broken pieces can never be put back together. So perhaps the best thing to do is not to have sex with an intellectual friend. Then again, what good is sex if you have no one to talk to after? Perhaps the two could go together? I doubt it. Maybe this is why Orson said I was the most exciting woman in the world, as he was never given a chance to find out how unexciting I might have been in bed. In silence I kept him and Rubirosa guessing.

Anyway, the curtain came down on Orson holding me in his arms tighter than ever as he kissed me harder than ever with his teeth in my bottom lip; I could not budge. When the curtain fell, Orson ran offstage right and I went stage left with just enough time to grab an apron and return on stage with it as I sang, 'Hungry little trouble, damned in a bubble, yearning to be, be or be free . . . All that you see, is all about me, hungry me . . .' (words by Orson, music by Duke Ellington). The blood was running down my chin, my mouth was swelling up, rendering it almost impossible to get the words out. I felt my mouth dribbling, but did not believe it could be blood. I took the end of the apron to wipe whatever I was feeling dribbling down my chin while still singing. Blood spattered on the corner of the white apron, and the sight of it brought on the pain as my eyes translated to my brain that I was wounded. The whole play thereafter consisted of me profiling myself to the audience as I dabbed with the apron and felt my mouth swelling up more and more. But the play went on.

When the final curtain came down the bows seemed to go on forever. I had a feeling Orson would dart away as quickly as he could, and he did. I ran to his dressing room and caught him just before he could get inside and close the door. The cast were hysterical as they watched this five-feet-two-inches-tall creature pound Orson on his giant-size humungous chest, her feet rising off the floor as she demanded, 'Why did you bite me?'

Orson took both my hands in his and picked me up till my feet were off the floor again, saying 'I got excited.'

We all laughed, but Josh came through the corridor, saw this, looked at my swollen face and asked, 'What happened?' While we were still laughing, Orson quickly went into his dressing room and closed the door. Josh, Mary and I went back to my dressing room but when I told Josh what had happened, he dashed off cussing through the corridor towards Orson's room shouting 'I'll beat the s____ out of that son-of-a-bitch!' Josh calmed down quite easily when he realized that Orson was at least twice his size.

Our limited engagement was played out with Orson very often moving in front of me whenever I had something to say. It must have been a strange performance for the audience to watch as I had to dodge Orson on stage in order to be seen. Though it was hectic at times with Orson covering me up, I had a lot of fun trying to out-trick his mischievousness.

We took *Faust* on the road. Our first stop was Germany, where we were billed as 'An Evening With Orson Welles'. The first half was *Faust*, with Orson, Michael and me. Intermission. Then Orson had planned a peanut concert with me doing a few songs before he was to come back doing a scene from *Richard III* ! His make-up and hunchback for this part sometimes took longer than usual and I would have to adlib another song or two until he was standing by ready. I wrote two songs for this spot. Since we took a pianist along with us (Sandy), we were both prepared to be on as long as it took Orson to ready himself. I wore a gold and silver striped slinky dress and very high gold and silver slippers. The outfit, given to me by Balenciaga, was enough on its own to make one stand up and take notice. As I was leaving the stage in the centre fold of the curtain which was dropped behind me, Orson would often push me back from behind saying, 'Get back out there, heffa! Can't you see they want you?'

I adored Orson, in spite of himself. For all his unkind treatment of me he was still a great guy. I might have been overwhelmed by who he was, by his talent as an actor, by his overall personality – who knows? But I was also afraid of him: I never knew what he was going to do next, on stage or off. After Paris he started acting a bit strange – or stranger –

making me more and more nervous, but I took everything as a joke which I am sure kept me from going completely batty. The more I laughed at or ignored his pranks, the more he became confused by me and the more angry he became, fuelling himself up to play more pranks.

There were lots of American army personnel in Germany at that time. An American newspaper critic had said, 'Orson may think it's an evening with Orson Welles, but it's really an evening with Eartha Kitt.' That almost buried me. Though we were staying in the same hotel across the hall from each other, Orson would not acknowledge me if we happened to come out of our rooms at the same time. If we were by chance in the breakfast room together, he would pretend not to see me. If we were invited to a cocktail party at the request of the theatre management, to Orson I was invisible. I could not figure out why he was behaving like a seven-year-old boy, but I thought it would pass. What did I do to anger him? There was nothing I could put my finger on that put me at fault, so I tried to ease my discomfort by letting it go without questioning it.

We went on to Belgium, a very successful trip. The last night there some of us were called to Orson's room for a closing night dinner: the usual Dom Pérignon and Beluga caviar, soup-to-nuts-type Orson Welles dinner. I slept haphazardly that night, excited to think that he was no longer angry with me, that I had come through so well. The next day I got a message to go on to Rome. A ticket and instructions came with the message. I was to take a plane to Rome where a car would meet me to take me to Lake Como where Orson would be waiting. The company was to go on to Rome too, I supposed. I did not see any of them as I was leaving.

When I got to the hotel in Lake Como it struck me as very fancy for a little schnook like me. Why was Orson giving me all this? I was greeted with great cordiality by the management as I walked into my room. It was a suite large enough for the whole company to stay in. Flowers were everywhere and 'Eartha Kitt' was written on every bunch; even the huge bathroom was covered in roses, gardenia, orchids and the like. I thought perhaps Rubirosa had appeared on the scene. Not a sign of Orson. He's probably here but busy, I figured. I made myself comfortable and waited for a call or something to happen. Nothing happened. Four days later and still no Orson. I went rowing on the lake, I walked around the hotel gardens, read, slept, ate, dozed, and wondered. No Orson.

I was very much into Agatha Christie, my favourite mystery writer along with Edgar Allan Poe. So I sank into my comfortable eiderdown pillows and comforter with one of her novels. I think I was at this hotel about a week before I was called to Orson's room – a beautifully

decorated suite to fit a king. A dinner table was set for two with Dom
Pérignon champagne and Beluga caviar on ice. Flowers were in the
centre and Orson was on the balcony overlooking the gardens. A waiter
was standing behind a chair waiting for me to be seated. I sat, and
waited for Orson to come into the room. When he finally did, he just sat
opposite me saying nothing. I made no move, waiting for him to move
first. I watched him as he picked up a spoon and started the dinner.
Before I followed him, I waited for him to speak.

'They have cancelled our engagement here,' Orson said softly and
slowly. There was nothing for me to say as he continued, 'The producer
ran off with the money.'

I was not surprised to hear him say this, because the whole time I was
alone waiting I had a suspicious feeling. Orson handed me an envelope
when the dinner was finished with a ticket to return to Paris. 'This
envelope contains vital information,' Orson said. 'Hand it over to
the manager at the Edward VII Theatre personally. Guard it with
your life.'

He opened the door of the suite to let me out, saying, 'Guard it with
your life.' I went to my room feeling like Mata Hari, wondering what
this envelope contained. I was now part of a mystery, an Agatha
Christie mystery. I gathered my things up to pack in great anticipation
of an exciting trip back to Paris on the Berlin express, the mystery train.
My ticket was for a sleeper, first class all the way. I put the envelope in
my handbag. 'Guard it with your life,' rang in my ears the whole time.

At the station, the porter took my bags and placed them neatly away.
I stood watching him, holding on with dear life to my handbag. When
the porter left my compartment I removed the envelope and put it under
my pillow in case someone should try and steal it in the night. If my bags
were searched, the envelope would not be found. I thought of all the
mysteries I had read, and expected something to happen at any
moment. When the night porter came knocking on my compartment
door I pretended to be asleep. It seemed to me the best way to protect my
precious cargo was to remain in my compartment sleeping until the
train arrived in Paris.

It was about eleven or twelve at night when suddenly the train
stopped in the middle of nowhere. 'Passports please!' I heard a man's
voice saying. 'Passports! Passports!' I sneaked a peek through the
curtains at the window. I could see nothing but lights flashing everywhere. A knock came on my door: 'Passports! Passports!' I knew I could
not pretend to sleep through this, I had to show my passport. I got
scared. Why would they stop the train in the middle of nowhere and ask
our passports? They are coming for the envelope. I was sure. The knock
came again as I remained still and silent. What would I do if they

searched my suitcases and did not find the envelope? Would they take me along with them? 'Passports!' I heard again.

The porter must have opened my door with his master key since three or four men in uniforms stood looking at me. Thank goodness I had put my silk nightgown on just in case. I pulled myself up to ask what all the commotion was about and why we had stopped in the middle of nowhere. Then I saw the guns slung over the shoulders of the uniformed men. They were army men, they had ammunition. Now I became more scared and more nervous. The envelope was on my mind. That is what they really want, I thought, but I did not dare show tension. My handbag was at the foot of the bunk. I reached for it and searched for my wallet that contained my passport. At a time like this, of course, one can never find what one is looking for. When the wallet was finally to hand, I gingerly passed it to them, thinking they would look at it, clear me and go on their way. But when they closed the door, they took my passport with them. Now I was sure I was the reason the train had stopped in the middle of nowhere. I waited nervously, looking out the window. Now not only were flashlights scouring the vicinity but a huge fire was burning in the distance. A lot of fuss was going on around the train; men in uniforms were running around the carriages and even searching underneath them.

I did not want to open my compartment door for fear someone might force himself in either to get me, or the envelope, or to hide. I remained still but a nervous wreck. I just knew I would never reach Paris. My hands went under the pillow to check the safety of whatever I was hiding. 'Guard this with your life,' I could still hear Orson saying. I might just have to, I feared. The train must have stood in one place for hours with everyone lingering in the aisles and looking out the windows. I could hear the grumblings of the passengers as they questioned the mystery of the stopped train.

'Someone planted a bomb on the tracks,' we heard a uniformed man tell the passengers as he went to and fro returning our passports. An anonymous telephone call had saved the train and perhaps its passengers from being blown into oblivion.

The train screeched off and arrived at the Gare du Nord in Paris. I took a taxi straight to the Edward VII Theatre, found the manager in his office and handed him my hot possession with great relief to be getting it off my hands. The manager thanked me with a smile from ear to ear, not explaining anything about the envelope. I asked no questions.

Two days later, the headlines in the French newspapers ran: 'Orson Welles declares all Germans to be Nazis.'

13 Ad-libbing

Now out of work, I moved into a small hotel near the Champs Elysées and got a room with bath and balcony at seven hundred francs a day. Thank goodness the *petit déjeuner* was enough for me to survive on – two very large *café-au-laits*, two croissants, a large slab of sweet butter, marmalade and strawberry jam. I am sure this *petit déjeuner* saved my life, since I now had no money at hand. My three hundred dollars was just enough to pay the expenses I had incurred with Orson, and I was still sending what I could to Josh White and Mary Chase who had returned to America and were constantly calling me for money.

Then I got sick. I had broken out in spots that did not hurt but itched very annoyingly. Philippe, whom I had met at some point along the way, found me and took me to the American Hospital where I was told my X-rays showed I had polio. I did not believe the chart and told them so.

'You must believe the chart, Miss Kitt, it does not lie,' said a doctor.

'Well, I don't,' I said. 'I refuse to have polio. I was pretty ill as a child with whooping cough and pneumonia but I would never have polio.' I was right. The hospital called me a few days later to say they had read the wrong chart. I was ill, but they had no explanation of why or what it was.

As well as being covered in spots, I was bleeding very badly and soon I had lost so much blood I could hardly get out of bed. I lay in my hotel room for weeks, not having enough strength to do anything. Philippe came daily, bringing food and forcing me to eat. The spots spread all over my body, starting on my legs, moving over my thighs and then creeping up my body, getting more and more intrusive. No one could explain the illness to me; the doctors were lost for a diagnosis so they wrote it off as a nervous condition.

Bayeux came back to Paris and found me through friends. He had been called home to go on a three-month yacht trip with his family. He returned with a pocket full of money so he was able to take over looking after me when Philippe was called to Korea as a newspaper reporter. Bayeux bathed my body daily with slices of lemon. The spots gradually went away and in about six weeks or so I was on my feet again, though still rather weak. With the medicines and proper food Bayeux had bought, his pocket full of money went rather fast.

I was still on hold for the new club, Le Perroquet, but I had received no word from Fred and her brother as to when it was going to open. My money had run out, the hotel bill was mounting and there was no way of saving face when passing the hotel desk and the concierge. My embarrassment at owing so much money forced me to do something.

Bayeux had moved into my room to nurse me back to health. He always spent half the morning in the bath tub. I never knew why he took so long sitting in a hot tub of water but this was his main pastime. Bayeux was from a very wealthy American family and was cautious when his mother was in Paris to be sure that she was not made aware of my presence in his life. As a matter of fact, Bayeux, Jane Russell and I had a photo taken together on one of Jane's visits there. When I saw this photo some years later at his mother's house in Santa Barbara, on her desk, I had been cut out. When Mrs Kelloge, Bayeux's mother, got to know me she admitted she regretted having done this. She had by that time become displeased with the wife Bayeux had chosen and decided I would have been better for him. I don't think she would have objected that much to me in the beginning, but Bayeux decided not to take any chances in complicating things when his mother visited Paris. So I became invisible.

Bayeux was trying not to rock the boat as he waited impatiently for his mother's inheritance. Mrs Kelloge was on her third husband, I believe, a Mr Baker, who was Bayeux's stepfather. Bay said his stepfather paid him to stay in Paris away from home – perhaps because Mr Baker was jealous of him, Bay being as handsome as he was and, it was my impression, Mama Kelloge's favourite son. Bayeux had a love-hate relationship with his mother. She must have been a real beauty and had vast riches which, according to Bay, she never really shared with them. He talked about all the paintings and worldly goods sitting or hanging in the house and all the land that could be sold and shared among them but which his mother hoarded. She probably thought Bayeux would drink it all up the same as Bayeux thought she was doing. His annoyance at all this made him drink more.

I adored Bayeux. He was intelligent and extremely funny. The more he drank, the funnier he became. Politics was his favourite subject; the situations politicians put the people in were so ludicrous to him they should all be got rid of. No matter what country or ruler, to Bay they were all idiots and puppets. Everything to him was seriously funny. I was interested in Bay not only sexually but in his intelligence and humour, which made him all the more exciting. He had become to me the Orson

Welles and Rubirosa that I had experienced intellectually and culturally but not sexually. With them it was an intellectual intercourse which was extremely exciting in itself – a kind of excitement that I did not want to be screwed up with the actual sex act itself. You really take a tremendous chance when you have a sexual affair with someone you enjoy being with so much; with someone who is witty and charming and who you never tire of being with. Sex can kill it and the relationship is very often never the same again. Better to stay guessing rather than take this dangerous chance. But in this case, I never lost interest: Bayeux was everything – a good sex partner, and a witty, charming, considerate, gentle man – except for the time when he tried to drown me in the bath tub in South America having had one too many, but that's another story.

Since I had to do something about my financial status, I decided to force Fred and her brother either to pay my expenses and living costs or give me freedom to accept other contract offers. Although I was still in a very weak state, I got dressed up in my finest finery with a brown suede coat trimmed in fur and a brown suede shirt-like dress to match, suede high heels, make-up to kill, and my hair rolled in curls on an upsweep. Bayeux took me to Carroll's about four in the afternoon when we knew Fred and her brother would be in getting ready for the night's show. We walked in. I had now worked myself up into a fury. Fred was wandering around the bar upstairs when I found her.

'Fred, we have to talk,' I said. I would have called her by her last name but I never knew it – to everyone she was just 'Fred'. Fred who was always dressed like a man but with a skirt. I knew she was a lesbian but since she was so beautiful I did not want to admit it. To me such a beautiful woman should never waste herself or deny herself the pleasure of a man. Maybe she did both – I don't know and I did not want to know.

Fred and I sat down at a table where I told her my problem. 'Fred, I have no money now and I must find work. I cannot wait for Le Perroquet to open any longer; it's been months now,' I almost cried. My back was against the wall, forcing me to show my claws.

'*Attendez, Kitt,*' said Fred, '*Il faut pas être fâché.*'

'I am not angry,' I said, 'I am hungry and can't pay my hotel bill.' I was trying to stay angry.

'*Mon frère, il est dans le bureau, parlez avec lui,*' Fred said, going towards her brother's office. Bayeux and I waited, with him getting more nervous by the minute.

Fred's brother came into the bar saying, in English, 'Kitt, you must be patient. Le Perroquet is opening, but you know how French builders are – they are very slow and we have no control over them.'

'You have no control over me either.' I raised myself from my chair as I said this, getting really keyed up.

'Only a week or so more, I promise you . . .' the brother said, trying to calm me down.

'How can you promise me when you just said you have no control over the builders?'

'Yes, but . . .' the brother tried to go on.

Before he could make up something to appease me with, I rapidly pulled off my beautiful suede fur-trimmed coat and flung it across the bar, knocking over everything in its way, to Bayeux's and Fred's and her brother's surprise – and mine.

'No! I don't want any more promises. I will give you two more weeks for Le Perroquet to open or I am accepting offers,' I said, *very* calmly. 'Then too, my hotel bill is now over ten thousand francs. I would like it to be paid and another ten thousand to live on, and if Le Perroquet is not open in two weeks, all my expenses are on you. Now I would like it all in hand before I leave here: ten thousand francs for my hotel bill and ten thousand france to live on, please!'

I was calm and precise, my words were clear and steady. I stood firm and majestic, and Bayeux had another drink. Fred's brother returned to his office and came back with ten thousand francs for my hotel bill and ten thousand francs to live on and ten thousand francs just in case; and Le Perroquet opened in two weeks.

I opened to a star-studded audience. Anyone who was anyone was there, including Rita Hayworth and the Ali Khan. I had received a completely new wardrobe from Jacques Fath, who adored my body. Jacques told me he would have liked me to be one of his models, but unfortunately I was not tall enough. Through him I could have, for nothing, any clothes that he couldn't sell. This evening I had a white silk satin dress trimmed with egret feathers, with a matching coat. Shoes made especially for me by Perugia were paid for by Fred and her brother. A Hollywood-type dressing room was built and decorated especially for the 'café-au-lait vedette', as Fred called me. I had prepared a new act of Spanish, French and American songs with the help of the Cuban band leader and Hugh Shannon.

This was my first time singing 'C'est Si Bon' in Paris. In my nervousness at such an important opening, and realizing how many VIPs there were, I forgot the lyrics and ad-libbed practically the whole song. It became so funny the audience could not stop laughing. I am laughing to this day since that ad-lib is what remained, was recorded by RCA and won five gold medal recording awards. I don't get any royalties for the ad-lib.

The opening night was extremely successful. Again the critics received me as 'the best thing that has happened in Paris in twenty-five years'. I was on my feet again. Now I was recognized as the great café-au-lait dancer-singer-actress, and my popularity began to spread to other countries. The clairvoyant's prediction of a third body of water seemed to come true when I was invited to return to New York, but I was too scared to accept the offer. I had been away from America now too long to know what America was all about. So when Mr Marouani suddenly came back on the scene (presumably forgetting his threat) and offered me a contract in Istanbul, I accepted it. My contracts were becoming for me not only a means of earning a living but also a way of getting the education I had never had.

I only played about a month at Le Perroquet because Fred said she wanted me to be the 'special artist' for the club. It would be Eartha Kitt's home base. I would only be there from time to time on rare occasions, perhaps three times a year, and I was to be paid three times my starting salary. This was a hell of a lot of money to me, handed over each night in a no-agent, no-tax envelope.

I would have liked to return to America, as there *is* no place like home, but there was really no place for me to return to in America. I no longer knew America. I had no family now and only God knew where all my friends had gone; and I don't think I felt friendship towards anyone of real value at that time anyway. I was always a loner and now I was, with Aunt Mamie gone, really alone. There was no family tie of any kind, no one to tell me where and where not to go or what and what not to do. I was a free spirit to do as I pleased – no one to answer to so no one to hurt.

Istanbul? Arabian Nights? I'll go. An exciting new culture to experience. I was given a round-trip ticket to the strange world of Turkey. *Always* have a round-trip ticket. I left Bayeux in Paris and took the plane to one of, if not *the* most fascinating country in this world.

14 'Usku Dara'

To see Istanbul from the air with all the fascinating mosques and strange-looking buildings was like a scene from *Arabian Nights*; it felt like we were a flying carpet of passengers floating over the city. On my arrival I was met by the owner of the Karavansari, Mr Omar Kibar, and his assistant, who took me to a modern hotel where I was to stay. The Nicholas brothers, who had been working at the Karavansari for some time, were waiting to greet me in the lobby. After a warm welcome, I was taken to my very humble room where I bathed, unpacked and dressed to be taken to the club to see the Nicholas brothers' show.

I sat on the upstairs balcony with Mr Kibar and his friends and watched as Harold and Fayard Nicholas got a fantastic reception. I wondered if it would be the same for me. I did not have to open for some days. It is always better to rest after a journey before delving deep into anything, if possible; I was lucky in this case that the management felt the same way. In the meantime, on the days I was free, I was sleeping most of the time (regretfully – I have always felt extremely guilty when wasting any hours of the day sleeping). Since I knew no one and the Nicholas brothers were not to be seen until late afternoon, I found nothing to do but stay in my room, waiting for something to happen. If I wanted to do something I was told by Mr Kibar to call the Karavansari and he would send someone to help me, but I was too shy to call, and too shy to wake up Harold or Fayard, so I waited meekly. When it was time for the Nicholas brothers to go to work, I was invited to go along with them and have dinner at the club and I gratefully accepted. This went on for about a week, until the time came for Harold and Fayard's last show and their departure from Istanbul.

I went along to the airport with them. Harold and Fayard were talking to me as the customs men went through their luggage. 'Where did you buy this?' asked one of the customs men. Neither of them knew what to say, so they looked at each other and then at me, like a scene from a classic Hollywood comedy, as the man said, 'Do you have a receipt for this?' The brothers produced the receipt. The customs man took it, along with the diamond rings they had bought for their girlfriends or wives or whatever back home – never to be seen again.

The game was apparently this: the American (or whatever foreigner) was asked, when buying jewellery or other valuables in Istanbul, to produce his or her return plane ticket and passport number. The salesman would then call the airport customs, telling them the plane information and passport number. The customs people would be on the lookout for the passenger appearing and they would then confiscate the jewellery, give it back to the salesman and split the money.

Fayard looked at me and said, 'Oh well, easy come easy go.' We laughed, but were cut short when they informed us you could not take Turkish money out of the country. If you have any on you, you must hand it over. Fayard and Harold looked at each other, then turned to me: 'Open your handbag, Kitt.' With that they emptied their pockets and wallets into my handbag, dropping about six-hundred-dollars-worth of Turkish money into it, laughing as Fayard said to the man, 'I'll be damned if you make a fool of me twice.' I bade them goodbye and watched them go through the gates, returning to a world we knew more of.

Since I had no money of my own, this was like a gift from heaven. I took a cab to return to the city. With so much money in my hands I had a burning desire to go shopping. I asked the driver (in German – he spoke no English) to take me to the shopping area. When I saw a department store that interested me I stopped the cab, got out, let him take some money from my opened hand for the fare, and went into the department store. I bought a very Turkish-looking blouse, jacket and shirt. As I was paying I noticed a crowd of people gathering outside. I did not take much notice, except to think someone important must be nearby. The important someone was me. When I tried to leave the store the ooohs and aahhs made me cringe; old people were bowing in front of me; some of the people were trying to touch me; the hem of my skirt was grabbed, lifted and kissed; some were reaching to touch my hair that was in curls, forming a French-style bun in an upsweep. My long thin earrings which dangled to my shoulders were snatched – thank God they were only clip-ons.

The crowd got thicker as I tried to push my way through in search of a cab. The manager of the department store came out to help me. At times like these, of course, there is never a cab or a policeman in sight. An American-style car stopped and its owner came through the crowd, took me by the arm, put me in his car and drove me to the hotel. Along the way he explained that the crowd thought I was the beautiful Egyptian princess they read had come to Istanbul. They were fascinated by my colour and my style of dressing – I was the most beautiful thing they had ever seen, but they were confused as to why I was alone. I did not know that young girls were not allowed to go out alone; it is considered sinful. My rescuer was virtually the only American in all of Istanbul; he was there checking on the problem of the water system. He dropped me off at my hotel telling me never to go out on my own. 'You must be escorted,' he said, 'by a man, a big man.' With this he was gone, only to be seen at times in the bar at the Karavansari.

My call for rehearsal was at about four p.m. the next day. Mr Kibar's assistant picked me up. I rehearsed and opened at midnight. The room was filled with Turkish VIPS, and it was the noisiest crowd I had ever experienced; no one listened, all were blabbing, eating, laughing and drinking. It was also the most embarrassing experience: my chic Parisian Jacques Fath gown of white silk satin got wetter and wetter by the second from nervous tension. The louder the crowd got, the softer I sang. After six or seven songs I ran off stage in tears, heading for the nearest exit. Mr Kibar was standing in front of the exit I had chosen for my escape, the door firmly closed behind him.

'I am sorry, Mr Kibar, they don't like me. You don't have to pay me, just send me back to Paris,' I begged through my tears.

'Are you mad?' asked Mr Kibar. 'You get back on that stage, they love you,' he boasted.

'But they are all talking, they're not listening,' I cried.

'When they don't talk, that's when you are in trouble. They are saying how beautiful you are and are translating what you are singing. Get back on stage!'

I did, and finished my hour-long programme.

Now I was a big hit in Istanbul but had no one to share it with. The next morning I tried to call Bayeux in Paris. It took three days to get through. In the meantime, Mr Kibar ordered a bodyguard to be at my beck and call – the most handsome Turk you'd ever want to see (he was also one of the bartenders). I was in my hotel room all day every day until I was called for by the bodyguard who drove me to the Karavansari about five or six p.m.

There were very few cars in Turkey at this time. Very often we had problems getting through with a vehicle because the Turkish farmers would squat in the middle of the road with their camels and donkeys, blocking the way, eating, drinking and shooing the cars away. They were rebelling against the progressive modern 'civilization' invading their country. I thought it was fun. I can't say I blamed them either: I came from a primitive world so I enjoyed their rebellion. I too have not seen much civility in this 'progress'. I wanted to squat with them, but it was not the done thing, according to my bodyguard. We drove through alley-ways dodging the banana peels, coconut shells and stones that the Turkish farmers sometimes threw at the car.

My days were boring, but the nights were fun. Meeting the important people of Turkey was very interesting. I never knew who we were going to have dinner with from night to night. Mr Kibar introduced me to a very attractive lady whom we dined with one night. She invited me to her home for a visit and lunch.

'We are told no one can ever learn our language,' she said to me over Turkish coffee, 'It's a very strange language, but I think it's mostly because people are lazy that they don't bother to try,' she went on. 'Are you lazy, Kitt?'

I was stumped for a reply. I took my coffee and walked around the room looking at the art objects, her beautiful collection of paintings, her plants, the marbled floors and mosaic walls, the chandeliers, trying to avoid answering. The lady followed me, noticing my interest in this museum-like house and its antiques. She started telling me about the house's history and the objets d'art.

'Are you a lazy child?' she asked again. I did not know how to reply to this. 'If you are not lazy, Kitt, I could teach you a Turkish song, a very simple one. It's an old one, must be over a hundred years old. Everyone knows it. I could teach it to you. That is, if you are not lazy. And you can put it in your show tomorrow night.'

Sweat came to my forehead, my knees weakened, my throat dried. 'Tomorrow night?' I asked, sipping my coffee.

'Yes, it's simple. You will surprise the people. We won't let anyone know; you will just burst into it without any announcement.'

'But I'll have to rehearse it with the pianist,' I argued.

'No, if you rehearse it with him he'll tell. We can't take that chance. I will teach it to you, you'll just start singing it. Since he knows it, whichever key you start in, he will join in. Surprise, surprise!'

I adored this lady. She was very comfortable to be with, no pressure. But she had now pushed me into a challenge. 'I'd better start cooking the dinner,' she said out of nowhere. 'My husband, the admiral, will be coming home soon on one of his rare visits. He spends more time on his ship than he does with me. Sometimes I think he loves that ship more than me.'

We both went into the very elaborately modernized but still old-fashioned kitchen. I helped her when I could as she taught me the song.

When I got about half-way through my show the next evening and felt confident enough, I stilled myself in a moment of silence to get my nerves together:

'Usku dara girdirdirikin, al de da beria mur,
Usku dara girdirdirikin, al de da beria mur.
Kia te bemin bin kia tibin, ele kara sur,
Kia te bemin set te reze uzen, ete eir sharmur . . .'

The pianist shakily followed me in the same key, then joined in the singing. I was grateful for his help. When I had sung the whole song through – at least, as much as I had been taught – the audience joined in with laughter and clapping to the beat. The applause was tremendous and I ended up laughing my head off in nervous pride. This was another dare – a Turkish dare. The admiral's wife came every night to hear me sing my Turkish song about a little town adjacent to Istanbul where in the olden days the women used to woo their men along the banks of the Bosphorus. Now I became even more popular with the Turkish people; to them I really was a princess.

I was free on Sundays, and on one of these days off my bodyguard took me to visit his sister at her summer house on an island in the Bosphorus. My bodyguard was handsome and a gentleman of good manners and courtesy, but this Sunday he drank a lot. So much so that on our return he drove the car off the ferry, went about five or six blocks, stopped at a red light and passed out over the steering wheel. No matter how much I tried to wake him, he went further and further down, down, down, slumping more and more into a limp nothing. I pushed and shoved and shoved and pushed, trying to pull him back to life, but he was out like a light. The traffic lights turned green and the car stood still. The lights turned red. I pushed and shoved, and my bodyguard slumped even more. Four men who were gathered on the opposite corner started walking towards the car. I could not drive. Besides, my bodyguard's body was now slumped under the steering wheel and could not be moved. 'No young girl, especially a pretty one, should be out alone . . .' I remembered. My first thought was to lock the doors. Now at least they can't get in. What if they break the windows? Oh God, please help me.

I managed to crawl into a position on the opposite side of the bodyguard where with my whole weight I could push him to the other side of the car. I pushed and shoved until his body made enough room for me to get behind the wheel. Now what do I do? Mother where are you? God please help me! The key was in the ignition. I turned it, and the engine started. I put my foot on whatever there was to put one's foot on. Nothing. Now Eartha, the thing you put your foot on at first did not make the car move, so it must be the other thing. I was mumbling and muttering to myself. The four men were getting closer. You better make this car move, Eartha, or you're in a lot of trouble. I was thinking fast. The light turned green, the men were closer, maybe not more than four feet away. I pictured myself being dragged from the car and taken to some secluded harem, never to be seen again; or worse, be found on the sidewalk with blood strewn everywhere, unrecognizable except for my passport (perhaps even that would never be found). It was in my handbag. 'Never go anywhere without your passport.' The words and pictures flowed through my head like notes on a piano roll. If I did get this thing started, how in the world would I stop it? Get it started and worry about that later. The light turned red. Never mind the light, go, for God's sake go!

The car shot from its position like an arrow from a bow, going through red light and all. The men's hands were left flailing in the empty air as they tried to make a grab for the car. Around the bend the car went, jolting to a halt and leaving my heart in my mouth. I thanked the gods, my mother, and even the devil in my happiness to have escaped. Afterwards I thought that maybe those men had been coming to see if I needed help. Still, better not to have chanced it. I was thinking back over the whole event when my bodyguard lifted his limp body into a normal position and asked, 'What happened?' I did not bother to explain that I had had only five seconds to learn how to drive. He would not have believed me anyway, so I let it go.

My engagement at the Karavansari was to be for two weeks. As the two weeks were drawing to an end, I started psyching myself up to return to Paris. When I finally got the phone call through to Bayeux he said he was waiting for me, that he missed me, so to hurry up. I was pleased that Bayeux was anxious for my return but I had received another offer to stop in Athens for ten days or so on my way back for an engagement at the Constantine club, and I had accepted it. 'Well, maybe I can meet you there,' Bayeux said. 'We can come back together.' This made me more anxious to finish my two weeks in Turkey, but when I asked Mr Kibar what time my flight to Athens was he said, 'But you are staying another two weeks here.'

'What do you mean?' I asked, getting annoyed. 'I am to open at the Constantine two days after closing here.'

'No, we have changed plans. I decided to keep you for another two weeks. I have called Tavel and Marouani telling them this is the case, so this is the case.'

I had given Mr Kibar my plane ticket for return arrangements, so I was helpless in that department. There was no money in my pocket either. As usual, with my trusting spirit, I assumed Mr Kibar had sent my weekly pay to Marouani's office in Paris. Mr Marouani had told me he had arranged it thus, as all my expenses and hotel bill would be taken care of by the Karavansari. This was true, but I received no pocket money whatsoever, and I had spent the six hundred dollars in Turkish money that I had been given by the Nicholas brothers.

I said, 'If that's the case, can I have some pocket money, please?'

'You don't need any money,' Mr Kibar said. 'If you need anything tell your bodyguard, he will bring you what you want; but you don't need any money.' He was emphatic.

'And Mr Constantine in Athens?' I asked.

'He has been taken care of as well.' Mr Kibar had seemingly taken over completely.

In my lonely hotel room I called Bayeux to let him know. This took another three days. The days passed slowly. My hotel room became more lonely than ever. I tried to call Bayeux again. All lines were busy and I couldn't get through. My loneliness was getting the better of me. 'If I can't get through to Paris can I get through to America?' I asked the operator. I had no idea who to call in America because I had lost all contact with American friends, but I just wanted to talk to America even if it was only the American operator – just to hear America. I knew I was on the other side of the world; *in* another world, completely another world, a strange world, a fascinating world, a world at least a hundred years lost in time. Some of the people still wore veils; some women's faces were never seen outside their homes. When the Turkish operator said, 'You cannot call America from here,' I knew I was not only in another world but on another planet. The operator explained that you had to call Athens, Athens calls Paris, Paris calls London and London calls America. Oh well, life is not complicated, but telephonology makes it seem so.

So here I was in my lonely hotel room waiting for something to happen. A knock at my door surprised me.

'Yes?' I asked.

'A package for you, Miss Kitt,' said a porter.

When I opened the door I was handed a package about the size of a shoe box neatly wrapped with a gold and black ribbon over gold and black paper – no note. I opened the package to find jewels of all shapes and sizes, from rings to necklaces. What a funny joke, I thought. The Nicholas brothers must be teasing me over 'C'est Si Bon': '. . . *des bijoux, jusqu'à ici . . . grand, grand Cadillac car . . . tous les choses comme ça. . . .* ' I laughed and looked at myself in the mirror as I tried on one piece and then another.

I went to the club that evening with the earrings on and a bracelet to match. I am not one for jewellery per se, but I was going along with the joke. Mr Kibar looked at me sheepishly as I sat down at our usual dinner table.

'Beautiful jewellery,' he said with a slight smile.

I laughed jokingly, saying, 'Yes, a rich Maharajah sent them. Isn't that cute?' I was playing games with Mr Kibar, who said nothing more about the jewellery but went on to take the dinner order. The joke with the jewellery went on for some time. I wore a different piece or pieces every night to the admiration of all whom I came in contact with.

Then I went to jail. Mr Kibar's lawyer called one day to say I had to be in court. I had committed no crime that I knew of and had not behaved badly in any form or fashion, so what was this all about? When I asked the lawyer he said, 'You are here illegally.' This to me was not a joke. 'You need to have a work permit to work in Turkey. This work permit you do not have,' the lawyer continued.

'I thought it had all been taken care of by Mr Kibar,' I stated.

'Well, in a way he has taken care of it, but to get a work permit you must come to Turkey, get the job, leave the country, the work permit would be sent to you, you return and go to work,' said the lawyer.

'Thanks a lot,' was my reply. 'What do we do now?'

'Since you are already here and working with no permit, you have been sued by the Turkish government, so we go to court and we argue the case; you being a special case, you get your work permit, we win the case . . .'

'And we all live happily ever after,' I finished his sentence.

'Yes, I suppose you could say that,' said the lawyer.

'What happens if we don't win the case?' I asked.

'Don't worry, we have ways of winning.'

I wondered what he meant by that, but as usual I trusted. There was nothing I could do but trust. We did not win the case – not at first. I was told by the lawyer not to say anything in court until I was told to. 'Yes' or 'no' were to be my only replies, according to which direction his head would turn. Three days of arguing in Turkish: the lawyer, the judge, the jury. No permit. I was put under lock and key in my hotel room, not allowed to leave except, ironically, for work. Of course it did not occur to me to call the American Embassy. If I had done, I might have been in even more trouble because now not only did I not have a work permit or a plane ticket, but the lawyer had also taken my passport. All was now in their hands. Then too, I was afraid the hotel operators would not let my calls go through anyway. So I sat waiting for something to happen, but still went to the club and worked.

The permit finally came through, making it legal now for me to remain in Turkey. The extra two weeks went by slowly, too slowly. I prepared myself again to leave Istanbul to fulfill my engagement in Athens before going on to Paris, only to have Mr Kibar say, 'You have been extended another two weeks.' He smiled after saying it. 'You need a police release statement to leave Istanbul. We have put in a request for this, but they said it would be about two weeks before it can be obtained, so you have two weeks more to play at the Karavansari.'

'But Mr Constantine!' I cried. 'He is waiting for me in Athens.'

'He has been notified,' said Mr Kibar.

So another two weeks began.

I had noticed a very distinguished gentleman who often sat at our table. Mr Kibar had introduced me to him, but I paid little attention. Even though he was supposed to be a very important person he was treated like one of the boys. When my last two weeks came to an end, I was again told I could not get the police release; I had to remain in Istanbul until these two little pieces of paper were given. It transpired that the distinguished gentleman and Mr Kibar were in cahoots with each other. It was this man who had sent the box of jewels, the jewels I took for junk jewellery and a joke. They were all real: rubies, diamonds, emeralds, pearls, all real. As long as I kept them I was innocently giving the distinguished man the right to visit me at any time. I was unwittingly accepting the position of concubine. If I gave them back I would be refusing him and the obligations of this position. Then I could get the two pieces of paper I needed to leave. Mr Kibar did not want to get on the wrong side of the distinguished gentleman and having me stay at the Karavansari seemingly for ever was certainly to his advantage. Mr Kibar thus had strong reasons to keep me there, so he had never even applied for the police release. I did not know this until Marouani called to say Mr Constantine was going crazy; he had advertised my engagement in Athens for nigh on two months and no Eartha Kitt had shown up. Now he was kicking up a fuss because he was constantly being put in the embarrassing position of having to make excuses for me not appearing.

Naturally, on learning the jewels were real I did not want to give them up, but since the alternative was to be a concubine or a member of a harem I had little choice in the matter. Then I learned from my bodyguard that he also worked for the Turkish secret service: he had been ordered to guard me especially closely when I got to know the wife of the naval admiral. I suppose I might have been considered some kind of Mata Hari, getting secrets from the admiral's son whom I also got to know, though I only ever saw him at his mother's house, where we often dined. I reluctantly returned the jewels and waited for my police release papers, which finally came through after a stay of about three months at the Karavansari.

15 New York Via the Acropolis

Mr Constantine met me at the airport in Athens and took me to the Hotel Bretagne. I rehearsed with the orchestra that afternoon, and the show went on. I was to be in Athens for about two weeks. I was very happy with Mr Constantine, I saw and worked with my native-tongue Americans, and I felt comfortable. For stimulation I had my books by Socrates and Plato, which led me to the ruins of the Acropolis where I would sit with my loaf of bread and glass of wine, a piece of onion and slice of cheese, or whatever else I could afford at the time to help me think and absorb as I overlooked the city of Athens and all its philosophy. I touched, I felt, I saw, I wondered. How can I make these spiritual stones become a part of me? Will I ever have the thinking intelligent 'ism' of the philosophers' minds? Can I place my hand on this stone of the Acropolis, can I pass through the statues of the thinkers of that civilization and gain something from that intelligence? I sat and thought and cried over my lack of knowledge and felt so stupid I wanted to vomit.

The engagement was okay, nothing great; at least, not for me. I felt alone, unnecessary, and non compos mentis. I felt I was in the wrong place at the wrong time. Some days passed and then Bayeux came, making me feel protected from my loneliness and self-doubting. I felt I was okay in the arms of my man; he would take care of everything, he would be my father-protector. Bayeux stayed in the bath tub all day long. I went into the ruins of the Acropolis to study, to search for knowledge, alone. I walked the streets of Athens, alone. Whenever I saw a building with a tablet saying 'Here slept . . .', 'Here was born . . .', 'Here lived . . .', I touched the walls in search of knowledge, hoping that knowledge would rub off onto me.

My father-protector was in the hot tub of his life when Johnny Desmond came along. There he came, through the pillars and stones, a brown paper bag in hand. We sat for a moment or two in silent communion, he with his brown paper bag, I with mine. 'Do you come here often?' he asked, in the stupidest of clichés. I thought him so stupid then that I ignored him. But within a short while we had brought out all the contents of our bags and packets and were sharing them as we overlooked the city of Athens, trying to capture knowledge in order to become aware of all that surrounded us in the before, the now, and the here-to-come. We walked together to the hotel where we parted, he to his room, me to mine. In my room Bayeux sat for another day in the hot bath tub.

My engagement came to an end after about two weeks and I had to collect my fee. 'Call Mr Constantine,' Bayeux said. I called the club. 'Bring a shopping bag,' Mr Constantine's secretary said. I had no idea what this meant, but I did as I was told. I took a shopping bag to the club into which my drachmas were deposited. Then Mr Constantine took me to the bank to have them exchanged into gold coins. He told me that if I was caught leaving the country with these coins, I would be put in jail with the key thrown away – no judge, no jury, no justice, no anything. I put the gold coins into the pockets of my suit – six coins here, six coins there, six coins here and there and there and there. . . .

'Ah, Miss Kitt, we are so happy to see you! Thank you very much for the "Usku Dara" song. Both countries recognize the rhythm of each others' ethnicism, no matter what the words may say. Thank you . . .' The customs man went off into a monologue about the camaraderie between cultures. If any one of them had touched me and heard my gold coins rattling against one another, I might not be telling this story today. After signing autographs I was passed through to the other side of the world thanking the gods that perhaps I might be able to pay my existence for another few days, weeks, months – a year?

Bayeux was my man then; he was all I thought a man should be – my friend, my lover, my father, my protector. On our return to Paris (his ticket to and from Athens had been paid for by Tavel and Marouani who wanted to keep me happy) we were now together, I in my place, he in his. We went out to dinner with my gold coins which I entrusted to his pockets, thinking he would take care of it all. In the restaurant bar he was telling the story of our experiences in Athens: how rancid the olive oil was on the salads; how rotten the food was in the Hotel Bretagne; how wonderful the real people in the countryside were for coffee, tea, and honest hospitality; how the farmers would invite you in for a meal, etcetera.

'Here are some of the coins we brought back,' Bayeux said, passing the coins along the line of people. They never came back. Bayeux, in his drunkenness, never noticed that the coins he passed along the bar to be inspected by his friends came back in the form of American pennies. Back to poverty. Find your way out of this one, Eartha. Seems I am always finding my way out of the trouble my 'friends' put me in: the closer the friend very often the shorter the knife.

Now, my money was gone, but I thought Tavel and Marouani would have the money that Mr Omar Kibar was to have sent from Istanbul.

But it was never sent. 'When she returns to Turkey, she will be paid,' Mr
Kibar told Tavel and Marouani. With interest I would say the Karavansari now owes me a lot of money, but Mr Kibar is dead, so collection
might be a bit difficult. Anyway, 'Usku Dara' got me out of poverty, so I
guess we are even.

I was asked to return to America for 'La Vie En Rose', a swanky night
club in New York. This time I decided to accept through the William
Morris agency. My photographs and clippings were sent, I received an
aeroplane ticket and went.

At the first rehearsal the manager came to me and said, 'Hey kid, I
hear you sing in seven languages,' his big cigar hanging from the side of
his mouth.

'Yes I do,' I answered.

'Well, get up on the stage and sing in all seven.'

I hurriedly did as I was told. We rehearsed, and opened to a
star-studded room.

For the ten days before the show opened the publicity department,
handled by Virginia Wicks, was very inventive. A full page ad in the
daily newspapers read: 'Learn to say "Eartha Kitt"'. People were asking,
'What's an "Eartha Kitt"? Is it a garden tool?' The last day, opening
night, the ad simply read: 'Eartha Kitt, Tonight, La Vie En Rose, 8:30
p.m.' I wore a white silk gown trimmed with egret feathers, my specially
made open-back shoes from Perugia, and I was scared to death. It is
wonderful to have success, but home is where I really wanted it. I
suppose in my subconscious I wanted to prove to all those who had
abused and rejected me that I had talent. God, I wanted so much to be
accepted at home.

I think I started in English, at least that would have been the sensible
thing to do, but when I took a glance at a beautiful blonde, blue-eyed
lady sitting with four very handsome distinguished-looking men I knew
I was in trouble. She paid no attention except to glance up at me once in
a while in curiosity, I guess; nudging her men to give her a cigarette,
then a light, then some more champagne. Then she folded her arms and
stared up at me; then she rested her chin in her hand, leaning her elbow
on the table. When I was about the fifth language into my repertoire, I
heard her say, 'Now really, what is that, an educated nigger?' Before my
programme was over she and her four men got up and left. There was no
great excitement after I finished. The applause was polite; not really
honest, just polite. No one except Virginia Wicks and perhaps one
other person from the William Morris agency came to my dressing
room. They were almost in silence. No one had anything to say to me.
They knew I knew, and what could they have said anyway?

I don't like to read the critics until some time later, and I particularly did not want to read what they had to say about this night. I went to the club every night and did my two shows with only a few people in the audience. The two-week contract was terminated after six days. The management found a good reason to let me go since I had fallen on the overly waxed stage, gashing my chin open. It happened so fast I could not protect myself and blood spattered everywhere, including into the audience; my reflexes didn't work that night – perhaps my subconscious mind was helping me out of my embarrassing situation. I was taken to Lenox Hospital in the wee hours of the morning, had cat guts sewn into my chin, pulling the open flesh leaves together, and with the cat gut strings hanging from my six stitches I went back the next night and did my two shows, after which I was told not to return the following week.

I was once again staying with Mama Foster, the mother of the girl who threw me the rehearsal garment; the same room, now for twenty-five dollars a week. The six hundred dollars I thought I was to be paid by La Vie En Rose was collected by the William Morris agency and passed on to me minus their share, but it did not last long. Oh yes, Mary Chase had suddenly shown up on the scene at my rehearsal, claiming to the management that she was my manager and I am sure she collected whatever she thought she was entitled to.

Here I was again, back in poverty. I paid Mama Foster a week's rent, bought some canned food and stayed in my room with a constant headache. Obviously I had a slight concussion from the fall, making me feel lethargic, not to mention shamefaced and unwanted. I assume it is natural not to receive any phone calls at a time like this because everyone else is embarrassed as well. What do I do now? Mama Foster was not in during the day. She was working somewhere and I don't think she knew what had happened. Not being interested in the entertainment world and not associating with anyone in it she could not have had any idea what I was going through. I was extremely restless and unable to pay my room and board. I had to do something, but what?

I must have stayed in my room for about six weeks before I got up enough nerve to pick up the phone. I called the William Morris agency. I did not know exactly whom to call personally at the office, but when I finally managed to remember a name on the contract I had signed for La Vie En Rose I said, 'Hello, my name is Eartha Kitt . . .'

'Who? Who? What-dja say ya name was, kid?'

'Uh, Eartha Kitt,' I answered.

'Eartha Kitt? Never heard of her.'

Perhaps he *doesn't* know who I am, I tried to figure. The next day I gathered myself up as best I could. I'll take myself down there and show them who I am. Since it was this agency who had requested me to return to America, someone would recognize me. I only had about fifteen cents in my pocket. I took the subway to 59th Street and walked to 1700 Broadway where the office was located. I did not have enough nerve to take the elevator up, and just stood in the lobby pleading with myself. The fear of an embarrassing rejection made me go first to the phone in the lobby. I was put through to the only name I knew.

'Yes?'

'My name is Eartha Kitt. Could you please give me twenty-five dollars until I find something?'

'Sorry kid, never heard of you.'

I leaned my body against the wall of the telephone booth and cried until my head ached. I pulled myself together and started walking back to the 59th Street subway, with my head slung as low as I could get it and still see where I was going, not wanting to be recognized by anyone. I felt someone following me. Please God, don't let anyone recognize me, please God. My whole being reverted back to those childhood days in the South: the ugly duckling, no colour, bastard child; nobody wants you; if your mother gave you away what do you expect from anyone else? She didn't want you, so why would anyone want you? You have no family, and you don't know anyone in New York who would help you. What are you going to do? And you're hungry, with only a nickel in your pocket – can't do much with that. My mind was going crazy. Someone is following me. I don't want anyone to recognize me, I am too ugly to be seen. I was being whipped again, I could feel the peach tree switch on my bottom, I could hear the voices of my childhood: 'Yella gal! Yella gal! Yella gal!'

I turned to look in a window so I could see the reflection of anyone following me. If there was someone following me perhaps my actions would send out the vibrations that I did not want to be seen. The reflection showed a man coming closer, taking off his hat and saying, 'You are Eartha Kitt, aren't you?' I said nothing, moving away from the store window, trying to get rid of the reflection, refusing to have eye contact. I wanted to become invisible, melt into the cement, get lost in the crowd. Walking alongside me he said, 'I was at your opening night . . .' My whole body tightened in disgust. I could not hide, could not become invisible, and did not dare run.

The man, with his hat still held in his hands against his stomach, continued: 'I know what happened, things did not go right. But you must not be discouraged. You are a great artist. There are those of us who know that. Please do not be discouraged.' I was too annoyed to cry, yet I wanted to. I was also annoyed because someone was being kind to me and I did not know how to accept it in my ugliness. Then too, could I trust his kindness? Was he just being kind to be polite or did he really mean the words being spoken? We arrived at a turning point at 59th Street.

'I'm going east from here, where are you going?' he asked. I could not answer because I had no idea where I was going or who I was, with only a nickel in my pocket. 'Well, I'll say goodbye here.' He turned, and was about to go in his chosen direction when he said, 'Oh, by the way, my name is José Ferrer.'

I returned to my room in the apartment, still with one nickel left in my pocket. Mama Foster was not at home so I sat in my room looking at my ugly duckling self in the mirror, smiling in ecstasy. Someone thinks I am wonderful. Someone wonderful thinks *I* am wonderful; the first live actor in the first real Broadway show I ever saw; the one who gave me that wonderful feeling of being alive; the one who had me hypnotized as I walked from the theatre after seeing *Cyrano de Bergerac*; the one who I am sure embedded in my subconscious the desire to be in the theatre, though fear of my aunt and lack of know-how ensured that the desire never really surfaced until that day when the girl who was sent by Miss Dunham to look for make-up took me to the school and the dare of the kids made me audition. I began to feel beautiful about myself, though I still did not know what to do. I did not want to call the William Morris agency. What would I say to them? They don't even remember my name.

I thought hard and long all night and day for days and nights until, 'Kitty, you're wanted on the phone,' Mama Foster said through the door. A man's voice on the line said, 'My name is Max Garden. Could you come down and audition for me? I own the Village Vanguard in the village.'

The one thing I am really shy of is auditions, but we arranged the day and time. I dressed up in my finery, took my piano parts in hand and, after searching through my pockets and handbags for a dime, took the subway down to the Village Vanguard, where I auditioned with the same songs I had sung at La Vie En Rose and was given a two-week engagement. 'I cannot afford to pay you what La Vie En Rose paid, but I can offer two hundred and fifty dollars a week, okay?' Max Garden said. Naturally I accepted.

Max Garden must have found me through the union who must have told him I was signed with William Morris. To get a contract legitimized it has to go through an agency, and you have to have a membership card with a union; no unionized contract, no work. The union and the agency must work together and everybody gets paid, like it or not. So here I needed to get the William Morris agency arrange a contract for me with the club.

'How can you accept his offer at half the price you were working for before? You can't do that, you have to maintain your original price,' said the agent.

'I'm hungry. Are you paying my bills now?' I could barely answer such stupid thinking. Wait by the phone until you're called? If they can't remember your name how can they call you?

I opened singing the same songs I did at La Vie En Rose (which was only something like twenty blocks away) and became, as they say in the business, an overnight success. Now, if you are successful at the Village Vanguard you automatically get two weeks at the Blue Angel uptown, which is (or was) owned by the same people. I was held over at the Village Vanguard for another two weeks when the bill included John Carradine reciting excerpts from Shakespeare and other classics. I absolutely adored John Carradine. I don't think he was ever recognized as the very fine character actor he was.

Friday was pay night. The agent (whose name I will say I have forgotten as he has become a very important producer in Hollywood and has made a big film with Shirley MacLaine) was waiting at a table for my show to finish. After he collected the cheque (which the office took, giving me ninety per cent later) he asked if he could do me the courtesy of taking me home to 128th Street at Convent Avenue. I accepted. He caught a cab and was playing very much the gentleman to begin with.

'You're a pretty good artist, you know that?' he said, and moved a little closer. 'And you're beautiful.' He moved a little closer. I clung to the walls of the cab trying to escape, hoping he would get the message that I was not that kind of girl. His body pressed me tightly into the corner of the cab as he began to crawl all over me like I was a whore, pressing his lips against mine; the only way to defend myself was to put my knee in his private parts and bite down on his lips as hard I could, remembering my Orson Welles experience.

The cab driver saw what was going on in the back of his cab through his rear-view mirror. He screeched the cab to a halt, throwing my attacker to the floor. With every abusive word in the English language, and some I don't remember ever hearing before, my agent-attacker opened the cab door, crawled from the cab, managed to straighten himself up, and slammed the cab door, spitting out abuse as the cab driver drove off with me still clinging like a spider to its side. At a red light the driver asked, 'Are you all right, Miss? I hope I did the right thing?'

'You did for me, but I don't know about him. Are there any more cab drivers like you, sir?' I said, trying to be funny to calm us both down.

During the time I was at the Village Vanguard I met Harry Belafonte. I thought he was very handsome and someone I would have liked to get to know better, but at that time our relationship remained quite formal.

He seemed to be too busy catching little white flies, as he proved to me later in Philadelphia where, getting up from my bed, he said, 'I don't want you to take this seriously. No black woman can do anything for me.' There went my heart right into my feet. Perhaps this is why I still walk with a limp whenever I see Harry Belafonte, who is now married to Julia Robinson, a nice Jewish girl who they passed off as an Indian to avoid racial complications.

I went on to the Blue Angel where I was supposed to have a two-week engagement. It lasted twenty-five weeks. It was here that I was spotted by Leonard Sillman.

16 New Faces

Leonard Sillman was best known as the producer of the show *New Faces* which he had been in charge of since 1934, bringing to the public eye such figures as Tyrone Power, Imogene Coca and many others who became very famous in succeeding years. I had no idea who Leonard Sillman was when one of the agents in the variety department of the William Morris agency called to tell me I had been asked to come down for an audition for the latest *New Faces* revue that Leonard was trying to get backing for. When I told the agent I would love to do so (despite my loathing of auditions), he made arrangements and took me to the theatre. I sang a little French song, 'Bal Petit Bal', which was part of my repertoire from Paris, then a belting number. I was a nervous wreck.

Auditions: a number is called out; if it's yours, it's your turn to be either rejected or accepted. Or the word 'next', and you are in the arena feeling like a Christian about to be fed to the lions. Then there's the agony of waiting days or maybe weeks to find out if you have been rejected or accepted. 'Don't call us, we'll call you' has to be the torture of the century. So if, like me, you have to do something like this that you hate so much, you sometimes get mad and act belligerently, leaving people with the impression you are being difficult, when in fact you are only trying to defend yourself from an uncomfortable position. I have often had to check myself on the spur of the moment because I realized I was giving the wrong impression. I am not angry, I am scared.

I saw no faces in the empty theatre that would give me a feeling of comfort or welcome. Leonard Sillman came down the empty theatre aisle. 'We'll call you,' he said, as he took out his black cigarette holder to refill it. The agent and I left the theatre through the stage door. 'I don't know why you'd want to audition for Leonard Sillman anyway, he hasn't had a hit since 1934,' said my representative. So I'm trying out for a failure, I thought to myself, thanking the gods that moment was over. I continued my nightly performances at the Blue Angel. I saw Leonard Sillman's face from time to time with different people, but he never approached me personally. He just came and went.

Some time later my agent told me I had been asked to do some auditions at people's homes on my Sundays off. This was for backers. The pianist, Ronnie Graham, and Arthur Siegel were to accompany us.

This kind of audition is not too bad, because you have others riding in the same boat with you. Through these auditions enough money was put together to produce *New Faces of 1952*. Rehearsals began. Since there were those, like Ronnie Graham, who had been working with Leonard Sillman for some two years, they already had projects which they knew would be part of the revue. I was the one they had to find material for. Ronnie Graham, Arthur Siegel, June Carroll and I sat around looking at each other for what seemed like weeks; no one could figure out what to do with me. Meanwhile I was telling them of some of my experiences in Europe – mainly Paris and Turkey, but especially Turkey because of the jewels, etcetera. And London also, where I worked at Churchill's for about a month and my mail went to Winston Churchill by mistake. I received a batch of fan letters from Sir Winston one time with 'I presume this is for you' written on the back of the envelope.

The nightclub Churchill's was a very interesting place. Since I am not much of a socializer, I minded my own business; I did my shows, went to my dressing room in between sets, and to my modest apartment after. Harry Meadows, the owner, often tried to get me to socialize with the chic and élite customers but I seldom gave in, except for one night I remember very well. This night, having to go through the audience to get on the stage, I passed a table of very distinguished men and heard:

'She is beautiful.'

'I wonder what nationality she is?'

'She must be from Indonesia.'

'Ah, she's nothing but a nigger.'

The place was so crowded I could hardly get through, allowing me to hear everything this group was saying. I had been beautifully received at Churchill's so far, and was therefore very much at ease, with never a thought of colour. Hearing this, I became so embarrassed I could hardly start my songs. I tried to pull myself together but my feelings were so hurt that I only managed about three songs before running off the stage to hide myself in the dressing room. Mr Meadows came up to tell me he was sitting at this table and hoped I had not heard.

'Some people are stupid about some things over which we have no control,' he said. 'Come down and finish your show.' But seeing that this would have made me too uncomfortable, Mr Meadows said, 'Well, come on down and meet them. Perhaps that will show them you are not "just a nigger".'

This statement made me cry and laugh at the same time. I was confused as to what he really meant. Did he mean: since you are beautiful, you're not a nigger? Or did he mean: you're a nigger, but you are beautiful? Or did he mean: you're a beautiful nigger and that makes everything all right? I decided to accept the offer of meeting Mr Meadow's friends. I felt that by facing the situation boldly and without animosity I could do more than I could hiding in my shame, and perhaps I could bring out their shame – if they had any.

Mr Meadows took me downstairs and introduced me to the distinguished men. There was silence at first when I sat down but then one of the men asked me to dance. I accepted. We returned to the table, and eventually we all had a turn dancing. It turned out to be one big evening of fun and laughter until the wee hours of the morning, when one of them offered to escort me home. Just as I was about to go into my apartment I turned and asked, 'Now do you think I am "just a nigger"?' Flowers flooded my apartment the next day.

Discussing this and other experiences with Ronnie and the others, we eventually came up with a song. We called it 'Monotonous':

'I met a rather unusual fool
While on my way to Istanbul,
He bought me the Red Sea
For my swimming pool.
Monotonous . . .'

Now we had the song, but what were we to do with it? (That is, other than sing it.) The choreographers watched me rehearsing the song for about ten days before finally saying, 'We don't know what to do with you. What do you do?'

'I can't tell you what I do,' I replied, 'I can only show you.'

'Then show us,' they said.

Now I was stumped. I had no idea what to do with this song, but I knew I could not walk across the stage, sing four lines and say 'monotonous' for eight or ten verses, as was being planned. I was afraid the whole thing would then really be monotonous, for the audience and for me. Since I was stumped for an ingenious idea I went along with what I was told to do: walk across the stage and sing 'monotonous' until you get to the other side and hope for the best. Boring.

We opened in Philadelphia. The show as a whole went extremely well, but I was not satisfied with the response I received. I knew I could do better, but how? Think Eartha, think. The opening night party at someone's swanky home was the usual thing. Since the show was obviously successful for all of us seventeen 'new faces' we were happy and delighted. I was delighted too, but with reservations. What more could I do that wasn't already being done? There must be a way. I saw Leonard Sillman and Mr Chrysler chit-chatting in a corner. Walter Chrysler, our main backer, might be the answer. I walked over to them.

'I would like to have six chaise longues,' I said, 'please.'

'What are you going to do with six chaise longues, Eartha?' Mr Chrysler asked, through his laughter.

'I want them to sing "Monotonous" on,' I answered. This made them laugh more.

'You almost stopped the show tonight, Eartha,' said Leonard. 'What more do you want? Wait till you get to New York, you'll be great,' he continued.

'But if I had six chaise longues I know I could do better, Mr Chrysler,' I pleaded, throwing the ball into his hands.

'We'll play it as it is now and during rehearsals in New York we'll see,' said Mr Chrysler. It was left at that.

Our stay in Philadelphia was wonderful for all of us. We then went to New York where Mr Chrysler said, 'We won't give you six chaise longues, Eartha, but we will give you three. Do you think you can manage with that?' I was ecstatic to get any at all, and made no pretence over my happiness. Three chaise longues were placed across the stage and as I sang 'Monotonous' I crawled in cat-like style from one to the other and with opened claws said 'monotonous' to the audience, ending in a passing-out faint, bringing the house down in applause that lasted so long I was embarrassed in pride. Eventually Ronnie had to write another verse for an encore. Even the little French song, 'Bal Petit Bal', which I sang in my toreador chanteuse outfit with balloons on a string, stopped the show.

I was on my way up. We recorded the album *New Faces* for RCA. I was now doing *New Faces* eight times a week, including matinées on Saturday and Wednesday, and the Blue Angel at night from as soon as I got there until about two a.m., two shows nightly. And then came John Barry Ryan the Third (whose sister, the Countess of Airlie, was Lady-in-Waiting to Queen Mary). A young man was constantly sitting alone at a table to my left during my second show, night after night for a very long time. I saw him but paid no attention, except to wonder why he was always alone. Usually it would be older men sitting alone, but they would inevitably make a move of some kind to be introduced. As a matter of fact, one older gentleman who had gone through this same exercise had made himself known to me by sitting with a black ribboned box saying 'Cartier' obviously on display on his table, making me curious all through the second show as to whom it was for. The lone older gentleman brought it to my dressing room with the maître d' and said, 'I am an old-fashioned millionaire and would not only like to give you this gift, which is not much, but I also would like to give you the deed to my yacht standing in the harbour in San Francisco. It is made of all-Japanese teak wood, and has a crew of seven.' Of course, I took the gold bracelet that the box contained but since the yacht would cost about seven thousand dollars a week to run and I knew nothing about boats, I declined it (to have taken the yacht and sold it would have been sacrilegious).

But this young loner never made a move in my direction; he just sat and stared. At times he would be sitting at the bar in the lobby when I left to go home. One night, as I was about to say goodnight to the maître d', I was told that the young loner sitting at the bar was most anxious to meet me. 'Do you know him?' I asked.

'Yes. His name is John Barry Ryan the Third and he is a very nice person.' I accepted the introduction. When he asked, 'May I take you home?' I looked at the maître d' to see if this was okay. When he nodded his approval, I accepted. As we got into John Barry Ryan's fancy two-seater I was impressed that such a young man should have such an expensive automobile (I guessed it was expensive, but I knew little about cars at that time). All the way home I was worrying about how I was going to get out of the pay-off but I needn't have bothered because when we got to my front door he said, 'I know all about you. You never have to worry about anything again as long as you live. I will take care of you. I will see you tomorrow.' He returned to his fancy two-seater and drove off.

I had a little studio apartment on the ground floor of 270 Riverside Drive, which I had found through two boys who had come to see *New Faces*. They had come to my dressing room for an autograph. We got into a conversation and I told them I was looking for an apartment. They told me that they were going to move out of theirs but it was in a building where negroes were not welcomed. The two boys explained to me that they would pass their lease on to me when they were moving out and told me to call the Housing Department if a problem came up. So I had taken over the apartment. Since I had nothing to move in furniture-wise, my occupancy went unnoticed. The two boys had left me their bed. Jimmy Komack from *New Faces* gave me some blankets and an old radio, a few pots and pans, towels, sheets and the like, making me feel cosy in my very first self 'owned' apartment. It was my little nest.

There was a knock on the door one morning, and the problem started. 'My name is Mr Zimmerman. I own this building and I'd like to know what you are doing here.' I thought of what the two boys had told me, but I did my best not to let on that the boys had no intention of returning; I was afraid to get caught in a lie and make a fool of myself. Before I could say anything Mr Zimmerman went on, 'I know those boys have moved out and are not coming back. You know there are certain buildings in New York that do not allow certain kinds of people to live in them. I give you ten days to get out and find yourself another place. I will be back in ten days. See that you are gone by then. In the meantime, if anyone asks you what you are doing in this building, tell them you are the maid.' He left.

I was not stunned by this. I was expecting it since the two boys had told me to be prepared and call the Housing Department if necessary. I have always believed that problems can be solved with a face-to-face confrontation, even though a deep hurt may be seething inside. But I was shocked at Mr Zimmerman because he was Jewish; I felt that he and I had more or less the same problems in life, and that he should therefore have an understanding of my dilemma. The situation was unnerving since I personally had no lease (it was in the name of the two boys). I put the problem aside, knowing I would think of something later. Something will come to me. If you are in a quandary, hold on and the solution will appear in the palm of your hand. I have always taught my daughter Kitt this – God may not be there when you want him but he is always on time.

I went about my usual routine – the theatre, the Blue Angel, and home – with John Barry Ryan coming most nights to escort me, never coming into the apartment or even hinting that he wanted to. Since I was careful not to give him the impression that I wanted him to, he remained the gentlemanly kind of man I have great respect for. But this left me curious about his intentions. Whilst I did not want him to tamper with the possibility of ruining things by making a romantic move, I could also feel my curiosity becoming more and more acute as our relationship became warmer and warmer.

Johnny was fun to be with: amusing, intelligent, and very considerate. He came to pick me up one day to take me to the matinée, after calling to say he would be in front of the building at eleven thirty a.m. 'My sister's birthday is in a few days. I would like you to help me pick out a present for her,' he explained on the phone. I was uncomfortable about picking out a present for a sister I had never met, but I was sure he would do the picking, using me only as a catalyst for his own taste to be approved of. We drove to the downtown area of jewellery shops. I did not ask any questions as to what kind of present he had in mind for his sister – I just went along with the game. Into a jewellery shop we went, looking at one jewellery case after another – diamonds, pearls, bracelets of gold, rubies, emeralds, etcetera. 'Do you see anything you think my sister would like?' asked John. Each piece of jewellery was more beautiful than the next but since I suspected in the back of my mind that John might be playing a trick on me, I decided to play the game straight and be discreet by choosing the simplest and probably the least expensive thing on the tray, since I do not like gaudy things anyway. If it *was* for his sister he would then say perhaps something like, 'No, why don't we choose this one?' meaning it would be more to his sister's liking and I would be safe. When I chose an emerald ring surrounded with diamonds, he asked, 'Do you really like that?'

'Yes, it's simple and elegant,' I said.

The salesman wrapped it up, we got into John's fancy two-seater and sped off to the theatre. As I was about to go through the stage door, John handed me the little box saying, 'This is for you,' and left. In my semi-surprised state I went to my dressing room remembering the words of our first meeting: 'I know all about you. You will never have to worry about anything again.' Time went by with John and me seeing each other at the club, sometimes between shows when we'd sit in the lobby bar in a corner with our favourite maître d' in attendance when he found time for us. The club was so crowded even I had to crawl on my hands and knees to get in at times since the lobby bar was the only way in and out. We all used to laugh hysterically when dashing from the theatre to the Blue Angel; John often picked me up for this race against time. On the floor like a cat I crawled to my dressing room, changed garments, and went on stage. Often John would be sitting alone at his usual table for the second show, waiting to take me home.

And on the tenth day Mr Zimmerman returned. I opened the door knowing it was him – I could tell by the knock. 'I see you're still here,' he said.

'Won't you come in, Mr Zimmerman?' I asked, dragging out the name 'Zimmerman' as far as I could to give him the message that I knew he was Jewish. 'Won't you have a cup of coffee? Please have a seat,' I hummed.

'I don't like coffee,' Mr Zimmerman said, 'I'll have a glass of milk.' I gave him a glass of milk and made coffee for myself.

'Well, haven't you found another place yet? Or haven't you been trying?' Mr Zimmerman asked.

'Mr Zimmerman,' I started saying, 'you know there are certain kinds of people who are not allowed to live in certain buildings in New York and these certain kinds of people have a very hard time finding apartments in certain areas.'

'There is always Harlem, why don't you try up there?' he asked.

'I don't see why one has to obligatorily live in a "zone" if one lives in a free democratic country. One should be entitled to live anywhere one can afford.' I looked straight at him. 'Don't you think so, Mr Zimmerman?'

I held onto his last name for as long as I felt the timing of my intended message would allow, hopefully forcing him to squirm in his pants in the knowledge that he and I were rowing in the same boat with the same pair of sick oars. How many times do we have to row ourselves across the river Styx before finding solace in a comfortable acceptance? I am sure Mr Zimmerman's milk was curdling in his stomach as he said, getting up, 'Well, I'll give you ten more days. I am sure you will have found a place by then.' He quickly opened the door himself and left.

The *New Faces* album was recorded. The show was going strong, my stint at the Blue Angel was being extended every two weeks, my popularity was rising. My bills were being paid but nothing was left over for extras like furniture. I only got about three hundred and fifty dollars a week for *Faces* and about one thousand five hundred for the Blue Angel, so with taxes, rent, agents' fees, public relations' fees, union fees and the like, I could only just hold my head above water. I saved money by taking a bus in between shows to 270 Riverside on Wednesdays, sometimes for dinner at home. Since I did not remove my make-up, sitting on the bus in full regalia I became a show piece. An elderly lady sitting next to me decided to attack: 'Young lady, why do you have so much make-up on? Don't you know you look like some kind of prostitute? *Are* you a prostitute?' This stopped me from riding the bus – at least between shows in full regalia.

The gossip columnists were now mentioning that John Barry Ryan the Third and Eartha Kitt were an 'item'. Why, I do not know because we were never out on the town together (except for at the Blue Angel), and since I had no idea where John Barry Ryan was and never used my relationship for publicity, I wondered why this was so important to gossip columnists. But many of them paid porters, waiters, doormen, cab drivers and the likes for 'items', so who knows how this one came to their attention?

At that time I had a gap between my two front teeth that, on certain words, would cause a slight hiss or a whistle. Alice Ghastly said to me one day, 'Eartha, if you ever need a good dentist I would recommend the one I go to on Central Park South.' I decided to have this space filled in since I did not want to have a whistle as part of my speech pattern. I made an appointment. My two front teeth were ground down to make room for caps to be put on. A price was decided beforehand and agreed. Then the dentist convinced me that the teeth on each side should also be capped for a more uniform look. A price was decided beforehand and agreed. When the temporary caps were on I waited for the permanent ones to be prepared. When they were ready the dentist called saying he wanted eighteen hundred dollars more.

'But we agreed on the price before. Why are you now asking for more?' I asked.

'Your teeth were harder to grind than I thought,' he said.

'But where am I going to get eighteen hundred dollars more? I'm not making that kind of money,' I pleaded.

'You have a very wealthy boyfriend, ask him for it,' the dentist answered.

I was flabbergasted, but my teeth were tied, so to speak. I would not dare ask John for anything. I knew I had to get myself out of this. I never mentioned it to John. I did the shows with the temporaries, begging the dentist to finish the job. I had always felt that doctors, lawyers, teachers, and dentists, like mothers, could always be trusted; and here I was, trapped with ground-down teeth capped with plastic temporaries that may wind up in the lap of my audience at any moment. I never said anything about it to Alice Ghastly because I did not want her to feel badly that she had recommended me to a corrupt dentist, while my teeth were rotting more rapidly by the day. How does one clean plastic caps, especially after two or three weeks?

I kept calling the dentist to finish the job. 'When you bring me another eighteen hundred dollars I will,' said he. I finally called the William Morris agency to explain my predicament. I was immediately sent to a supposedly more reputable dentist who re-did the four teeth at a cost of about a hundred dollars each. Since he too had my teeth tied, who knows if he was or was not taking advantage? At least the job was done in a relatively short time. I made a claim against the original dentist with the help of the second dentist, forcing the former to lose his licence to practise in the state of New York for unethical practice.

John Barry Ryan had now been to my apartment during the day when he came to pick me up to drive me to the theatre. He saw how bare it was and sent a television set, some paintings for the walls, a throw rug and some curtains, and decent pots and pans, silverware, dishes, glasses, and a kitchen table set. Things were coming together nicely. Mr Zimmerman returned on one of his regular visits.

'I see you're still here.'

'Come in, Mr Zimmerman,' I said. 'Have a glass of milk, sit down.'

'Oh, so you like this apartment?' he asked. Watch it, Eartha, I thought; this may be a trap.

'I beg your pardon?' I asked, thinking as fast as my brain would allow me to on an empty stomach.

'Would you like to have this apartment?' he asked.

'Mr Zimmerman, why would anyone want this apartment?' I rambled. 'Look at this kitchen: it's too small and it needs painting. It leaks under the sink where there is a hole in the wall; the floor badly needs repairing. Take a look at this whole apartment: it's in the back overlooking a giant wall with an alley way so small not one ray of sunlight can be seen; the ceiling is about to cave in; the whole thing is dark and dingy and depressing. Who would want to live here? But since certain kinds of people cannot live in certain kinds of buildings in New York, you, Mr Zimmerman, must know how difficult it is to find decent places. That's why I am still here, Mr Zimmerman.'

I could not find enough fault with the apartment; and I was looking to find any and everything I could in case he was trying to trap me.

'Well, I guess we should fix the hole in the wall, mend the leaks, dress up the ceiling. And what colour would you like on the walls?'

'Anyone who would live here would like the colours to be as bright as possible, to cheer it up,' I said, still trying to avoid the trap. Mr Zimmerman studied the whole apartment methodically.

'Oh yes,' I said, 'about this nothing-nothing bathroom: it must have been made for midgets.' I hoped he had a sense of humour. When he sorta-kinda laughed I felt the message had penetrated.

'You may have the apartment. We will come in and fix things up for you,' Mr Zimmerman said, as he went towards the door.

'And the lease?' I asked.

'I'll have a lease made up. What is your full name?'

I was exceedingly happy; the whole problem had been solved through a meeting of the minds, without the prestige of a name. Mr Zimmerman did not know who I was.

He did as he had promised and sent his people to fix up *my* little apartment. John Ryan helped furnish it. Then Mr Zimmerman offered me the one-bedroom penthouse apartment, decreasing the rent by forty dollars, which John Ryan bought new furniture and paintings for. I made a glass room Japanese-style garden atmosphere. I was given two cats by Tex and Jinx, two radio personalities who were very popular at the time. I named the cats Tex and Jinx; they were adventurous cats, and led a life unnervingly similar to the Tex and Jinx who had given them to me. Maybe one day I will write a book about my cat tales. . . .

17 Show-hopping

New Faces ran in New York for a year. John Barry Ryan and I were now really strongly into our relationship; I became so attached to him I never wanted to think of ever being without him in my life. We were being mentioned regularly in the gossip columns though we did not frequent restaurants and clubs; we just used to drive around the city or walk the streets sightseeing. I would go shopping with him in stores of his choice. 'Wait here for me,' he said one day. He disappeared into a shop, returning with what turned out to be my first mink stole.

I received so much jewellery from John that it became embarrassing; I don't think he ever came to see me without bringing a gold something – a bracelet, a set of pens, even a yellow diamond ring. I finally said to him one day, 'Johnny, you don't have to bring me gifts. I like you – *you*, Johnny – without all the extras.'

'It's the only way I know to say I love you,' he answered.

I could not change his ways, no matter what I said, so I left it alone and he continued to shower me with gifts. Until one day when he reluctantly but happily said, 'I'm going away. I have been asked by John Huston to come to Egypt to be his assistant director.'

I was not at all happy about this, but could not bring myself to tell him not to go, that I was afraid he would not come back. 'I didn't know you were interested in doing movies,' I said, trying to think of something to ease the pain of him going so far away.

'My mother is a friend of John Huston's and she said it would be the best thing I could do. John Huston could give me a good training. I could learn to be a good director from him,' John went on, ecstatically happy at the thought of his new job.

'Assistant director to John Huston – sounds great. How long do you think you will be gone?' I asked, half expecting him to say 'forever'.

It was much the same to me when he said, 'Oh, I suppose a few months, until the film is finished.'

There is nothing to do when 'old' money is at stake. Old money usually wants to merge with old money; keep it in the family. It does not like to be challenged by a different cultural or ethnic influence, especially when the other culture is also a different colour.

I was getting to the point of expecting John to call the cards on our relationship. He had been hinting at it for almost a year. We had been so much to one another; I thought nothing could separate us. We were great for each other in every way – sexually, intellectually, humorously. 'You will never have to worry about anything again. I will take care of you.' His words haunted me. Now there was a thorn in my heart and I did not know how to pull it out.

John left for Egypt, leaving me with fantastic memories of a wonderful experience with a great guy whom I felt lonely for every day of my life in his absence. I went on day by day with my work in *New Faces* and my twenty-five weeks at the Blue Angel, waiting for John Barry Ryan to come back, riding on the rays of the eastern sun. After some months he did return, telling me there was nothing much for him to do in Egypt. He just stood around in the hot sun waiting for John Huston to tell him what to do, but John Huston just told him stories completely unrelated to the immediate project. After his return, John's visits to me became less and less frequent. Soon thereafter he was married to someone 'acceptable', and divorced in a relatively short time.

I went on to record for RCA, signed up by Dave Kapp, who was fired (he told me years later) because he had signed me to a five-year contract. RCA told Dave Kapp I would never sell a record: 'She is an actress-dancer, not a singer,' he was told. I don't know what they thought I was doing on *New Faces* and at the Blue Angel. RCA released the most sophisticated and foreign language song of my repertoire to prove they were right; the record would not sell and they would be able to get out of the contract. The opposite happened: 'Usku Dara' was released and went to the top of the charts in a matter of days. The combination of Turkish and my voice was so out of the ordinary that the public's curiosity was roused to the extent that I became the only woman in the popular music department to make money for RCA in twenty-seven years.

When I went to the studio to record, a white chauffeur-driven Rolls Royce was sent to pick me up and a red carpet was spread out on the sidewalk to welcome me; red roses were everywhere, even in the recording room itself, and Dom Pérignon champagne was on ice for all of my musicians – the number of them varied between thirty-five and sixty-five. These were wonderful times, with Henri René, my arranger-conductor, who I really felt great with. As long as he and Mannie Sacks and Hugo Winterhaulter were by my side, I felt safe and wanted and respected and protected. We were a happy group for years but when Mannie Sacks died, Elvis Presley and his management came onto the label and we were sacrificed for Elvis; he was singing like a black then, very much in the Little Richard style, but getting the recognition Little Richard never got.

I was lucky to have Henri René and Mannie Sacks behind me – not to mention the public, who made me the hottest recording personality of the Fifties, despite RCA's belief that I would 'never sell a record'. But the black people said, 'Oh, she thinks she's white,' which is ironic seeing as they accepted Elvis thinking he was black, until they saw his photograph on his records. I was accepted by the whites, the international whites, but it took some twenty years on the American scene before I was accepted by the blacks.

In the 1960s I took the same show I was doing at the Plaza Hotel Persian Room to the Apollo Theatre in Harlem; agents and friends told me I would have to change my repertoire because the audiences of Harlem would not understand anything I was singing. 'You have to come down to the public,' I was advised. I took this to be an insult to the people of Harlem and went in with exactly the same repertoire, foreign languages and all. I was still extremely nervous that they would not accept me though, because one of the black magazines had a story on me that was excellently done, praising me for being a highly intelligent self-educated person, but the cover headline read: 'Why Negroes Don't Like Eartha.' I was therefore very happy and relieved when the queue to see me stretched from Eighth Avenue to Seventh Avenue for the whole two weeks I was there. I guess Mr Shifman, the owner of the Apollo, was happy too.

The Civil Rights Movement was just about coming into its prime then, with Martin Luther King at the helm. The Black Panthers were on the rise as well, but I was with Martin Luther King. Every penny I made from my Apollo audiences went to the Martin Luther King organization in support of the Civil Rights Movement. I had been threatened by the Black Panthers in the elevator of the Palmer House a month or so before. Four of the football-type muscle men caught me in the elevator, telling me they wanted me on their side. I rejected their threats. 'Okay, Kitt,' they said, 'We will get you in Harlem.' This made me even more hesitant about accepting the contract offer for the Apollo, but I took my chances and hoped for the best.

There was a rally on Seventh Avenue in front of the Theresa Hotel, where those of us who were with Martin Luther King were called on to make speeches in his support. I was booed and hissed and had rotten tomatoes and the like thrown at me by members of the Black Panthers who had mingled with the crowd. When I finished my speech in support of Martin Luther King I returned to the Apollo Theatre to finish my shows for the evening. I was followed by members of the Black Panthers who spewed insults at me all along the way, hoping I would perhaps run away or find protection in a shop. I walked as slowly as I could, window shopping, saying nothing, standing my ground alone which seemed to anger them the more; but I remembered President Roosevelt's words when I was a child during the Second World War: 'There is nothing to fear but fear itself.' Mama, please ask God to protect me. I walked slowly through the front door of the Apollo Theatre, alone, with no harm done to me except the verbal insults. I was told later that the store windows on both sides of the front entrance of the Apollo were smashed with stones thrown by members of the Black Panthers. I called the Plaza security officers to stand guard at my hotel suite because my daughter Kitt and Mama Foster were there, and I was afraid for Kitt.

My attitude towards the Black Panthers was that nothing could be gained with hatred; that Martin Luther King's idea of pulling people together with sit-ins and pressure on our government to pass laws for equality for all was the right way, rather than the Black Panthers' way. My argument with Malcolm X was the same. As a matter of fact, I had a lively discussion with him in the BBC studios the Sunday before he was killed (by one of his own people) where he told me he was thinking of changing his tactics and going towards Martin Luther King's way. We were asked to have a debate on BBC television, but I think Malcolm felt it best not to. Perhaps he had already been warned not to change his tactics. I adored Malcolm X but not his tactics. We had known each other as kids in the streets of Harlem and had had many discussions about the black American problem, but I believed in Gandhi and Martin Luther King and God and the Ten Commandments and the Bible: 'Do unto others as you would have them do unto you.' Equality for all, and jobs, jobs, jobs, of equal pay and opportunity for all.

New Faces went on for a year in New York and then we put it on the road; a few months in Detroit, a few months in Chicago. By the time we got to Chicago, RCA had released several of my records. 'Santa Baby' and 'C'est Si Bon' had hit the charts, enabling *New Faces* to have a longer run with each release. What was to be a month or so in Chicago ran into six months. Each time Leonard announced the end of the season, RCA released another record and an extension run had to be planned. I received a twelve thousand dollar royalty cheque from RCA, and the first thing I did was buy twelve pairs of shoes and a bicycle and a supply of food for a month (I still remembered those days in New York when I picked the garbage cans, slept on rooftops, and rode the subways from one end of Manhattan to the other when I was running away from Aunt Mamie's cruelty).

Ronnie Graham walked out of the theatre one day; he put on his costume, took it off again and left. Leonard Sillman saw him leaving, came into the theatre and made the announcement that Jimmy Komack, Ronnie's understudy, was to do the show and that he,

Leonard, was going to report Ronnie to the union and have him suspended from doing anything for a year. Leonard asked for a vote in support of his decision. I could not believe my eyes when all hands went up. 'I see Miss Kitt did not raise her hand,' said Leonard, 'May we ask her why?'

'I think it's wrong to suspend someone who supported you and stood by you for two years, probably without pay or even a thank-you. Ronnie has lost several close members of his family recently and you, Mr Sillman, just know this has taken a great toll on him psychologically. I don't know too much about Ronnie's emotional problems, but I do not feel it is right for us not to support him now.'

The cast was very quiet. Leonard said, 'I'll call my lawyer.' Leonard told me later that his lawyer said I was right, but Leonard nevertheless went on the Jack Eigen television show that night and told the public Ronnie was very unprofessional in his behaviour and that he was going to see that he was punished. A contest developed between Leonard and myself when Jack Eigen's people called me to ask if I would come on the show and give my opinion: one night Leonard would be on attacking Ronnie, the next night I would be on defending him. This went on for two weeks or so, until Ronnie was reinstated in *New Faces* because the fans were on our side. I don't think Leonard ever forgave me.

Charlie Morrison, the owner of the Mocombo in Los Angeles, had been requesting a contract for me to play there. I had made a promise through the William Morris agency that I would accept when *New Faces* closed; but the success of the records kept *New Faces* going strong and I kept putting off the 'Mocombo' offer. Charlie Morrison flew into Chicago.

'Please Eartha, you have got to help me out. I can't get liquor credit any more. I owe forty thousand dollars to the liquor people and I cannot keep the club open unless I can get alcohol. Who wants to come to a club and not have a drink?' Charlie pleaded.

New Faces had been contracted for the Biltmore Theatre in Hollywood after Chicago. 'Mr Morrison, I promise you when we come to Hollywood, I will play the 'Mocombo' – if I can do both.'

'Anything you say, Eartha,' said Mr Morrison happily, 'But if you put your name on this contract now, I can show it to the liquor people. That would make my credit good and I can stay open.'

This was done and Mr Morrison left Chicago a happy man. The result was that I had to do the Mocombo after the *New Faces* curtain went down at about eleven o'clock. There would be a police car waiting to rush me the ten or fifteen miles from the Biltmore to the club while I changed my clothes in the car; I would dash on stage as Arthur Siegel waited patiently to accompany me on the piano. Arthur was also the pianist for *Faces* and had had to make the mad rush there as well, but at least he didn't have to change his costume. I adored Arthur, and we both had a lot of fun doing these Mocombo shows.

Now I was making records during the day, doing *New Faces* from eight to ten thirty at night, the Mocombo from eleven to two thirty a.m. and the *New Faces* film and publicity, and I got the flu. I got the flu so badly that I was vomiting in the wings; but since the show must go on, I went on. That is, until my secretary, René Morrisey, called the doctor to my dressing room because she realized I could not go on. The doctor wrapped me in a blanket, put me in his car and put me to bed in my little bungalow at the Garden of Allah, telling my secretary to be sure I stayed there until Monday with antibiotics and hot soup. The doctor told Leonard that if I kept going I would risk getting pneumonia and I would be no use to anyone. He also called the Mocombo and cancelled that night's shows. It was a Saturday, which meant I also missed the second show of *New Faces*. The headlines in the Sunday papers read: 'Eartha Kitt's Walk-out On New Faces Gained Her No Friends.'

Leonard Sillman was annoyed that he had to return that night's sales so he called the newspapers telling them I had walked out – not that I was ill, but that I had walked out. There was nothing I could do to correct the story – the damage was already done. Besides, who believes a star anyway? So, as usual, I left it alone. God has his ways, and what goes around comes around; I don't know anyone yet who has done me harm and harm did not come back on them. Leave it alone Eartha, God will take care of it.

I was making about two thousand five hundred dollars a week at the Mocombo, about six hundred dollars a week for *New Faces* (graduating from three hundred and fifty), and I received a week's pay for the film – six hundred dollars – and a contract for four per cent of the profits, which of course I was never given.

I was asked to perform in between shows one night for the King and Queen of Greece at an affair hosted by Dick Powell and June Alyson. My choice of songs was decided by the affair's committee – 'I Wanna Be Evil', 'The Blues', and 'Old-Fashioned Girl'. I did my songs, took my bows, acknowledged the King and Queen, and ran to my awaiting car. Dick Powell ran down the stairs shouting, 'Eartha! Eartha! you must come back. The King and Queen want you to do an encore.' I was hysterical with laughter, only half believing him, but his persistence convinced me so I did two more songs, returned to the Mocombo and finished the night, a Saturday. The Mocombo had asked me to extend my stay, so Arthur and I were there rehearsing on Tuesday afternoon when I was called to the phone.

'Eartha! What did you do to the King and Queen of Greece?' a man's voice asked.

'What you you mean? What have I done?' I asked in surprise.

'This is a *Los Angeles Times* reporter,' said the voice. 'Mayor Poulson's monthly meeting was today. He said you shocked the King and Queen of Greece. What did you do?' The voice became more excited.

'What are you talking about?' I asked, getting excited myself.

'Mayor Poulson said you are risqué, un-American and vulgar and should have never been asked to perform for the King and Queen of Greece,' said the reporter.

'All I know is, the committee chose the songs they wanted me to sing and that's what I did. As far as shocking the King and Queen, I don't know what you are talking about,' I answered.

Headlines: 'Eartha Kitt Shocks King and Queen of Greece, says Mayor Poulson.'

Headlines: 'Eartha Kitt Risqué and Vulgar in Front of King and Queen of Greece.'

It turned out that a trio of girls had sung a song called 'Chicken in the Barnyard', about how farmers smell under their arms after pitching manure, accompanying it with the relevant gestures. This is apparently what Mayor Poulson was referring to, but when a reporter raised his hand at the Mayor's meeting to ask what he thought of Eartha Kitt, the Mayor said he thought the whole evening was risqué and un-American. This gave the newspapers freedom to say what they thought would sell; since Eartha Kitt was the hottest thing in town, they had carte blanche. The story went on for about two weeks until the King and Queen were found on a yacht somewhere in the Pacific. They were wired to give their opinion about Eartha Kitt; the reply they gave said, 'We don't know what all the fuss is about. We thought Eartha Kitt was wonderful.'

That was the end of that, but my salary went up from twenty-five hundred dollars a week to ten thousand. Charlie Morrison, his wife Mary and I were sitting at a table one night in between shows, when Charlie suddenly jumped up and ran towards the entrance where a thin young man was standing, looking as though he was in search of someone. I looked to see where Charlie was running to. I saw the young man and my whole being went crazy. They both walked towards our table. The feeling I had at this man's presence was indescribable. I had no desire to fall in love after my disappointment over John Barry Ryan, but it hit me in the face like a bat out of hell; the closer he came the stronger the feeling was wringing my heart. I did not want to see his eyes, fearing I would definitely be going where I did not want to go.

'I've been looking for you,' the tall thin man said, standing next to our table, close to me. Charlie Morrison asked him to sit. He sat next to me, never looking at me directly. 'Now that I have found you . . .' He fiddled a bit on his chain.

'Eartha Kitt, this is Arthur Loew Junior; Arthur Loew Junior, this is Eartha Kitt,' said Charlie, introducing us.

'I know who she is,' said Arthur Loew Junior.

18   *Taking Buffalo by the Horns*

I had no idea who this Arthur Loew Junior was. I never connected the name with the Loew cinemas all over the country. I laughed when he said 'I've been looking for you' – who would or could believe a line like that? Yet it was better than 'Do you come here often?' Though I was nervous and scared of my feelings towards him, I felt comfortable in this man's presence.

Charlie asked him where he had been, since he had not been around the Mocombo for some time. 'I've been with my mother driving over the Swiss Alps,' he said. 'That's where I heard your voice on my car radio,' he continued, turning briefly to me. He never looked at me directly; there was a shyness about him.

'What are you having, Arthur?' Charlie asked him.

'Scotch,' Loew said. 'I told my mother I was going to find that voice when I got back to America,' he added, looking in Mary's direction.

'How is your mother?' asked Mary.

'She's okay,' answered Loew.

His drink came. He raised his glass to me, saying, 'Farley Granger said you were out here somewhere.' He acted a bit nervous, reminding me of Danny Kaye. I had a desire to laugh, to giggle, to chuckle; I felt warm with the feeling I had known him before – at some other time, in some other place. Loew was my kind of man; a man with a wonderful sense of humour, a travelled man, a man who was aware; a curious man, intelligent and fun. I wondered if he was kind, if he was gentle, if he was considerate. I knew I wanted to be with him, to see him again. In just a few moments I knew he was everything I had ever wanted in a man. I excused myself saying, 'I'm sorry, I have another show to do,' hoping he would not go away. He didn't.

My second show was sung for him. My love songs I felt for him, my humorous songs I hoped were amusing him. He was quiet for me, he was still for me; but his face was without expression. He puzzled me and he haunted me. When my show was over I went to my dressing room and changed, returning to say goodnight to Mary and Charlie, hoping Loew would still be there. He was. 'I'll take you home,' he said. I looked at Charlie and Mary.

'Yes, Kitt,' Charlie said, 'he's okay, he's one of us.'

Loew drove me to my bungalow at the Garden of Allah. As I walked away from the car thanking him, I hoped secretly that he would ask to come in for a cup of coffee or something – and then I hoped he would not, at the same time. Since I liked him so much I did not want to spoil my chances of a future relationship. I was in a quandary, with my heart leading my head. Being the gentleman he was, I heard him say as I was putting the key in the lock, 'I'll see you tomorrow.' I wanted him. I wanted him for now, I wanted him in my tomorrows, in my nights, in my company. If a night can ever be long, this night went on for ever. I wished with all my being that tomorrow would bring him back, and it did.

There he was at Charlie's and Mary's table as I came on stage. The room was packed but I only saw him, I only felt him; he was the only person in the room. I looked at my pianist Arthur Siegel with smiles and giggles of joy, but Arthur had no idea what I was feeling. He was only aware that something unusual was happening when the vamp to introduce my opening song went on longer than usual. I was extremely happy in the hope of a wonderful relationship with this man. My senses told me that he was the man to have my children with, he was the man I could be happy with, he was the man I could trust to be kind and gentle, who would not desert me; the man who would be strong and defy all that might want to hinder us. The show was exceptionally good. I was in my glory, especially when he again took me home saying, 'I'll see you tomorrow.'

'I'll see you tomorrow' went on for about ten days to two weeks before I found out who he was. By now I was so much in love I could not bear to be away from him for a moment.

The *New Faces* engagement at the Biltmore Theatre was over and so was my contract with the Mocombo. The film was done, as was the next album for RCA. We moved on to San Francisco for about six weeks, where we became an instant hit. Then Sammy Davis Junior came upon the scene. One of the girls in the show, Pat Washaver, came into the theatre one day and was standing in the stage door entrance talking to a small black boy with pressed hair. As I ran upstairs Pat said, 'Kitt, this is Sammy Davis.'

'Very nice to meet you,' I said, 'Would you please run and get me some coffee?'

Since Sammy was standing in the stage doorman's area, I took him for the errand boy. A few minutes later, Sammy Davis returned with coffee to my dressing room; he smiled as he said, 'Here's your coffee.' Pat Washaver laughed her head off when she explained who Sammy Davis Junior was and saw me crippled with embarrassment. I had never heard

of the Masterson Trio, which annoyed Sammy no end when we got to
know each other.

Sammy got my address and phone number from Pat. I was at the
Huntington Apartments just across the street from the Fairmont Hotel
where the Masterson Trio was playing. Sammy had his manager call on
me to ask if I would come in to see the show. I went in for the late show
and had the biggest surprise – Sammy Davis, with his dad and uncle,
were about the greatest entertainers of this kind I had ever seen (except
for the Nicholas brothers, who were my favourites, along with Bill
Robinson). I adored them, especially Sammy, so I accepted the invitation to visit Sammy in his hotel suite. There I found comic books on
both sides of his bed piled up level with the bed; cameras of all sorts,
records and record players were everywhere; his bedroom was cluttered
with what to me was junk. I thought Sammy was a great entertainer but
I wondered about his intelligence. What kind of mind did he have?

When the little party of the evening was over, Sammy walked me
across the way to the Huntington Apartments. The next day he called
me to ask if I would have dinner with him before my show. As we walked
into the restaurant the maître d' said, 'Miss Kitt, how nice to see you.'
Nothing was said to Sammy – he was not recognized. When we were
seated Sammy said, 'I don't get it. I have been in show business since I
was four years old. You have been on the scene only a year or two and
everybody knows you and they don't know me.' I pretended not to hear
him and went on ordering.

Sammy and I saw a lot of each other during the San Francisco run of
New Faces. I thought Sammy was a lot of fun to be with but he was also
exhausting. He gave the impression that he was looking for something
but he did not know what it was. He wanted success, yes, that was
understandable, but even that was haunting him. He wanted to be
recognized by all and this was not yet the case; he was not yet able to
achieve this on his own, though his talent was certainly obvious.
Something bothered Sammy and when he was with me it seemed to
bother him even more. He walked me to the theatre after dinner one
evening and as we parted he said 'So long'. I was crossing the boulevard
when I heard Sammy yelling to me through the traffic, 'One of these
days I'm going to be bigger than you are!' As I entered the theatre I was
laughing uncontrollably at the sight of Sammy Davis Junior stopping
the traffic with his yelling. I can still see him standing on the corner of a
San Francisco street yelling, 'One of these days I'm going to be bigger
than you are!'

Sammy called me to ask if I would accompany him to a brunch one
Sunday at a Mr Maxwell's apartment. Mr Maxwell owned a small
museum of beautiful paintings, and his apartment was swarming with all

sorts of objets d'art. After the brunch, we had a look round and discussed the art with Sammy clinging close behind, hanging onto every word. I thought it was very cute to see Sammy like this – in search of knowledge. Mr Maxwell and I had a great time discussing the different artists. Sammy was silent but listened intently. When we left, Sammy asked, 'How do you know so much about art?' I did not bother to answer because I did not take the question seriously.

The next day Sammy came to my apartment with a pile of books under his arms.

'Look! Look, Kitt! I bought all these books on painters.' We investigated the artists.

'Look at this painting, isn't it great?' he asked.

'Yes, Sammy. Do you know anything about these painters?' I asked back.

'No, I just look at the pictures,' he said.

'Don't you think you should read the books as well as look at the paintings, Sammy?' I asked.

'Oh, you have to read them too?' We both laughed.

I had bought a Lincoln Continental – yellow with black leather upholstery; a plaque reading 'Especially Made For Eartha Kitt' was on the inside of the door. After our shows one night I drove Sammy to the top of one of the hills overlooking San Francisco and the Golden Gate Bridge in her beauty of lights. It was very romantic, but I had no romantic interest in Sammy; my desire was for Arthur Loew. Being a one-man woman no one could touch me. So there was no interest except I thought Sammy Davis was a very nice, amusing person even though he was exhausting to be with. There was always that nervous tension surrounding him, of having some place to go and not knowing how to get there. He was silent as we sat in my car looking at the beauty of San Francisco.

'I'm going to be bigger than you are one of these days,' Sammy was saying softly. 'I'm going to learn how to drive a car and have one of my own, one of these days. I'm going to know about paintings too, one of these days. You wait and see.'

'You'll have to do more than read comic books and play with toys,' I said, in the same tone he was using. I took him to the Fairmont Hotel where he sheepishly went in, turning halfway round to say, 'I'm gonna be bigger than you are one of these days.'

'You'll have to do more than read comic books and play with toys,' I singingly repeated as I drove away.

The run of *New Faces* came to be extremely successful, with Leonard Sillman constantly telling us we were going to close after such and such a time, then picking up more and more dates on the success of my records with RCA. I signed a contract for a venue in Buffalo when I thought the show was going to close, and after the show had been extended a few times I was made to fulfil this engagement as the management could not move it again.

Buffalo for a week. My secretary, René Morrisey, accompanied me. The engagement went well; the maître d's were extremely happy, which meant the audience was a monied crowd so good tips were had by all. I was in my dressing room between shows when one of the maître d's came to ask me if I would join a table of prominent men. A Mr Snow was the asking party. 'I am sorry,' I said, 'but I do not frequent the place I am working in, it kills the impact of my show.' The maître d' became a little nervous but I paid no attention. I was putting the finishing touches to my make-up when there was another knock on the door and the same maître d's face appeared in my mirror.

'Uh, Miss Kitt,' he stammered, 'Mr Snow insists you come to his table, please.'

'I am sorry. It is not my policy to do that. If I am seen mingling at tables before the show, the mystery is gone,' I answered.

'Please, Miss Kitt, Mr Snow is a very important person. He may get angry.' The maître d' was getting more nervous.

'Sorry, please tell this Mr Snow I thank him very much but my policy is my policy. No.'

The maître d' stood silent and still for a moment before departing. Again, a knock on the door, the same face in the mirror, this time with a bottle of champagne on ice – my favourite, Dom Pérignon. 'Please, Miss Kitt, Mr Snow sent this with a stronger request . . .'

'Who *is* this Mr Snow?' I asked. 'If this Mr Snow is so important and so persistent, tell him he can come up here to visit me. I will not go into a room in which I am working. Thank you.'

The maître d' turned slowly to leave. 'I will try and bring him to you,' he said, very, very nervously. I was having fun with the whole idea. I knew this very important Mr Snow would come to my dressing room since he seemed so anxious to meet me. René looked at me and saw the mischief in my eyes; she played the game. I put on long black netted hose that were for one of my costumes; René had a long black cigarette holder, which I borrowed. I painted myself up more heavily – not too exaggerated but enough, I thought, to tease. I lit a cigarette in the holder, put my black netted legs up on the dressing table and sat in a leaned-back chair to wait for the knock on the door. Sure enough, there was the knock, and the same face appearing in my mirror, followed by a tiny little man with four giant-sized escorts. I leaned my chair back even more as the maître d' said, 'This is Mr Snow.' He beckoned to the tiny little man.

I took a puff from the cigarette and blew it slowly into the mirror. 'How do you do, Mr Snow?' I purred. Mr Snow held the back of my chair with both hands, squeezing the chair's back as he said, 'Very nice to meet you. Will you come and join us at my table, please?'

'I am sorry, Mr Snow,' I said, blowing smoke into the mirror without turning round. I watched the reflection of the four men and the maître d' as they nervously shifted from one foot to the other. 'I never frequent the place I work in, it spoils the impact.' I could feel Mr Snow's hands tightening as I shifted the crossing of my black netted legs.

'I am sorry you feel that way, Miss Kitt,' Mr Snow said, 'I am sure we will see each other again. Please, enjoy your champagne.' He and his four giant bodyguards left with the maître d'. René and I laughed heartily at the joke we had played. We were still laughing when the maître d' returned to say, 'Miss Kitt, I think you had better leave by the back entrance tonight. You have just rejected the Number One head of the underground in the Buffalo area.'

'What underground? What do you mean, "underground"?' I asked in my stupidity.

'Try Mafia,' he answered.

Since I did not want to show fear I left boldly by the front entrance, but as René and I walked to the hotel my heart was in my mouth. Fortunately it was my closing night, so I was able to get out of town – fast.

I returned to San Francisco to finish my run with *New Faces* before returning with it to Los Angeles for a return engagement at the Biltmore Theatre and the Mocombo, not to mention a return to Loew, hoping I would be able to carry on where I had left off. Since there had been no word from him I thought perhaps he had forgotten me, but there he was on opening night at Mary and Charlie's table. We continued where we had left off.

19 An Innocent Fool

Loew and I were now being seen at Chasen's, a restaurant which a lot of stars and people in show business frequented. The gossip columnists were picking up on our every move and we had become an 'item'. I was not in the habit of reading the gossip columns, so I had no idea what was being said about us. I have never been a real 'show biz' person, and have never been interested in publicity. I did have Virginia Wicks as a public relations person, which I accepted on the condition that there were no lies; I cannot remember lies, so I tell the truth, no matter what. I did not know that you pay a public relations person two hundred and fifty dollars a week (that's what it cost then) to keep your name in gossip columns by feeding them stories about your private life. Virginia was making up a scrap book of my clippings which I might glance through some time later, but usually I was making my own publicity without knowing it.

The Hollywood gossip columnists such as Hedda Hopper and Sheila Graham were all for the relationship between Loew and myself. They said they had never seen Loew so happy. He had cut down on his drinking and was in his office at MGM more often, getting serious about work. Though Loew never said he loved me (I guess some men can't), I felt he did: he showed it in so many ways. I was meeting members of his family, even from his mother's side, who stayed out with us until the wee hours of the morning (in spite of their motto, 'Never after ten p.m.'). We were happy. I was happy. At last I had found someone who would be with me forever. We had no problems that I was aware of.

Loew's uncle used to come to the house we had on Miller Drive in Los Angeles. It was Loew's house but I had moved some of my things into the second bedroom. Ethel the housekeeper and I had a good friendship. I also got on well with Loew's uncle, who used to come round every morning after Loew had left for MGM. We would chat about his life – the uncle seemed to know all about mine from the newspapers. He was a very funny man and very easy to be with. Apparently he was the black sheep of the family. He would sit behind the bar, drinking whatever he was drinking, saying, 'If Arthur doesn't marry you, he's crazy.'

'What do you and my uncle talk about all morning?' Loew asked me from time to time.

'Ask him,' was my reply.

I was in Los Angeles for some time before my next project in New York with Leonard Sillman. I had promised to do *Mrs Patterson*, a new dramatic play with music. In the meantime I had contracts for a club called El Rancho in Las Vegas, twice a year – six weeks every six months, with cancellation clauses for Broadway. Loew and I became so close we were never seen without each other unless we were working. I would drive myself from his house to Las Vegas on my own. One day I set out for the six-hour drive, leaving Loew, who had told me he was going to Arizona to buy a piece of property. I was not in my bungalow at the Garden of Allah long enough to unpack when I saw Loew's car driving up. 'What are you doing here?' I asked. 'I thought you were going to Arizona.'

'I am, but I was missing you so much I decided to take the long way there,' said Loew.

Loew had a lawyer friend whom I had met a few times. At one point this lawyer was giving Loew and his father, Mr Loew Senior, the same bill – he was charging both Loew Junior and Loew Senior for the same job. Loew said he knew this but since the lawyer was having a hard life at the time, he would say nothing to him about it; but when things got better for this 'friend', he was going to let him go. Loew's kindness was often taken for weakness and he was often taken advantage of. He never wanted to hurt anyone. Being the boss's son was not a very comfortable position at times. He wanted to be a producer-director, I think, but when he came up with a film project he said he was always given the weaker stars at MGM because they knew he would never cause a fuss if he could not have who he wanted. Loew was often frustrated when he came home but seldom discussed his problems. When he did he made everything seem so funny no one took him seriously.

I had a birthday in the last week of my stay in Los Angeles at the Mocombo. Charlie Morrison had arranged a birthday dinner for Loew and me and some of our friends. When I sat down at the head of the table, on my plate was a tiny package wrapped in blue paper with a blue ribbon and bow. When I opened it, there was a tiny gold angel with fresh-water pearl wings and ruby eyes. The card was from Loew: 'You may want to be evil but I think you are an angel. Arthur.' I was so happy I cried and laughed at the same time. Loew was not really a gift-giving person, though whenever I went away there was always something on my bed when I returned; never expensive things, just small tokens to say 'Glad you're home.'

It was closing night at the Mocombo after my third return engage-

Dining with Azikiwe at his home in Nigeria, 1958.

Visiting Nehru at the palace, where the food was a great disappointment to me.

St Louis Blues, 1958. I am wearing an Edith Head dress. *(Paramount Pictures Corporation)*

Anna Lucasta, with Sammy Davis Jr and Rex Ingram.

With Nat King Cole during the making of *St Louis Blues*. He was one of my favourite people, but his wife did not approve of our friendship.

I was always reprimanding Sammy Davis Jr for reading comic books instead of real literature.

In Nigeria, at a formal ceremony to open a palm oil mill, I was shocked that the local people had been fenced out and I passed as much food to them as I could through the fences. The security guards were not too pleased!

Chatting to the King of Swaziland in 1971 at a ceremonial 'Dance of the Virgins'.

'What a sweet man!' I loved appearing on the Harry Secombe show in 1962. (*Jeremy Grayson*)

I am presented to HRH Queen Elizabeth II at a Royal Command performance in the London Coliseum.

Beluga caviar, my favourite!

Shopping in Africa.

Playing with pigeons in
Milan, 1968. Mother
McDonald was with me and
she took this photo.

Keeping fit on the lot
between takes, during the
making of *St Louis Blues*.

Freda Paine, Jayne Kennedy and I were chosen as the three most beautiful black women in the world for the cover of *Jet* magazine.

Being kissed by Wendel Corey after the curtain calls for *Jolly's Progress*. That's Mr Loew Senior on the right of the picture.

ment, by popular demand. Every night before this, Loew would wait for me and we'd go home, but this night he came to my dressing room and said, 'Meet me next door in the restaurant. I'm having dinner there with Frank Sinatra and some friends.' This was a very odd thing for Loew to do. I felt uncomfortable about it, but since closing nights mean packing up etcetera, I took it for granted this was the reason for him not behaving in his usual manner. It was no more than five minutes after Loew left my room that a man whom I shall call RS, someone I had met somewhere along the line, came in the door.

'Kitt, Kitt, you've got to help me!' cried RS, 'I'm having a terrible time with my girlfriend. She is threatening to leave me, you gotta talk to her.' I had met RS's girlfriend and I liked her, but I could not figure out why he would think I could keep her from leaving him.

RS's family were fairly well-to do and he was a handsome blond, blue-eyed macho type. I had no interest in him at all; to me he was just another hunk with nothing much to offer.

'What can I do, RS?' I asked, wondering about his motives. 'I don't know your girlfriend well enough to have any influence over her,' I continued, rushing to finish my packing to get to Loew as soon as I could.

'Please Kitt, she adores you and will listen. I don't want to lose her. You gotta help me,' he pleaded.

Like Loew, like Eartha, I never want to hurt anyone, and when I see someone in trouble I can't just walk away without at least trying to help. Stupid me.

'Where is she?' I asked, thinking at least I'd try – nothing to lose.

'Oh, she's just next door in the restaurant with some friends. It won't take long,' said RS.

'Which restaurant?' I asked, hoping it was the same one Loew was in. The restaurant he named was not the one Loew was waiting for me in, but two or three away in the opposite direction. 'Okay, RS,' I said, 'I'll talk to her, but I have to tell Loew.'

'You don't have to worry about Arthur. I've told him you'll be with me for a minute or so.'

Stupid, stupid me. Who would have ever thought a plot was at hand? I had never been at ease with RS, especially not now, but I went along with his request. My things were all packed to be picked up the next day. RS took me by the arm and led me outside. I started to go into the restaurant I knew Loew was waiting in to let him know what was going on, but RS held onto me, threw me in his car that was conveniently parked in front of the Mocombo and locked the doors saying, 'We have to hurry before she leaves.'

The car zoomed off in James Bond Style, ignoring all red lights and not slowing down in any form or fashion. 'What are you doing, RS? I thought you said your girlfriend was . . .'

I could not finish the sentence before he said, 'Oh, it's not far, only a minute.'

The car was turning into a residential street north of Sunset Boulevard. Then it went into a driveway – RS's house.

'RS, what is this? Loew is waiting for me,' I said angrily. 'What kind of trick is this?'

'Come on Kitt, she's inside.'

Knowing I was trapped, I went inside the house with the idea that I could phone the restaurant and tell Loew where I was and what had happened, but when I analyzed my predicament and this craziness, I wondered if Loew would believe me. I kept begging RS to take me back to the restaurant where Loew was, but he paid no attention to my plea. He got a drink instead.

I thought RS was the bastard of the world when he pushed me down on the sofa and tried to force me into making love. When I fought him he asked, 'What's the matter? Are you in love with Arthur?'

'Yes, I'm in love with Arthur,' I said.

'You must be a nutcase, then,' RS said. 'The girls tell me he's not very good at making love.'

'I'm in love with the man, RS, not the way he makes love. Besides, what business is that of yours?' I was so mad I could spit. 'Where is the phone?' I asked, thinking I'd take my chances and explain to Loew. There was no phone in sight. As I looked around for it I noticed the curtains were all opened. This made me more curious about RS's motives. I was so uneasy that he finally said, 'Okay, okay, I'll take you to Loew.'

When we reached the restaurant Loew and his friends had left. When I came back from looking for them, RS was standing by his car waiting, as though he knew Loew had gone. The ploy was successful. When RS asked me where I wanted to go, I knew he had planned this to keep me away from Loew long enough for him to think the worst. The damage was done and I felt like the fool of fools. 'Take me to Loew's house, please,' I said. When I reached the house on Miller Drive, RS drove off leaving me on the doorstep; he did not even say goodbye. The ploy was successful. I had no key and though I rang the bell there was no answer. How could I ever explain this to Loew? I walked around the yard praying for an answer.

Just before this, *Confidential* magazine had run a big story on me: 'When Eartha comes to Hollywood, she and Arthur Loew Junior set up white and tan housekeeping.' There had never been a meeting between Arthur Loew's mother and myself, and now I began to wonder why. I had met all his family, even his sister and her husband, but not the mother. I knew something was brewing; I had felt it from time to time but could not put my finger on it.

I never asked Loew about his mother; I assumed she would come upon the scene one day, but it never happened. I was so much in love with Loew I never thought anything could or would come between us. But here I was again, with the only son of an extremely wealthy white American family. He was the only hope for the continuation of the family name and money. All this was a lot of nonsense to me, but I knew that was the way it was; I just hoped it wouldn't be a problem in our case. Wishful thinking.

I was sick to my heart walking around Loew's gardens. I was sick to my heart fearing I had lost him in an act of innocent stupidity. I knew all this had been planned, but how could I explain that his friend, a friend of his family, had done the trapping? I was going to leave the next day for New York and wanted to have Loew understand that I was innocent of any wrong-doing, except that I had been stupid in my trust of others. The fact that practically all of my songs were saying the opposite didn't help. By dawn, I was so exhausted I could not hold myself up any longer. I got into the back of Loew's car and slept there until Ethel, the housekeeper, came down from her apartment over the garage. I went into the house with her and continued sleeping until Loew came down. Loew saw me on the couch, said nothing, went into the kitchen and came back with a cup of coffee. I joined him at the table in silence, searching for a way to explain the night. Finally I said, 'I'm sorry about last night but RS made me go with him . . .'

Before I could finish the sentence I could sense I was putting myself into an ever-hotter frying pan; I was even lighting the fire with my own match. I realized nothing could explain me out of the previous night, so again I just said, 'I'm sorry.'

'That's all right,' said Loew. His whole attitude had changed. His body language was telling me that he thought the worst and that he was in a trauma over it. Since I knew no words could help me, I went upstairs to pack and prepare to leave for New York. My few things at the Garden of Allah were packed already; I needed only to pick them up and pay the bill on the way to the airport.

This day I can truly say was a day of tears that drained me to weakness. It was not the tears so much as the fact I had been made a fool of. 'The closer the friend, the sharper the blade.' The saying was assuming a painful significance. I cannot find words for the hurt I felt when I heard the front door close and Loew's car drive away. Without a word he was gone. My plane was leaving that night. Up to the last moment I called MGM only to have the operators tell me that Mr Loew was 'not in his office'. I tried to console myself with the thought that one day he would find out the truth; he must know I would not play games. God help me that he loves me enough to realize this. I tried very hard to be strong and not show that my heart was dangling over a sharp-edged sword.

In New York, rehearsals started for *Mrs Patterson* a few days after my return. Lots of attention was given to the play as it was written by a black person, and was therefore the introduction of a black playwright to Broadway. I was most anxious to do the play because of this, and also because it happened to be a *good* play, with incidental music. 'Tea in Chicago' was one of the numbers, about a fourteen-year-old girl who wanted to be like the folks on the hill whom her mother worked for. Rehearsals went well. Loew eased my anxiety when I finally managed to get through on the phone, saying everything was all right and he might be able to come for a visit to New York. I had no idea this was a ruse to appease me.

That animal instinct was there though; the tone of his voice was guarded and a certain freedom of expression was missing. I could feel an undertone, an uncertainty, of not wanting to hurt – but the tone of his words made me know he was trying to get something across. There was something he had to do but he did not know how to do it. It was all there in his voice. 'Perhaps he has found out the truth of that night,' I stupidly thought. But, of course, RS would not admit to Loew that a plot had been hatched and that he was in cahoots with someone else to carry it out. I found out years later that Mama was behind it all. I was suspicious of this, as I had travelled that path before; but how can you say to the man in your life, 'I'm suspicious of your mother plotting against me'? Especially as the whole situation had been designed to make me look guilty.

Each time I spoke to Loew on the phone he promised he would call back on such and such a day, which he did. This kept me hoping that RS, to rid himself of his guilt, had told Loew the truth. I still felt that the love Loew and I had for each other was stronger than any outside influence. Insane thinking, insane dreaming. Wishful, wasteful hope. One son, one line. I only hope RS got paid well.

James Dean sometimes answered the phone on the occasions when I was able to get through. James told me what was going on at the house and in the studio; he told me that Loew was being strong against the pressure and he believed he would conquer. I had met James Dean in a dance class given by Syvila Forte, an ex-Dunham dancer who had a school in New York where we all went for lessons and muscle toning. Her husband had come to me asking for help to keep the school open, so I was paying the rent and most of the expenses for the school, thinking that through Syvila Forte I was helping to keep the Dunham technique alive.

Meeting James Dean, the up-and-coming number one screen actor at this time, led to a relationship that no words can explain. I became his teacher of stage presence and his confidante. We were soul brother and sister, so to speak. We seemed to have a spiritual contact that is so rare in any relationship, whereby we could be with one another, just walking along New York streets or in Central Park, with no words spoken between us for hours but we knew what the other was thinking. Sometimes we would just look at each other and laugh at something we were sharing in our mental conversation.

James was in the MGM stable, and was in Hollywood to make *Giant*. He and Loew had become extremely good friends, and when this problem arose between Loew and me, James was spending most of the time at Miller Drive. So James knew and James relayed information to me. But he did not tell me everything until much, much later.

20 Doctor Miracle

Rehearsals for *Mrs Patterson* finished in New York and we opened in Detroit. It was very successful, and after the remaining kinks were ironed out, we went on to Chicago. We were only supposed to be there for a month but stayed for four, I believe, playing to full houses every night and getting great reviews. Calls to or from Loew happened once a week or so. Almost ninety per cent confident that everything was okay between us again, I threw myself into my work, wanting to be at my best at all times. But with such heavy schedules, little sleep, and Leonard Sillman on my back all the time – 'Be careful going home, don't get run over, here's another present' – I got the same sickness I had had in Paris: I started to haemorrhage. No one could explain why, but I was losing so much blood that it sometimes took me a whole day to get out of bed and drag myself to the theatre. Only my maid Okey knew how sick I was. I did not allow her to say anything to anyone because I knew how Leonard Sillman would react; just like he did when I got the flu in Hollywood, when the papers said 'Eartha Kitt's Walk-out on New Faces Gained Her No Friends'.

Leonard Sillman was a selfish person who had no feelings about you personally; he only cared about the box office (which of course is understandable from a producer's point of view, especially when a show relies entirely on one star). I knew I had to stay on my feet, that the show must go on, but I was getting weaker and weaker by the day. I used my weakness to inject more dramatic intensity into the young character I was playing, which worked and brought standing ovations of about ten minutes for the last scene. This scene sees the mother returning home to find her young child just about to run away to catch the train to Chicago, where she thinks she can make a better living and become as elegant as the daughters of Mrs Patterson up on the hill. This scene alone made me so weak it took me sometimes fifteen to twenty minutes to pull myself back. Okey always had fresh orange juice or grapes or beef bouillon for me to take immediately after so I could muster the strength to meet people. I never went out, only to my hotel apartment where I would force-feed myself to build up strength, praying to God I would come back to normal and the bleeding would stop. It didn't.

After about six weeks of this I was yellow-skinned, my hair was falling out, and I was scared. One matinée day I dragged myself out of the building to go to the theatre when I noticed a doctor's office across the street. I walked over, knowing I had to do something more than trying to get better by myelf. I rang the bell of the first doctor's name I saw. When I walked into his office he said, looking at my eyes, 'Eartha, don't you know what doctors are for? If you were not the kind of person you are you would be in your coffin.' After examining me he said, 'I don't know how you are even walking around. Not to mention how you are doing a show every night and twice on matinées. You have one third the amount of blood a human being should have.'

I laughed as he began to pump vitamins E, B, A, iron and I guess every other vitamin or mineral he could get into me with a needle.

'Eartha, I know this may not be the proper thing for a doctor to do, but with your permission your producer should know your condition. I think I should have a meeting with him. You need a rest, a rest of doing nothing for two weeks.'

'No, doctor,' I said, 'we only have two more weeks here. As long as you give me the vitamins that should be enough to build me up, don't you think?'

'Eartha, you need two weeks of rest, nothing but rest.'

'I can't close the show for two weeks, doctor,' I argued.

'You have two more weeks here?' the doctor asked.

'Yes.'

'When do you open in New York?'

'A few days after leaving here,' I said.

'Sillman can give you two weeks before you open in New York. He must. Nothing is more important than your health. Anyway, it takes about two weeks before you get any real results from these vitamin injections,' the doctor continued.

'If that can be done,' I said, 'it would be better.'

I gave the doctor permission to speak to Leonard Sillman. He made an appointment for dinner after the show for the three of us. The doctor told Leonard what he had told me: 'She needs a rest for at least two weeks before you open in New York. She can either stay here in Chicago where we can take care of her or the same treatment can be continued in a hospital in New York. I have colleagues I can call who will take over. . . .'

'I can't afford to give her two weeks' rest,' Leonard interrupted. 'It will cost me too much money. Besides, there is nothing wrong with her; she just wants to be with her boyfriend in Los Angeles and is pretending to be ill.'

The shock on the doctor's face cannot be put into words.

'The lack of blood in her body is certainly not from pretending, Mr

Sillman,' he laughed. 'What do you think she did, empty herself of blood like you do a gas tank? Or hire a vampire to suck her neck at night?' The doctor and I both laughed. The image created by his words was very funny.

Leonard did not think it funny at all. He got up from the table and left, saying, 'She's not sick, she's just pretending. I'll get Doctor Miracle to take care of her in New York.'

The doctor looked at me and asked, 'Who is Doctor Miracle?'

I shrugged my shoulders, saying I had no idea. I had never heard of a Doctor Miracle, but assumed a doctor was a doctor, one who has the miraculous powers to make everything alright. On our return to New York I was put in the care of this Doctor Miracle, who told me I must come for an injection of strong vitamins twice a week, Tuesdays and Thursdays, without delay. If I did not take his advice, he would not be responsible for my health.

Mrs Patterson opened in New York to great critical acclaim for Eartha Kitt. When I went to the theatre the morning after the opening, the front of house on 41st Street was covered in blow-ups of the reviews; I was hailed as one of the greatest artists of our time. I could not recognize this person as me. I walked up and down the pavement outside the theatre, reading the critics' blurb, wishing Mama could be there to share in my glory. But this glory was for Eartha Kitt, not for Eartha Mae. As Eartha Mae, that unwanted urchin child of the cotton fields who survived in the dirt and the forest with the animals, I was proud to have a friend who was now becoming an important actress as well as a singer. Being a singer was one thing, especially on records; you learn the songs, go into the studio and sing them until you feel it's good enough to sell to the public. But in front of an audience, there are no producers or buttons to help you – you are on your own.

To be acclaimed now as a great actress was really a coup, particularly as my character had to sustain the whole evening. No strings can be pulled to help you on these occasions: the greatest directors in the world are left in the wings. Eartha Mae was happy for Eartha Kitt but sad for herself. Eartha Mae, the urchin, the rejected yella gal, began to feel neglected. Would she ever become loved and adored as Eartha Kitt was, and recognized as a 'worthwhile'? I stood across the street looking at the marquee, watching people go in to buy tickets and the expression on their faces coming out. Eartha Mae was hiding behind – no make-up, hair tied up, old clothes; anything that would not attract attention. She hid among the ordinary people. She was more comfortable there. She was more at ease when no one paid attention to her. She was always told she did not belong and was not accepted, so she felt no one would ever want her.

Eartha Mae was never supposed to have anything, and was now beginning to feel whatever Eartha Kitt achieved did not belong to her, it belonged solely to Eartha Kitt, the achiever, the survivor. I could feel the separation of the two of me as I stood in front of the theatre, analyzing both of us. I enjoyed the happiness for both of us but with reservations: Eartha Kitt was being accepted in the civilized world of luxury and comfort, but could Eartha Mae be accepted also? Eartha Mae is a child of the dirt, she knows how to survive there, she knows poverty and rejection. She thinks once given away she will always be given away. But she encouraged Eartha Kitt to carry on because she knew she would not have to scrounge for a living any more. She too can have a big house up on the hill; she too can have guests for tea dressed in fancy clothes with hats to match.

I wondered what the cotton plantation owner would think now? Would he let me through the front door of his house now? And would his pigeons still cry 'Nigger's a fool, nigger's a fool' as we thought they did? Eartha Kitt was a very happy artist but Eartha Mae wondered about it all as I walked through the stage door and into the dressing room. It was completely done over, and flowers covered every nook and cranny. The dressing room was always a sanctuary, the place where Eartha Mae could hide.

Mrs Patterson was sold out every performance. I continued my treatments of vitamin injections twice a week. I was making recordings and television appearances for Ed Sullivan and other popular television variety personalities, including Perry Como. With the care of Doctor Miracle I got my strength back. My hair grew, my nails grew, my skin returned to its normal colour, and the bleeding stopped. I was fine, I felt great. The phone conversations between Loew and myself were fine.

Since I felt so great I naturally did not feel the need for a doctor any more. I stopped going. About two weeks later, the curtain went up on my entrance, I walked onstage with my fake long walking stick in hand, started my dialogue, then stood like a dunce, silent, looking at the audience with nothing coming out of my mouth. I heard the dialogue in my head. I knew it backwards and forwards but I could not say it. I just stood there gazing into space. I knew where I was, I knew what I was doing, I knew the character I was playing, but I could not say the words. I heard my stage manager Marty giving me the lines. I don't know why he's doing that, I thought, Marty knows I know the lines. Why is he prompting me? I was calm as a cucumber, and silent and still. I saw the curtain going down, I heard the mumbling of the audience. Why is the curtain going down? It's only the beginning of my dialogue. Be still, I'll say the words in a minute. I'm acting, it's just that my timing is different today. It was all going through my head. I'll go on from where I left off. Where did I leave off? Oh yes, I've said that line, the next line is. . . .

The curtain hit the floor as Marty took me by the arm and led me to my dressing room. I heard Okey saying, 'I told you she was sick. She was sick in Chicago. They said she needed two weeks' rest but Mr Sillman said it was too expensive. I told you she was sick. . . .' I knew where I was, I knew each person who came to my room, but they all looked hazy, they were all in a fog. I was dreaming. I have to wake up, I must be on time for the theatre. What is my schedule today? Voices came from everywhere. I lay on my couch watching all that was going on around me. I was still. They were all looking at my sleeping body as my dreaming figures were moving in and out of my room. Someone was testing my pulse.

'I'm going to call a doctor,' Okey said belligerently.

'I'm going to call my lawyer,' Leonard said belligerently.

I was still, just staring into space.

'I'll have her back on stage in fifteen minutes,' I heard Doctor Miracle saying.

'No! No! Please don't let him touch me. Please don't let him touch me!'

I have no idea why I was so adamant about Doctor Miracle; suddenly I hated him. I was fighting those who were holding me, so as not to let Doctor Miracle near me. I was even kicking him away. Something made me suddenly afraid of him, but I didn't know what.

'You know it is illegal to administer medicine to someone without their consent,' I heard Okey say.

'Okey, Okey, please don't let them touch me, *please!*' I kept pleading.

'I'm only giving her something to calm her down,' said Doctor Miracle. 'She should never have stopped coming for her treatments. I told her, twice a week she must come for her vitamin injections.'

They were holding me down now, with my arms held firmly making the veins clear for the needle. A strap was tightened above my elbow, a vein on the inside of the elbow was found, and a needle was forced into it. When I was finally taken to the Doctors' Hospital later that night – after much discussion between Okey and Virginia Wicks who, as my best friend, was called in for advice – they found that the medication Doctor Miracle had been giving me consisted of vitamins mixed with high doses of amphetamine or 'speed'. When I had stopped going for my 'vitamin treatments' the speed had worn off, and this was the result. Doctor Miracle had kept many people going like this for years, and was known as the miracle doctor because, no matter what, he could get you on stage or back to work when other doctors prescribed rest. He was eventually found out some years later, and indicted with loss of licence. But a lot of damaged patients are still walking on a thread.

I guess my animal instincts told me his needles were loaded with danger, and the gods were telling my subconscious to fight him off. From the hospital I continued to do the show under the guidance of the doctors who took over my case. Like the doctors in Paris all these years before, they were unable to come up with a concrete diagnosis for the condition I had been suffering, but they suggested it was a kind of nervous exhaustion. The news that Eartha Kitt was ill in hospital closed the show after about a three-month run. I did not want the show to close, but there was nothing I could do to offset my hospitalization; the doctors had bodyguards take me to and from the theatre; I was not to do anything but the show; no one was to talk to me at any time except as characters on the stage – no interviews of any kind. Until this day I am wary of theatre doctors.

The two weeks' notice was put up on the stage door bulletin board. I called Loew to tell him I would now be accepting my usual six-week run at El Rancho, Vegas, in a month, so as soon as the show closed I would come to Los Angeles where I could rest for two weeks.

'I don't think you should do that,' he said on the phone.

I thought I was hearing wrongly. 'I beg your pardon?' I asked, in a state of shock, though I was almost expecting it.

'I don't think you should come to Los Angeles.' I could hear a harshness in his voice.

'Why not?' I asked, holding the phone closer to my ear to hear the truth in the sound of his voice. Even his silence was telling me it was over. I did not want to believe this. I pressed the phone closer. I could not think of anything to say, and I could not translate what I was feeling through the wires to Loew. Then the line went dead.

Putting the phone back in its place I could not cry, I could not think straight; something was disturbing the elements; this was not Loew. All the scenes of our recent past came back to me: RS's 'kidnapping' me on my last night in Los Angeles; *Confidential* magazine's headline about 'white and tan housekeeping'; Loew coming into my dressing room and saying 'I'll meet you next door . . .' and five minutes later RS appears. Was this the night Loew was going to ask me to marry him? Or was he going to take this chance to sever the relationship? Was his mother guilty of the plot?

I relived every moment of those last scenes. I walked through the tiny penthouse apartment that Mr Zimmerman rented to me for ninety dollars a week. John Ryan and I had fixed it up so beautifully, with plants everywhere and even a little oriental glassed-in area. I tended my plants as scenes of Loew and me together rehashed themselves in my mind. I wanted to cry but couldn't – I was numb from hurt. I walked out onto the roof wishing every star, moon and planet would help me. Mama, my heart is sick, please don't give me away again. My two cats, Tex and Jinx, meandered towards me as if they understood; they were caressing me when the phone rang, taking me back inside. I picked it up expecting it to be Loew. Perhaps he wanted to talk about it, perhaps he had changed his mind. 'Yes, you must come to Los Angeles,' he would say, 'I love you too much to let anything come between us.' Perhaps he would. . . .

'It's Jamie,' said James Dean down the phone.

21 James Dean

'Loew is in his room, Kitt, and they have all moved in. The house is very dull and no one says anything much to each other. Loew is extremely quiet – stays in his room drinking most of the time. The operators of MGM have been warned not to allow calls between you two. His mother is here now too.' James continued, 'I heard her say, "He will marry that girl over my dead body."'

Knowing I could not fight for my position from so far away, I could not do anything but listen.

'That article in *Confidential* magazine put the crunch on the whole thing. When the whole family accepted you, she was left alone to destroy the relationship; she told Loew if he married you it would be the death of his grandfather.' James was talking in a very soft tone. Loew's grandfather was in his late seventies, and had had several heart attacks; he lived in the tower of the Waldorf Astoria and rarely went out. So the pressure was on. The one man I wanted to be the father of my child was being emotionally blackmailed. What could I do? I wished Loew would defend his position as a man who was not afraid to reach for happiness, to fight for it. But the plot had weakened my position to fight and I was three thousand miles away with a show to do. There was no way to defend myself, so I had to let it go. Perhaps the truth will out in time and all will come as it should, I kept thinking.

James continued to tell me what was going on. James knew how heartsick I was, he knew Loew was hurting. He told me Loew was in his room drinking for six weeks while the mother was inviting Marissa Pavane, Joan Collins, or any of the other young mares in the MGM stables, trying to get Loew interested – anything to get him away from Eartha Kitt. 'He'll marry her over my dead body' kept sounding in my ears as I listened to James. He also talked about his own problems. James was doing *Giant* at the time with Rock Hudson and Elizabeth Taylor. He was now becoming *the* number one actor for the screen, but he told me how unhappy he was working with Rock Hudson and Elizabeth Taylor.

'How can you create a character when you are working with plastic?' he asked. 'I feel nothing from these people. You can't become an old person just by putting make-up on your face and grey stripes in your hair.

You have to be old, you have to think old, you have to imagine old, then you become old.'

I could hear James's frustration and anger; he was really growing old in his fights with the director, George Stevens, who James claimed catered only to the plasticism of Rock Hudson and Elizabeth Taylor. James was not at all happy with his performance in *Giant*. 'I had nothing to grow on,' he complained. 'I had no support from anyone. I could not gradually mature the character as I wanted to because the others were not maturing with me. They were the same from beginning to end, just with grey hair.'

James had often spoken to me before of these frustrations in Hollywood. We would ride up and down Sunset Boulevard on his motorbike, from one end of the Strip to the other, often stopping to rest on a park bench around Sunset and Vine, or Hollywood Boulevard and Vine, or in the downtown area where the night people roam. People-watching: winos and junkies, workers, street cleaners, night watchmen, prostitutes. We watched for character study, most of the time in silence. James and I had such a strong spiritual contact I could hear what he was saying even when he was silent. We felt that his contact between us was of a different place in a different time; that we had travelled the same path together many times before. Our souls were mates, our minds so much in tune with the other.

I could truly understand James Dean's frustrations with Hollywood – the Hollywood that Orson Welles hated, where, he said, 'They don't make films, they make commercials'; where 'The artist has no place because there are no thinkers, let alone intelligence.' Hollywood, where they cater to the lowest common denominator; where intelligence has no place and real artists die from frustration at being prostituted. Artistic intelligence does not run very far on the money path in Hollywood. James Dean, being both an artist and intelligent enough to know what he needed, could never be at peace with himself in the plastic, commercial world of Hollywood. But his frustration gave him the material to enhance his artistic abilities. So when he tore up a studio set in horror at seeing life-size posters of himself gloating at him everywhere, from floor to ceiling and ceiling to floor, James knew no one would understand why. Art is true only when art remains true to itself, and James wanted to be true to himself and to his art; he would not stand by, like so many others, and watch it be prostituted.

As I listened to Jamie's problems, I thought that perhaps something could be done about them in time, and encouraged myself that it could be the same for me. *Mrs Patterson* closed after the two weeks designated. I packed my things and was in Los Angeles a few days later. I took a suite at the Sunset Towers, and called some friends who invited me out for dinner. I dressed in my favourite Don Loper outfit with the secret wish that I would run into Loew. I sent out so many electronic vibes, I'm surprised I didn't fuse myself. After dinner, the group wanted to go to Cyrano's on Sunset Boulevard, a swanky nightclub in competition with the Mocombo. Cyrano's had good food and entertainment and late hours. My back was to the door as the four of us ordered. I was holding the menu in front of me when the hairs on the back of my neck began to send messages. I could feel a wonderful, strange, sensual sensation. He was there, I knew he was there. I could feel him. I was too afraid to look away from my menu. He was coming closer. Or was I going mad?

'Eartha, I'm having a little party at my house after we leave here. Would you like to come?' Arthur was speaking to the back of my head. I did not want to turn around, but I did. 'I'd like you to. See you there.' And he was gone.

I was very uneasy for the rest of the evening until we arrived at Loew's house, the house that was our nest. James Dean opened the door and we fell into each other's arms, hugging each other like there was no tomorrow.

'Jamie,' I said, 'what have they done to you? I can't feel you, your spirit is gone.'

Jamie laughed, saying, 'Ah Kitt, you're on one of your voodoo trips again.'

My escorts went in different directions as I found a place in what was my favourite room in the house, the study. I sat on the long wall-sofa, waiting for something, waiting for Loew to come and sit next to me, waiting for Loew to show me the real reason he wanted me here. And soon something did happen. Loew came and sat next to me, took my hand and gently held it between us on the couch saying nothing; just holding, getting up, leaving, returning, taking my hand and holding.

At one point, Judy Garland came into the study. She stood in front of us, looked at Loew, and said, 'You bastard, you are so much in love with this girl you can't see straight, and you are too fucking weak to do anything about it. Arthur, when in the fuck are you going to grow up and be your own fucking man?' Judy left the room in what looked like a fury. Loew got up and followed her. Through the door I could see Judy and Loew continuing the discussion.

Jamie came into the study and sat next to me. Neither of us knew what to say to the other, but we did not need words anyway. The guests gradually left. When it was obvious I should be doing the same, I was still sitting in the same place waiting for Loew to return, perhaps this time saying something to encourage a future between us. My escorts came to the door of the study to ask me if I was ready to go. It was beginning to seem out of place for me to stay any longer, so I got up to leave. Jamie walked me to the front door where Loew was saying goodnight to Judy and the others.

'I'll call you tomorrow,' Loew said to me. 'Sunset Towers, isn't it?'

'Sunset Towers,' I answered.

Jamie called up the next day to say they were waiting for me. I took a cab to Miller Drive, where Jamie opened the door. Again there was no soul when we hugged. I did not say anything, but it did haunt me a bit. I did not see Loew – I assumed he was upstairs. I had only been there for a short time when Jamie said he wanted to collect some records from his place. We took his Porsche and drove over Mulholland Drive to Jamie's house. We collected the records and drove back over Mulholland Drive. Jamie was driving very sanely; he knew I was leary about Mulholland Drive – a few of our friends had never made it over this road. It was about the most dangerous route between the San Fernando valley and Los Angeles proper. No one plays with Mulholland Drive. For no reason I can find to explain, I said softly, 'Jamie, I don't like this car, it's going to kill you.' Jamie laughed as he calmly took the curves to finish our journey back to Miller Drive.

The whole day passed and Loew was nowhere to be seen. Jamie and I played records and playfully took a dance class around the pool. When we got tired of that we played the conga timbo drums to accompany the records. Loew never came down from his room. Jamie drove me back to the Sunset Towers. He held me to say goodbye: 'Give him time, Kitt. He's got to get rid of a lot of shit that has been hanging over him for years. Give him time. He loves you. He's trying, Kitt, give him time.' With this encouragement, we parted.

I left the following day for Las Vegas. My show was to open on Tuesday at El Rancho and this was Sunday. My musicians would be waiting in Las Vegas for rehearsals. I didn't want to leave Jamie – he was my only binding spirit to Loew, and he had said he was going somewhere to be in a car race. I didn't want him to go in this car race. Was this from selfish reasons, or was it that I was sensing danger for him? Either way, I did not trust my instincts enough to warn him. But I had warned him, on Mulholland Drive when I had said, 'Jamie, this car is going to kill you,' though I had no idea why I was saying it. Jamie always thought of me as a voodoo priestess anyway, and laughed it off as he always did.

There were no days off in Las Vegas – seven days a week, two shows a night, each one an hour long. The following Sunday, one of the girls in the chorus line came into my dressing room announcing James Dean's death in a car accident. I was furious with her because I thought she was playing around. 'No, I'm not joking,' she said, 'I wouldn't joke about a thing like that. It's just come over the radio – James Dean is dead. He was on his way to a car race and crashed.' The girl was crying. The shock was too much for me to believe. I wanted to call Loew and ask if this was true. I didn't. One of the stage hands brought a radio to my dressing room where the death of James Dean was verified.

I was so angry. How could you be so stupid, Jamie? How could you kill yourself? Why? How could you desert me like this? Jamie, don't let this be true. Jamie I need you. . . . The stage make-up on my face went in all directions with the line of tears that carried my angered sorrow. I was angry that he left me; I was angry that I no longer had him to hold onto. I was angry that he had so much inside of him; so much was happening, so much was coming together. So much of him that was so misunderstood, so much Jamie had to say. So much he had to do and no more time to accomplish or even challenge his own desires; no more time for us to talk in silence and wish away stupidity and mediocrity.

I mourn you, Jamie, not so much for your death, but for cheating me out of your presence in my life. How dare you cheat me out of your life? You took the only real friend I had, my own true love friend. Jamie, you cheated me. I won't let you leave me, I will hold your spirit with me. You won't leave me, Jamie, ever.

James Dean: probably the last of the Hollywoodites to fight for artistic value and integrity, knowing art cannot be expressed unless it's in action; for art means action. Without action there is no art; and the artist must be protected from commercial prostitution. When mechanical technology becomes more important than the living artist there is no longer art. An artist who is no longer allowed to think is no longer an artist.

James Dean: a giver who wanted to receive, to be stimulated, to be ignited, to be sparked in order to spark. The better the others, the better the you; the better the you, the better the me.

Jamie, how can you cheat me? No one here understands me; you are the only one – my line of communication, my line of understanding, my line of translating my feelings. You made me understand that all was okay in me, that I need not be afraid of myself or my ability to think and use my thinking to challenge others. You were a thinking artist, Jamie, along with the James Baldwins, the Ella Fitzgeralds, the Leontyne Prices, the Paul Robesons, the Sugar Rays, the Marian Andersons, the Booker T. Washingtons, the George Washington Carvers, the Bethunes, the Katherine Dunhams, the Billy Mays, and all those who had to struggle to protect their integrity and beliefs.

I truly miss you, Jamie.

22   Into Africa

My life went on in its usual form – cabarets, recordings, and so on – with the hope that Loew would return always in the back of my mind. I had no desire to get interested in another man; I was waiting for Loew. I had bought a house on East 92nd Street. Since blacks could not easily buy into that area, I bought it in my accountant's name and he sold it back to me for one dollar. It was a duplex of three apartments, two of which I rented because I preferred the house to pay for me living there. I intended to buy up the whole of the south side of 92nd Street. Much to my agent's surprise I wanted to own land instead of diamonds and fanciness. It seems if the artist has monetary security this puts the agents in fear of you perhaps not needing work – stay broke and you'll have to keep working for less than you're worth.

I beautified the back yard, laid in brick, and made an embankment for an apple tree, a wild cherry tree, and vegetables. Downstairs was turned into a Hollywood-type bathroom, dressing room, bedroom, living room with real fireplace, and a small kitchen, which was all I needed. I was happy waiting for Loew. There was an alleyway between my house, number six, and a humungous apartment building. A tiny window looked into this alleyway, but the light was blocked by the apartment building. So when I was asked to pay light rent to the apartment building, naturally I closed the window up. Then I found I had to fix the sidewalk directly in front of the house; then I had to remove a staircase; then I had to make another staircase, and so it went, drain, drain, drain, until nothing was left. But I managed. While all this was going on I moved in with Virginia Wicks and her two children, little Chrissie and Mike, where I stayed until I was asked to take on an engagement of the Café de Paris in London.

This, to me, was an extremely important engagement. I prepared for it, as I always did, with my trio, as if I was preparing for a one-woman Broadway show. I had Pierre Balmain make an aquamarine silk satin dress that flared out at the bottom, with a train of chiffon coming from the left knee that I could remove at will. Since the Café de Paris had a staircase leading down from the stage to the dance floor, and another leading from the audience on the opposite side, I had Major Neville-Willing build a walkway to connect the two stairways so I could walk the room without too much upping and downing from each level. Turkish-style pouffes were placed in strategic positions for certain songs to be sung from. A train of chiffon was plucked from my right shoulder as I reached the bottom of one of the staircases and was left draping the stairs from top to bottom until the show was over. My make-up was very cat-like, with aquamarine eye shadow, and my hair (extremely short still, a result of the haemorrhaging) was combed into bangs. As I entered the stage with only a bastard-amber spotlight, the effect was startling. Lord Snowdon captured it in a photograph which he took when he came with Princess Margaret one evening, and which he used in one of his books.

This is where I met Chris O'Donnell; Major Neville-Willing brought him to my dressing room to introduce us. Chris and I hit it off immediately, and had a lot of fun together. I remember one occasion when Otto Preminger came in for the second show and asked me to his table. I was courteous and accepted, despite my suspicions about Otto, who had once auditioned me for his film *Carmen Jones* and then insisted that my voice be dubbed. I thought that would be cheating the public, and refused to play the game, so he used Dorothy Dandridge instead. The night Otto came to the show so did Chris, and he was waiting for me in my dressing room afterwards. I did not have much patience with Mr Preminger, who was behaving as though I was going to be his target for the night. The champagne flowed, Mr Preminger mauled, and I was bored. I made some excuse to go to the ladies' room and disappeared with Chris into the night.

I adored Chris but felt an air of insecurity about him; it was as though he was waiting for something to happen, wanting something more than he had but not knowing how to make it happen. He took me to meet his mother Jo, whom I immediately adored, in her house in the countryside – a very fine old English estate which she had re-bought, having lost it during the war when she divorced her first husband. Chris had one of those most unattractive cars (God knows what it's called), with doors opening up like wings, instead of out like a normal door. I found this car the most uncomfortable thing to get in and out of, but Chris seemed to be so proud of it. He had a bragging attitude when he drove it; he was el macho, but I hated it. Pretentious things always make me feel uncomfortable, especially when they are not practical.

Chris's mother showed me around the house, and Chris walked me round the gardens. All was peaceful, calm and comfortable, and Chris's stepfather was easy to talk to and be with. Only Chris was a bit uneasy. This made me restless too. I did not know anything about his background, except that he was Huntingdon Hartford's nephew. As I looked around at the grandeur of the house and garden, I began to be haunted by the memories of the cotton plantation in the South; the memory scared me into feeling I could never be completely comfortable in this kind of world. The spirit of the house was good, Jo and her husband were great, but I could not get away from that old conditioning which told me I did not belong. Through the years I have realized that I am much more comfortable with the basics – simple, comfortable luxury. Give me a log cabin, a kerosene lamp and outside sanitation any day . . . as long as it's mine I'm happy.

Chris and I came back to London and went to his house on Pont Street. I left the next day for Sweden where I had been contracted to Berns Solenger in Stockholm. Naturally I expected to hear from Chris at some time, but he made no contact. My engagement was only for two weeks, so I did not have to wait too long before I could be back in London. Then I got word from a mutual friend that Chris had gone off with some Italian countess. Perhaps this was what he had been waiting for all along – after all, it's not every day that a layman can run off with a countess. The main problem with the gypsy life of an entertainer is that you have to go where the work is. It can be simple when the woman follows the man, but not the reverse; the man often resents the woman's position, especially if she has prominence on the bread-winning side. Often the man will simply not follow; if he does, he may find he never gets what he was looking for and wallows in the success of the woman until he self-destructs – sometimes destroying both. Chris was not selfish in this way, he just wanted to do his own thing.

My stay in Stockholm was very enjoyable. Prohibition was still current then, as it had been when I was there as a young dancer with the Dunham Company – when the sun never really left the horizon; when we did not know night from day; when we sat on park benches to dream and play in the midnight sun; when you could only get two jiggers of schnapps with a meal or a smorgasbord; where you would never see poverty or bums or drunks in the streets; where life to us was what heaven must be like. The city was so clean you could eat from the streets; the children were so curious they gathered around us in crowds at the swimming pool to see just how much blacker we were going to get lying in the sun.

My stays in Stockholm have always been pleasant, and I always look forward to returning. It was there I won a gold medal for my first Swedish television special, *Kaskade*, with Jan Namsjour (directed by Oke Falk). I never actually received the gold medal, but Sweden also gave me my first gold record with 'Where Is My Man?', so I take it we are even.

Life went on, with engagements hither and yon and back again, until I found myself back in America being asked by Lloyd Young to do a film in Africa with Sidney Poitier called *The Mark of the Hawk*. I could not immediately make up my mind about this offer, even though I thought it would be great working with Sidney. The part of the wife was extremely small and not much in the personality stakes, but I wanted to see Africa, any part of Africa. The film was financed by a religious organization so there was no money to speak of – just expenses to and from Nigeria and London. Since nothing much was happening except for my usuals, I went out with Lloyd Young and his wife to discuss the idea. We had a Japanese dinner and drank sips of sake. I had never had sake before, and felt no effect until we hit the air; I can really say my head was jolted into a twirling shock, something I would not like to repeat. We went dancing at Guy Lombard's. It must have been New Year, since I remember balloons falling from the ceiling and tiny horns being blown in my ear; 'Should old acquaintance be forgot, and never brought to mind . . .' This was a night to be remembered, not forgotten, because during it I promised Lloyd I would do the film. All my scenes were to be shot in London, but 'Only if you take me to Africa' was my deal.

We went. We stayed at the Catering Rest House Hotel, supposedly the only European hotel in the vicinity. It had little bungalows like the Garden of Allah in Hollywood, and a main building containing the restaurant and bar where we all met after the day's work. There was nothing for me to do all day so I was up at dawn to start enjoying the beauty of Africa. There are no dawns or sunsets anywhere else as beautiful as those in Africa. My little bungalow was surrounded by mango trees, my favourite; a little boy came each morning, climbed the trees, picked the ripe ones, put them in a basket and sold them to me, even though I could easily pick up the windfalls. But the boy was so adorable I could not resist paying him. No matter how many mangos there were left over from the previous day, I still paid the boy a dollar a day to let him feel how smart he was trapping a sucker.

My bed was covered with a mosquito net to ward off mosquitoes; and though we had had injections against malaria, we still had to take a batch of malaria pills each day. We did not know that gin and tonic would have served the same purpose. I rented a bicycle to exercise each day in the dawn sun, when I would marvel at the beauty of God in his or her glory as I watched the painting of the skylines fade into the glow of sunlight. I would listen to the sound of nature mingle with the wakening sounds of the people squabbling in the market places; see the beauty of the African faces in the expressions which marked their struggle to survive in a 'civilized' jungle of primitivity; see some of the realness of that civilization that had been carted to the western worlds of Europe and America through slavery; see where some of my ancestors came from. The way of life there was not too different from that which I had known in South Carolina – the blacks still struggling to hang on, with a few notable exceptions.

Since the heat of the sun was so great I dressed scantily in a bikini to ride my bike around, only to find photographers hanging from trees. I was eventually called by our producer, Lloyd Young, who requested that I not dress so scantily as I was upsetting 'the natives'. When I was not being hounded by photographers hanging from trees, I was starving at the Catering Rest House: the food was terrible, so I only ate on Thursdays, the day when the food was African – curried rice with chicken sprinkled with peanuts and bananas. I looked forward to these African dinners, but was less enthusiastic about the vultures sloping around outside the restaurant windows, waiting for whatever was left to be thrown to them. I have never seen such ugly, vicious-looking birds in my life, and though they were fascinating to watch, I was scared by the knowledge that they would eat *anything*.

Sidney asked me to go for a walk with him one Thursday night. It was calm and romantic, the moon was full. Only the sound of the crickets could be heard. The night was soft and gentle and right for romance, but with the wrong timing and the wrong man, a married man. We followed the dirt path over the hills and down the dales, where only the music of the gods could be heard. The sound of an organ was coming from a small primitive church and then changed to the beat of native drums which we followed. A group of men were gathered around a fire amusing themselves in dance and play. We stopped to watch for a while before retracing our footsteps on the path we came on.

'There is a tribe near here called the Ebos who worship bats,' said Sidney.

'I'd like to see them,' I said. 'I wonder where they are located?'

'Kitt, whatever you do, don't go looking for them; if the bats are disturbed, I am told the whole tribe will have to pack up and move with them,' said Sidney.

'Why?' I asked.

'Because the bats settle where there is food, and the Ebos follow,' answered Sidney.

We returned to the Catering Rest House. I did not sleep the rest of the night as I thought about the lifestyle of the Ebos. How can I find them? Sidney had also told me that if I disturbed the bats I would either be taken with the tribe or hacked to death. I became extremely curious about this. The next morning I asked my cabin boy if it would be possible to find the Ebo tribe. He told me he had a friend who worked for the newspaper who could act as a guide to take me to them, but I must be sure not to disturb the bats in any way.

The newspaperman came to take me to the Ebo tribe, his camera in hand. I had a small movie camera that I took with me. We arrived at the Ebo village – a nucleus of huts with a regular house made of wood in the centre. 'We must get permission from the chief before we do anything,' said the reporter-guide. We drove to the wooden house and knocked on the door, which was opened by two black Swatzer negroes; they were two of the most handsome Swatzers one could ever hope to lay eyes on. The chief was standing behind them, and said he recognized my voice from the radio (that screamed at them from morning to midnight). I explained to the chief through my reporter-guide that I wanted to see the bat 'shrine'. No one could go near the 'shrine' without the permission of the chief. Some words were exchanged, then I understood they were questioning why a young girl from the foreign land of our lost cousins would want to see a shrine of bats? When I realized that this was their question, I replied 'To understand my ancestors' culture better.'

The chief and the Swatzer negroes escorted me and my reporter-guide-translator to a set of three trees in a semi-circle. One tree with a burnt-out hollow held the replica of a cross; an area in front of the three trees showed signs of something having been burnt there, the remnants of a camp fire perhaps. Looking up at the three trees they seemed to be covered in some kind of fungus which formed fist-sized swellings. One would have thought they were three infested, cancered trees until a flutter of bird-like vermin moved from a branch and back again. They probably thought this was sufficient movement for the lost cousin, but I asked, 'How can we make them fly in abundance? I want to see them by the thousand.' The decision lay with the chief, who risked having the bats leave completely. He gave permission for a fire to be started where the camp fire area was. The fire was prepared with sticks, flower plant leaves, some kind of powder which was sprinkled over it, and then lit. A tiny flame eked its way out, causing a few more vermin to flutter from the fist-like swellings. My tiny camera was grinding away with dissatisfaction. 'Can you make more of them fly from the shrine?' I ventured, looking directly at the chief. He seemed a bit uncomfortable, but he was also eager not to disappoint his lost cousin. The order was given, and the fire was fanned to force the perfumed smoke up into the clinging bats. More fluttered out and back again; a higher band of smoke went up and more and more bats were on the wing. 'But that is still not enough,' I said. I wanted my camera to catch them in their thousands.

A few words were exchanged between my translator-guide, the chief and the Swatzer negroes. Two of them stood on opposite sides of the 'shrine' trees, and shot off the ground guns (home-made) they were carrying. The bats flew in their thousands from the trees; my camera was pointing up in the air to capture their every move. Then the rains came down. First the clouds came, the sky turned as dark as night, the sun disappeared; only it was not the rains. My camera was grinding in the sudden darkness not of a storm, but of bat spittle. Eventually the camera ground to a halt, covered in urine and dung. 'That was wonderful, sir,' was all I could think to say to the chief, who I didn't know how to address properly. The chief obviously saw my excitement at such an out-of-the-ordinary experience; an experience that an outsider might consider uncivilized, rural, primitive, but that to me was of a culture more real in its behaviour than ours. The following of the birds and animals would take you to food. What could be more real than that? I instinctively did that as a kid in the fields and forests of South Carolina, so to me this was all very natural. But how could I prove to Sidney Poitier that I had found the Ebo tribe? That I had made the bats fly and was still here?

I needed proof. The film and photographs would take too long to develop, and Mr Young was leaving for London the next day to be with his family for Christmas. I needed immediate proof.

'Sir,' I said, seeking the attention of the chief, 'do you think it's possible for me to have a bat to carry back to the Catering Rest House?' The chief did not speak my language, but his look made me know he had understood me before my translator-guide could spit the words of my request out. The chief looked at me strangely, warm in the appreciation of the joke he knew I had in mind. Why else would I want a 'rat on wings'? He sent the two Swatzers out into the forest, away from the bat shrine. A while later, we heard the sound of guns hither and yon, followed by silence. We all stood still, waiting. A rustle of footsteps was accompanied by the sight of the two Swatzers as they returned bearing a batch of bats swinging from the end of their ground guns. I was like a kid seeing electricity or a gas stove or inside sanitation or hearing a radio for the first time, so great was my excitement, especially since I had a lot of it on film. I was bursting to get back to the Catering Rest House to show Sidney and the crew what I had accomplished. The chief gave me one of the six or seven bats that the macho Swatzer negroes had brought back. Since bat meat is considered a delicacy, we all gained by the day's happening. The bat was put in the trunk of the car for me to take back to the hotel. I decided the joke would be on Lloyd Young – something he would remember on his trip back to London to be with his family for Christmas.

On my return to the hotel, I called my cabin boy. 'Can you find me a lot of Christmas paper?' I asked. The cabin boy told me there was none to be found around the hotel, but I could get some in a shopping area nearby. I took a taxi which waited while I did the buying. I went back to the hotel armed with a roll of wrapping paper and some ribbons; with my cabin boy I cut six pieces of paper in the same size and wrapped the winged rodent gift with great care: one piece of paper, wrap and tie with a bow, another piece, wrap and tie with a bow, and so on. When dinner time came, I went to the restaurant where Mr Young was dining with the director and a few friends. I had left the 'Christmas present' on the coffee table by the fireplace in the bar, much to the interest of the crew who were having their usual drinks at the bar while waiting for a table in the restaurant. Sidney was giving his grandiose speeches as usual, eulogizing on the fabulous use of the English language. If Sidney had not become an actor, I am sure he would have been a preacher; he was always practising on anyone who would listen.

They gathered round my package, trying to guess its contents. I went into the restaurant to get Mr Young. 'Mr Young,' I began, 'I know you are leaving early in the morning for London to have Christmas with your family.' Mr Young looked up at me as I continued nervously, not knowing his sense of humour, 'And I found you a Christmas present. Of course there is no Fortnum and Mason here; it took me a while to find something suitable, but with a little help from my friends, I managed.' I was so insipidly sweet I almost vomited on my own words.

Mr Young looked at me with an expression that said 'Well, where is it?'

'Mr Young, I did not want to make an issue of it, so if you would come into the bar, I have left it on the coffee table.' Mr Young got up to follow me as he said,

'Gee, this is very sweet of you, Eartha, I had not expected any presents; I thought we'd do all that in London when we got there.'

'I just wanted to show you my appreciation for bringing me to Africa, Mr Young. I know you didn't have to, and it may have been my first and last chance to ever come to Africa.'

By this time we had reached the coffee table. Mr Young sat down, a Cheshire cat grin on his face in happiness at the thought that someone had gone to such lengths for him. One ribbon was untied, one wrapping was unwrapped, a wry smile played on Mr Young's face when he saw another layer of paper, another ribbon untied, another wrapping unwrapped; and so it went, with Mr Young becoming more and more frustrated until he finally got to the last layer. When he was halfway through getting this wrapping off, there was the bat lying on its back with its wingspread of about three feet, its eyes staring at the ceiling. Everyone who had gathered to see the surprise scattered in all directions when Mr Young jumped up like a jack-in-the-box and burnt a path back to his table in the dining room. Sidney Poitier jumped through the open shutter windows to join the vultures outside in laughing hysterics; the others returned to their respective places, laughing in horror and taking bigger gulps from their drinks or asking for something stronger.

I gave the bat to the bartender, who was greatly appreciative to receive such a rare delicacy that he said he would enjoy with his family. Mr Lloyd Young left for London early the following morning without seeing anyone. I did not hear from him until we came to London to finish shooting at Shepperton Studios, so I had no idea as to how my little joke went over, though I was told he never ate his dinner.

23 Bush Travel

I met Nnamdi Azikiwe in his house and he used to come often with his daughter to have dinner on Thursdays at the Catering Rest House. Azikiwe had earlier been jailed by the British government for alleged siphoning of British funds. He was a powerful person in Nigeria, fighting for funds for schools and hospitals and the general elevation of his people. It was rumoured that his imprisonment was an attempt to demean him in the eyes of his people so as to weaken his position. According to him, he was not siphoning funds at all, but depositing them in a Nigerian bank instead of a British bank, so he could better control the monies. The whole affair was used as propaganda by the British government and their political allies in Nigeria to disgrace Azikiwe. But the reverse happened; whereas he had the support of about sixty-seven per cent of the people before his imprisonment, while in jail his position became stronger as he became a martyr, giving him a further twenty per cent of support.

The only way to weaken his position now was to put him in such a high position he had no power at all. Azikiwe met me on a visit to London and told me that he had been invited to run for the position of President of Nigeria, and he asked what I thought.

'Whom would you have to answer to?' was my question.

'Her Majesty the Queen and the British government,' Nnamdi replied.

'Would you and Her Majesty and the British government have mutual agreement on decisions?' I asked.

'The British would have the last word,' was his reply.

'Then why would you want to be President? Why not remain as you are, since you already have so much influence in Nigeria? Should not the "last word" be by and for the Nigerians, with economic equality for all, black and white, according to ability? Why be a President without power?'

'It is so rare that a black man can become President of his own country,' Nnamdi argued.

'A President without power, Nnamdi,' I meekly replied, 'seems to me to be a President without a country. You would be just a figurehead.'

He bowed his head in thought.

'But then what do I know about politics and power?' I joked, and we both laughed it off.

Some time later I was called to the Dorchester Hotel in London to have dinner with Azikiwe, who was there for very important government talks. Again he asked my thoughts on the subject.

'Well,' I said, 'at least you will be able to say "I am President of my own country".'

'Why don't you marry me? We can be President together,' he laughed.

'Nnamdi, you have a wife, a beautiful wife, a wonderful wife,' I answered.

'I need two wives,' he answered. 'One who has an international understanding of things, an understanding of different cultures; one who will stand by me and keep me unafraid of the white man. As well as the wonderful wife I have already.'

'Nnamdi, you have no reason to be afraid of the white man,' I said. 'You have a country that has something the white man wants; if he wants it and has the skill to get it, let him have it, but make him share it equally with you and your people. He may have the know-how, but you have the product. In this way you can elevate your people economically; you must train them for skills, school them, and build up their standard of living without begging for loans. You must be able to pay your own way. Right now, the young Nigerian goes away for his schooling and often, after a taste of the Western world, does not come back. If he does, he finds the girls, who have not had the same opportunity for higher education, are unequal to the boys and no longer good enough. If the British want what Nigeria has in oil or whatever, let them pay for it, rather than taking it out in the small hours of the night without telling anybody.'

A British oil hunter had told me that this was happening, when I went into one of those private areas where Nigerians were allowed to work but not live or socialize in; the British had discovered oil and were sneaking it out in the midnight hours, and would not tell the Nigerians until they absolutely had to. In the meantime they were preparing homes for their families to come over. When the wives and children arrived, fences and barbed wire were immediately erected to protect them and their houses. When there were no fences or barbed wire, there had been no problem with the Nigerians; there was a feeling of mutual trust. But now it was as if the British were telling the Nigerians they no longer trusted them, that they expected them to rob their houses. I was reminded of my childhood down South.

It's funny, but when you're considered a beautiful sex symbol, you're not supposed to be intelligent enough to realize what's going on around you. I remember one of my agents saying once, 'Don't think, Eartha, just sit on your chaise-longue and sing "Santa Baby". Please don't think, you're rocking the boat.' It's because I *do* think that I do things like go into places where only white people are allowed to live, whether in Nigeria or in South Africa; it has always embarrassed me, but it has been worth it for the learning experience. It is worth facing the lack of equality in order to be able to change it. No, we are not all born equal, that's a fallacy; some of us are born at a disadvantage, but that doesn't mean we should not all have equal opportunities. All of us should have the chance to become equal, be it in skills or in thinking; all of us should have the right not to be oppressed, except in cases of criminality.

If other civilizations have made the same mistakes before, why are we digging them up to learn from them? If history repeats itself, why are we not learning from it in order to avoid repeating the stupid things man has done to man? That is why I admire the primitiveness of the Ebo tribe, for instance. They follow the bats for food and, like all nomads, they have never confiscated the land; they only take what the soil has to offer, moving on to new areas where there is food in order to let their former settlement rest and replenish itself at the hands of nature doing her unconfused thing. Our way of helping the soil is to 'enrich' it with chemicals instead of cow dung and natural compost; we should be recycling our waste and eating less. But then we should want less, which is impossible in a society that coerces you into thinking more is better, more makes you richer, more makes you know how powerful you are. More makes you feel important. More means power. No one tells you more makes you a slave to that more. We should remember the indigenous people and their ways; the American Indians, for instance, who believed that land can never be owned by man – it is to be used as God intended it, for survival, not for ownership. God owns the land. The white man doesn't listen to the indigenous people, the indigenous minds. Well, he should, because they know – they've been there before.

Amongst all the VIPs and the likes whom we met at dinner affairs and cocktail parties was a Mr Arinini. He seemed to have been the Minister for Sanitation and the Minister for everything else he could be minister for. His daughter and I got to know each other quite well. She told me about the bush people; how they never wanted anything to do with 'civilization', and had often stopped cars on the roadways, demolished them, and sometimes the people inside. I don't know how true the stories were, but human limbs had been found in different areas of the jungle where the bush people lived. To them machines were evil objects, and their presence created a feeling of malice amongst them. Mr Arinini's daughter was going through the bush country by car with a driver-bodyguard, and asked me if I would be interested in making the trip. Sounded fascinating to me.

'It's a rather long trip,' she explained, 'so we may have to stay with some of the tribal people overnight along the way, which may mean sleeping on dirt floors in thatched huts.'

Sounded fascinating to me.

One morning we left, with as little as possible, like two kids running away from home with nothing but a knapsack hanging from a stick flung over our shoulders. Of course there was no need for me to tell anyone where I was going, since if I did I might have been stopped (by my insurance people, if no one else). Moreover, since I had no family, I was only responsible for myself. We were going to an area where Arinini was chief. He was to meet us there. Along the way we stayed with a tribal family on the dirt floor of their hut. To me these were the real people, and it was fascinating to see their natural way of life.

Some days later we reached the area we were bound for. There was an unfinished cement block – just four walls – which represented the promise of the chief's return. As long as the 'house' was there, the chief would always come back. It was now all overgrown with weeds and overrun by rats and birds. A feast was prepared as part of the day's events; huge black iron pots were filled with chicken and beef to stew for all; in the corral of dirt, mangy dogs were sniffing at every pot and pan; food was dropped on the ground from the plates that were coming towards us in our place on the balcony, picked up, and returned to the plate. When the plates of rice and stew reached us, the look on my face must have relayed refusal because the son of Arinini who was sitting next to me whispered, 'You will have to eat it or they will feel insulted.' Not wanting to experiment with these people's emotions, I nervously ate the stew until my stomach refused to accept any more. My stomach became more and more agitated as I watched the mangy dogs grabbing at anything that dropped to the ground, as pieces of food returned to the pot or the plates, as a tribal dance kicked up dust all over the food.

The VIPs drank Scotch while the lesser members drank beer or palm wine. Palm wine was extracted from the palm tree through a rubber tube that drained the sap from a cut in the bark; it was then placed in a container where it would ferment in a very short time, becoming a wine. I was told that the longer it stood, the more potent it became. This was the least expensive means of getting high, but no matter how much of this or any other alcohol was consumed that day, no one got out of hand that I saw.

We stayed there overnight. I was put in a very comfortable room with a bed covered with a net to protect me from insects. The thought of snakes, rats, spiders, and scorpions kept me with my eyes fixed on the ceiling all night, with a lit candle flickering from a table in the corner of the room. The day's events passed through my head: the sight of children playing in a pond of water layered with scum and debris; the children walking several miles to and from school with little or nothing on, having to cross a muddy river with no bridge, risking exposure to a tiny worm that embeds itself under the toenail and wriggles itself to the brain, causing brain damage and death if not caught in time; I thought of all the children and adults who had to struggle through life with no hospitals or medical care to speak of. The ceiling of my room filled with scenes from areas I had travelled through. I saw the need for better health care and proper diet; all those swollen bellies showed the lack of knowledge about the importance of a balanced diet. Here, if you came upon a fruit tree, you would eat only that until your belly was full, with no thought of balancing it with anything else. And the bare feet, exposing the children to the worms (our company had been told to wear closed-in shoes, no sandals, especially in grassy or bushy areas) – all of this I saw on that sleepless night.

The next morning we were invited to a ceremony to mark the opening of a palm oil mill which was powered by stream water. The locals would pick the palm nuts, put them in a hole in the ground under straw and leaves to soften the shell which would then crack. The meat of the nut would be taken in a basket and carried on the women's heads for miles to market, where it would be crushed for oil. The oil would be bottled and exported as cooking oil to various areas of the world. This would take days of coming and going, and each trip only earned a few shillings. This new mill meant that the people could earn perhaps double their previous wages.

We all gathered around a table, the British and the Nigerians with the various tribal chiefs and representatives. A young lawyer who spoke most of the different dialects translated for us all. Each of the chiefs welcomed and thanked the British for building the palm oil mill, and the British answered by speaking of their happiness in playing a role in this project, etcetera, etcetera. What could have taken about an hour or so took about four because no one could understand the local dialects, even those who lived next door to each other (so to speak). One chief was argued down by his son, who claimed his father was now too old to maintain the position of chief and should not be taking this honour. A row blew up between them as we all sat in silence, waiting for them to deal with their own problems. Then another of the sons joined in to say neither his father nor his elder brother had the right to make these honour speeches, because he was the highest in intelligence so he should be the one to welcome the British to the mill. We all sat quietly, waiting for them to come to a solution. In the meantime, here we were with large quantities of food sitting in front of us – large boxes of biscuits, cheddar cheese, fruit, cokes, and so on.

The people of the village had been fenced out of this meeting; thin hands were coming through the cracks in the fence, reaching for whatever was on the table. There were also bottles of Scotch, fruit juice, and different kinds of soft drinks. I took some of the small boxes of crackers, biscuits and fruit juices and started to pass them to the crowd of hands; the fences were about to give in when I was snatched back by bodyguards. I could not bear to watch these people – especially the children – see so much food and not be able to share it. I remembered the hungry times of my childhood. So when the bodyguards pulled me back I still threw boxes of crackers and anything I could get my hands on to them.

When the ceremony was finally over, we went to see how the palm oil mill worked: it was a rather large object, with a vat at one end where the nuts were thrown in; then they travelled up a conveyor belt into another vat where they were heated, to separate the meat from the shell. The shells were carried to another part of the mill, dumped into a furnace, burned, and then used as fuel to generate the mill. Each different sound of the nut shells as they travelled along the tin belt formed a language for the people: if the sounds said the right words the mill and those who were responsible for it were all right. If not, well . . .

I was wearing two bracelets of gold coins (that the customs men had almost confiscated when I entered Nigeria). I always wore them rather than worry about leaving them in a hotel room, but sometimes they got me in more trouble than the worry. As I walked or moved my arms, the coins made a noise; with each sound the Nigerians oooooed and ahhhhhhed like a gospel choir. On this occasion I was scared to a state of nervous tension because I did not know what kind of message the coins were giving. I soon realized the more still I was the less oooooohs and ahhhhhhhs they made. Whatever the message, I'm still here.

When I finally returned to the Catering Rest House (after an absence of about ten days), everyone was very glad to see I had not been hacked up by the bushmen, and spent the next few days we had left there telling me gruesome stories about what could have happened to me for playing with my curiosity in this way. My search for knowledge first-hand has brought me more of an education than I could ever have got from a college degree; but it has also brought me close to danger over the years. My curiosity can never be satisfied. It's like reading a book on philosophy that refers you to another book on philosophy and another philosopher, or a book that has been translated that refers you to another translator. Truth is a theory that is constantly being disproved. Only lies, it seems, go on forever.

24   *The Way of the White Man*

We all returned to London to finish *The Mark of the Hawk*. While we were there, James Dean's last film *Giant* came out. Sidney Poitier and I were invited to the première. All dressed up in a Don Loper green and navy blue evening gown with coat to match I sat in the cinema and remembered my times with Jamie, especially the phone calls we had while he was making this film. I watched the film looking for the reasons Jamie had felt as he did. Perhaps Orson Welles was right when he said, 'No good films have come out of Hollywood since colour came in,' in that the focus became more what a film looks like than what it *is* like. The film première was over, and we were invited to attend a reception after, but I was numb from sorrow, and walked out of the cinema in a hypnotic state, dazed and missing Jamie. Tears rolled down my cheeks as I walked through Piccadilly Circus and along Piccadilly; my legs carried me along of their own volition. I just aimed myself in the direction of the Mayfair Hotel, which was like a second home, so my feet knew where to take me – like the mule that would bring Aunt Rosa's husband home, hanging off the cart in his drunkenness – but my heart and soul was with James Dean.

Ladies of the night frequented the area. They were very protective of me. When some sailors chose me for their target, I heard, 'Leave 'er alone, you nit, that's Eartha Kitt.' From the corner of my eye I could see a couple of the prostitutes assisting me along the way, walking slowly behind me until the end of their beat when another group of two or three took over. They seemed to sense I was not compos mentis and acted as my protectors all the way to the Mayfair Hotel.

The prostitutes at that time were more or less protected: they were brought in for health examinations every so often and had, I believe, a better chance of surviving and, most of all, a much smaller risk of passing on diseases. Too much goodie-goodie-ism can get to be danger-ous – when they were forced off the streets, for instance, they went indoors and since new 'moral standards' put them on the wrong side of the law, I imagine examinations are rare. There will always be prosti-tution, it is the oldest profession, so why not help them keep themselves (and their partners) clean? I went to my suite at the Mayfair Hotel and stayed awake until the sound of street vendors crying their wares and produce reached my windows.

When *The Mark of the Hawk* was finished, I had about a month to six weeks before I had to fulfill a contract in New York. I was not too happy about what was going on with the US government at that time. We seem to pick leaders for the wrong reasons. We are often voting *against* something or someone rather than *for* something or someone, probably because we seldom have real leadership material to vote for. When we do have a leadership figure, he is very often considered too intelligent, and the bottom line of his intelligence gets lost in the myriad of unthinking people. We are often too busy with 'What am I going to get out of this?' rather than 'What is the country going to get out of this?' We Americans very often tend to think as individual groups, not as Americans as a whole. The immigrants who came on the *Mayflower* and similar vessels say they are the real Americans, the ones who fled Europe in search of freedom from all sorts of oppression. They were the forefathers of the later immigrants who cried when seeing the Statue of Liberty that says, 'Give me your unwanted, your hungry, your poor'; but there are those of us who never saw the Statue of Liberty because we were already here as Indians, or were dragged here in the bottom of slave ships. And we have had a very hard time with hunger, poverty, and even being accepted as Americans. The Bill of Rights deals very vaguely with the American Indian and the negro slaves, if at all; the slave issue in particular was too sensitive to delve into – how can a piece of property have human rights? When the Bill of Rights was being thrashed out, slaves were argued to be owned property, not people (except perhaps for a moment or two), and then forgotten about until the gin mill came in and replaced them. As they were no longer needed as slaves in the cotton fields, they were freed; freed without a means of surviving in the white man's civilization, with no schooling and no trade; let out like birds from a cage that had held them for so long, without thought of gradual education, acceptance and savvy in such a vastly different world.

The Cherokee Indians (whom I have the blood of) went off on the Path of Tears, as did all American Indians, suffering from the greed of those who used equality only as a word written on a piece of paper – a word referring to equality among themselves, not to those of colour. I recall reading that Queen Victoria was sent a message from one of her generals who was fighting to obtain Africa as a part of the British Empire: 'Educate the Zulus and you will lose Africa.' Since it's hard to tell what tribe is what, the effect of this was that no black person was to be educated. But those immigrants who fled oppression and prejudice in Europe seemed to have brought it with them: they slaughtered and starved the American Indians; they even gave them blankets contaminated with the smallpox virus; they neglected the freed slaves (those who were not worked to death or had died on the slave ships).

Even in Australia they hunted down the Aborigines like flies to be swatted. When Australia celebrated its two-hundredth birthday recently, the Aborigines were there in the shadows saying, 'Remember us? We've been here for forty thousand years.'

One Aborigine chief once said to me, 'The white man is destroying himself and we will stand still with folded arms and watch.' I can see where people of colour are beginning to get even though: the Colombians are buying up Florida, the Arabs are buying up England, the Japanese are buying up America. And the blacks are standing still, for every time they make a move to become a partner they are backed up against a wall of poverty and neglect. The French are dropping bombs in the South Pacific that cause the natives of the islands to flee to France in search of medical care. When they ask the French if the bombs are harmless, the answer is always positive: 'So why are you not dropping them on yourselves for testing? And why are all our people getting cancer after these bombs are dropped? What are you testing?' No answer.

In New Zealand I asked if I could visit the Maori people. 'Where are they?' I asked, 'Are they on reservations like our American Indians?'

'Oh no,' said the white New Zealander who took me to the reservation – a place where only the Maoris live, a place sectioned off from the 'civilized' world.

I met them and was told some of their history by the beautiful chieftainess who showed me around her house. She gave me an ashtray made of sea shells that I still treasure. She is gone now. On my way back from this reservation to Christchurch (where I was in concert), I asked, 'What kind of education do these people get?'

'We choose the most promising ones in an IQ test and they are sent to very good schools,' said the New Zealander, 'Oh yes, we treat our people well.'

Like the Australian politician who said, 'We are good to our Abos, we give them money.' Money, which very often they do not understand. When they go shopping they just put their hand out with the money that they do not understand, leaving the shopkeeper to take what he wants. The Aborigines themselves told me stories of groups of uniformed men with guns coming into the Aborigines' area, raping thirteen-year-old girls, putting a gun to their heads and swearing to do away with their families if they told. I have been to see for myself the conditions of a group of Aborigines. I drove some three or four hours from Alice Springs with a cameraman, a sound man and an Aborigine who knew the area. We had to have a pass to get into the reservation from the post. Adjacent to the post was the 'supermarket', where Aborigines could buy food and clothing.

My curiosity took me inside the 'supermarket'. Food on the shelves was at least a week old, a head of cabbage that had been cut away had maggots eating paths to the inside; potatoes were shrivelled and dehydrated, and little else was fresh enough to think about eating. Clothes were hanging on racks like in a second-hand shop. When I examined the price of a navy jacket it said 'Thirty-five dollars'.

'What is the average monthly pay for a working Aborigine?' I asked.

'Thirty-five dollars,' was the reply.

When we entered the reservation I saw a sprinkler dripping water into a bucket of some kind. The Aborigine said, 'It takes about an hour for that sprinkler to fill up a glass.' There was no sign of water anywhere else that I could see. I was told the Aborigines are usually pushed onto waterless land. Tent-like abodes served as homes; a couple trying to make love could be seen sprawling on the ground in one of them; children were playing in the dirt, clothe-less; old mattresses were humped on their sides along the paths; cement blocks resembling small buildings overgrown with weeds could be seen in the distance, that the government had built for the Aborigines who would not live in them because, they said, they were 'Too uncomfortable. It's not our way; we want to build our own houses to live like we want to live. We know nothing about the white man's ways. We don't tell him what kind of house to live in.'

I interviewed some of them through an old man. I wanted to know for myself, to see for myself, to feel for myself in order to better understand both sides.

'Over there where that mound of rocks lies is where our ancestors are buried,' said the old Aborigine who was explaining to me. 'There is talk that we may have to move out,' he went on. 'The white man tells us he has found a better place for us; but we know it's because he has found something he wants.'

'What do you think it might be?' I asked.

'Opals, they are always looking for opals: black ones, white ones, blue ones. Money, that's all they want, money. Every time they move us on, they find something and move us again, and always where there is less and less water.'

I remember my visit to Canberra where I was asked to speak on the Aborigines' behalf in the House of Parliament. They were asking for a particular piece of land with water enough for all so they could build and live as they saw fit; all the Aborigine chiefs were there, representing different areas. When they told the Australian representative which area of land they were requesting, his words rang through the room like the bells of Notre Dame being rung by Quasimodo: 'You don't tell us what piece of land you want,' he said. 'We will tell you what piece of land we will give you.'

We all sat in silence, stunned, too stupefied by his words to find an answer. We all realized then how fruitless this coming together was, that talking to someone as insensitive as this politician was equally fruitless. In one body we all got up and left in silence.

We discussed the problems of the Aborigines outside the building before we parted in different directions, wondering what to do and how – to fit into the white man's civilization or fight to maintain our own culture? To live alongside their culture, and hopefully help them to recognize us, accept us, and exchange culture with us? Nothing can be won through guns and greed; they only breed hatred and one day someone will want to get even. We are all hostages to the crimes of history, committed in the name of God and economic power.

The film I had taken at the Aborigine reservation was left to be developed and it took me some years to get it back. When I did, it was so blurred and out of focus, not to mention edited to death, that nothing could be done with it. I am still wondering how this happened and why. But then I have always wondered and questioned my way through life; I have always looked for the whys of my existence. I decided now was the time to go in search of these whys. One place I had the strongest desire to see and experience was India.

25 *Dinner with Nehru*

I was a great admirer of Gandhi. To me, his philosophy was the only way to aspire to equality and partnership with the powers that be. I used to spend hours walking around Gandhi's shrine at Pallisades Park in Los Angeles on my way back from jogging on the Santa Monica beach. I sympathized with his thinking; I felt the presence of his spirit at the shrine; I walked around the lake there wanting him to touch me, to give me wisdom; I saw the beauty in him and hoped that it would always linger in all of us. It is so sad that there are so few Gandhis and Martin Luther Kings; how terrible it is that they get shot down for rocking the boat of economics; whenever someone comes along and tries to pull people together, the element of divide and conquer rises up like the wind on the desert sand.

When I applied for my visa to go to India, I asked the consulate if it would be possible to have dinner with Nehru, as I was very keen to talk to him. They said it was impossible.

'Nehru doesn't even have time for political persons, Eartha, so I don't think he would have time for you.' He smiled as he said it.

'All he can do is say yes or no,' I replied.

When the answer came back from Nehru saying yes, he would be delighted to have dinner with Miss Kitt on the day she arrives in New Delhi, it must have scared the devil out of the men at the consulate because I received a call almost immediately.

'Miss Kitt, we would like to take you to dinner, anywhere and anything you want. Is there anything special you would like to have? Anything?'

The tone of his voice made me suspicious, particularly as this did not strike me as the orthodox way for a consulate to behave over a visa application. I pressed the phone more closely to my ear to analyze his voice.

'Oh yes, we have your visa for India. We will have it when we meet for dinner. Now, where would you like to go?' he went on.

'I'm afraid, sir, I don't care too much for dinners,' I teased, seriously.

'What do you mean? You asked to have dinner with Nehru and you don't like dinners?' He acted a bit taken-aback.

'Dinner with Nehru, of course, I'd love,' I answered, with pictures of wonderful, real Indian food already forming under my eyelids. If real Indian food could be found anywhere, I thought, it must be in Nehru's house. I could see thousands of dishes laid out on a marble table, Taj Mahal style. 'But I really prefer lunch,' I went on. The man on the other end of the line was really getting confused.

'Miss Kitt, anything you want. Have you thought of anything special you'd like to have?'

'A hamburger.' I was silently laughing my head off. I knew something other than my visa was behind this, but what?

The consulate man picked me up from the Mayfair Hotel and took me to the commissary in the American consulate where the best hamburgers, American-style, could be found. I sat next to the wall, surrounded by three of the consulate men. The hamburgers were ordered. My mouth watered as we waited, for I had been away from America for quite a while and longed for a taste of home. The three men looked a bit uneasy; I could read a slight tension in their body language. One looked at me from across the table and asked, 'What do you think Nehru would be talking to you about?'

'I have no idea,' I said. 'Why are you asking? What do *you* think he'd talk about?' I was getting curious.

'We don't know why he accepted your request for dinner; to us it's rather strange, as he rarely if at all accepts this kind of request.'

So this was what it was all about! The hamburgers arrived, thick and juicy, that good old real meat beef that I had missed so much on my first visit to London, when meat was still rationed and all you could get was imitations. I remembered the window kiosks where you could buy a sandwich that was so small you could hardly see it – three or four tiny sprigs of watercress that one could thread a needle with, and maybe a thimble-size piece of salmon in between; the sandwich was cut so small that it could only be picked up with the thumb and index finger; there was just about enough sandwich, all in all, to fill the inside of one's navel.

As I reminisced about my days past in London, the men's voices were weaving in and out, with me coming back into the picture when I had to give a response. In my excitement over my Texas-size hamburger I had smeared so much mustard and ketchup over it that it was dripping everywhere when I bit into it. We all scrambled to grab napkins to catch the drippings, laughing all the way.

'Would you like something to drink?' one of the men asked.

'Beer,' I mumbled through mouthfuls, as I giggled my way through each bite.

They must have thought I was some kind of nut, but I was having a lot of fun playing games with these authority men. Anyway, the best way to enjoy a hamburger is with beer; at least the beer has other nourishments that the meat does not. A hamburger and a beer makes a very balanced diet (don't ask a doctor).

'Now, Miss Kitt, we don't know what Nehru might ask you; if he asks you about certain situations in America or Great Britain we would like you to be, well, diplomatic. We don't know if this will be the case, but . . .'

'What "certain situations" are you referring to?' I managed to ask through another mouthful, wiping my mouth, trying not to look like a complete slob.

'You know, he might be interested in how you feel about the black problem both here and in America,' said one of the men, who turned out to be from the British consulate, 'knowing very well about the Notting Hill Jamaican riots and so forth.'

'Do you have a black problem here?' I asked, as if I did not know.

'Not really, but you know how these things are, just like they are in America. Sometimes too many come in at one time to find crowded living conditions, difficulty in finding jobs and assimilating themselves in such a different world to theirs. At least in Jamaica it's always summer, so to speak, whereas here it's cold and damp. So, discomfort besets them, and anger . . .'

As his voice droned on, I remembered Enoch Powell's speech in the House of Commons when he had pleaded not to allow more Jamaicans in at that time. His statement was taken as racially prejudiced, but for anyone who listened closely, what he was really saying made sense: don't bring in any more racial minorities if you cannot place them in jobs and shelter; stop the influx until the situation is less tense. But we all know what happens when the press gets hold of an 'item'.

Anyway, here I was with a dripping hamburger as three men from both consulates tried to brainwash me into being diplomatic. The more they tried to appease me, the more annoyed I became. I suddenly stopped my sensation with the Texas-size hamburger, placed it down on my plate, and looked them all dead in the eyes.

'Are you paying my way?'

'No, but . . .'

'Are you paying my expenses?'

'No, but . . .'

'Therefore, since I am travelling as a free person in a free democratic world – supposedly – at my own expense, don't you think I should be free to answer in the manner in which I see fit, gentlemen?' They looked at each other in amazement. 'May I have my visa please?' The visa was handed over immediately. I smiled and said 'Thank you.'

The lunch ended more or less in silence, with them guessing how this free spirit was going to behave in the presence of someone with whom they were playing a game of political chess. I made arrangements for my trip, and booked a flight to India. The plane stopped in Karachi, where I stayed for about a week. Since there were no 'proper' hotels that I knew of in Karachi, I stayed with the missionaries, a family of three. My bedroom had a coal burner, there was very little hot water for bathing, the bed was lumpy; even after the prayer my food tasted pretty bad, but I was grateful for small favours, remembering the days I had picked the garbage cans of Manhattan and slept on the subways and rooftops. No matter what the conditions were like, everything here was beautiful to me. The family was warm and loving, and even though the climate was colder than the icebergs of Alaska, I was having a wonderful, beautiful experience.

I revelled in the beauty of the snow on the hilly terrain; the camel-drawn water wagons crawling along the almost modernized streets; the old world costumes mixed with a hint of a more recent culture; the little children's miniscule fingers weaving rugs in open spaces in the shopping area; the rugs spread out on the street where the camels dropped their dung (this is how they aged them, together with the passing traffic and feet running over them, and then sold them as 'antiques'). To see men dressed up as clowns playing a tiny whistle-like instrument and begging for money; to see and feel the real people of Pakistan – how many cotton-picking urchins from South Carolina could have this?

I had one of those round-the-world tickets, whereby you could disembark at any place and stay for a week or so, before catching another plane to carry on circling round the world. My week came to an end and I booked myself onto the next plane for New Delhi. I got packed and ready to leave when I was told my plane had been delayed on its outward journey by snow storms in Turkey. Now I was going to miss my visit with Nehru. I relayed a message to the British consulate in Karachi requesting another dinner date. When the message was received in London, I was considered a real nutcase and told it would now be really impossible to arrange. But again I argued that Nehru could only say yes or no. Again the answer was positive. At that point, they probably thought I was some kind of Mata Hari. When I arrived in New Delhi a few days later I had only enough time to bathe, change my clothes, and get into a waiting car to do a Stirling Moss to the palace. The car stopped in front of huge gates guarded by two rifled men. One opened the gates to let us drive through. Since, as far as I was aware, no one knew about this visit, I ignored the lone photographer walking along the walls; I took him for one who is always lingering around in the hopes of getting a story. I was not seeking publicity, so I paid no attention, any more than I had when I visited Einstein at Princeton University.

I had read about the theory of relativity – the splitting of atoms to create energy. I had also read Einstein's biography and was in love with his mind. I was writing *Thursday's Child* at the time in a small house I had rented on Santa Monica beach. I had just finished making *St Louis Blues* with Nat King Cole. With a deadline for the book constantly looming, my sleeping hours were few and my thinking acute; concentration was deep, forcing me into an ethereal state at times. The little house stood alone, fighting off the rushing ocean waves in its struggle to stand firm in the teeth of death as the sea threatened to carry it in its arms to another world. I often woke up in the early morning hours to watch the coming of the dawn; to see the sky painted by the hand of God and watch the colours change like a Van Gogh masterpiece – into yellows and blues and then into pale sunlight as the morning became stronger and the tides weakened.

This particular morning the waves were very angry, rushing up against the little house. I stood on the balcony, holding on. There was no one to be seen; even the seagulls were silent, hiding from the fury. I could see myself being carried into the ocean or flung into the air like Judy Garland in *The Wizard of Oz*. I thought I should have a last wish, in case this did happen. I ran back into the house to phone Virginia Wicks in New York.

'I am due back in New York for *Mrs Patterson* rehearsals in a few weeks. If you start now, perhaps you can find someone who can help me meet Einstein,' I said.

'Kitt, are you crazy?' Virginia asked.

'Of course I am. If I was sane do you think I'd ask you this?' I joked.

'I don't think it will be possible,' said Virginia, 'but I'll try.'

'All he can say is yes or no.' I said goodbye, leaving Virginia in a state of amazement at such an 'impossible' task.

On my return to New York I went into rehearsal for *Mrs Patterson*, always with the insane idea of meeting Einstein at the forefront of my thoughts. Virginia was unsuccessful.

The time came for me to make my annual donation to an orphanage of my choice. As I was looking at a list of orphanages, I decided the easiest way to decide was to run my finger down the list with my eyes shut. My finger stopped on the North Side Orphanage. As I wrote out the cheque I asked, 'Do you think the manageress or whomever would know someone who knows Einstein?'

'Kitt, you're crazy,' said Virginia.

'All you can do is ask and all they can say is yes or no,' I said, smart-alecky.

Virginia picked up the phone to tell them I had chosen them for my donation that year, and then asked them the sixty-four billion dollar question.

'Why yes, of course,' the woman's voice said. 'It so happens that Einstein's secretary is my best friend.'

Virginia had a look of shock on her face, as if somebody had walked over her grave. From the expression on her face, I could see my wish had come true. 'They know someone, don't they?' I asked. Virginia swallowed and meekly said 'Yes'. When she regained her senses she added, 'Eleven a.m., December eleventh.'

Mrs Patterson opened and on 11 December I drove to Princeton in my yellow and black custom-made Lincoln Continental, parked it across the street from Einstein's house, and knocked on his door. The secretary opened it, and when I entered, Einstein was standing at the top of the stairs in a grey Mickey Mouse sweatshirt, his hair pointing every which way, reaching for (or replacing) invisible atoms.

'Oh, how young you are! Why would such a young thing want to see such an old thing as myself?' he quizzed me in German. We sat on a long sofa facing the window overlooking the Princeton tower. The pigeons were circling around the tower in flocks. 'You see, every morning about eleven o'clock and every evening at four, they do their exercise. They are so disciplined; isn't it a shame human beings are not so disciplined?'

We spoke of the Berlin theatre, how great it was in its time, how beautiful Berlin was, how great Bach, Brahms, Mendelssohn and all those were, as we sipped tea and ate German cake. Me talking about the American musical theatre and theatre in general seemed so trite. I asked him to explain to me personally the theory of relativity.

'My dear, you are much too young to understand all that nonsense,' he smiled.

'But I want to know,' I said impatiently. 'I want knowledge now.'

'You are too impatient, my dear,' Einstein said calmly. 'You must learn to curb your impatience.'

I wondered if he really thought I was too young or that it was all too difficult for my small brain to comprehend. When I left I was so drunk with brain stimulation that I drove back to 270 Riverside Drive, locked myself in my tiny little Japanese-style penthouse and wrote without sleep until it was time for me to go to the theatre. This state of mind lasted for days; only my stage manager knew about my visit, and I think he felt the stimulation too. My visit became an 'item' after Leonard Sillman and I had had lunch one day at Sardi's, the artists' restaurant on 44th Street. The conversation must have been overheard by a newspaper plant as I read about my visit to Princeton some days later.

And now here I am walking through the gates of Nehru's residence in search of a closer touch of Gandhi. The door of the palace opened, and Nehru's daughter's face met mine in greeting. I was ushered in and walked down a long marble corridor. I stumbled as I tried to see everything along the way – the statues, the paintings, the artefacts, the beauty of the things; things of wealth, priceless things, a wonderment of things; a puzzlement of possessions. I was ushered into a room where more priceless possessions were on display. I sat uneasily where Indira Gandhi indicated, waiting. As I waited for her to return with Nehru, I glanced around the room, afraid to move, my eyes in constant search: a gift from President Eisenhower, gifts from the whos and whats of the world; everything an unreachable, everything an untouchable for the likes of me. I waited fearfully for her return with Nehru. I hoped I was properly dressed in my gold silk print Dior; I hoped my make-up was clean and not smudged from the heat and that my manners would be proper for such an occasion. Funny, I did not have this feeling of discomfort when meeting Einstein.

My patience was beginning to wear thin when suddenly the walls-of-Jericho-type doors opened, allowing two beautiful dogs to enter, followed by a white, wrinkled lady; a European lady, a heavily suntanned English lady. The shock of seeing her overwhelmed the entrance of Nehru, who followed close behind her. Stupified as I already was, I could not comprehend the presence – seemingly as hostess – of this lady. I was expecting an Indian leader's Indian woman.

'I am Lady Mountbatten,' the English lady said with a slight smile. I got to my feet to greet her. 'Please, remain seated,' she commanded. We both sat and looked at each other, trying to figure out what the other was all about. The dogs sniffed me in greeting and turned to greet Nehru as he came through the walls of Jericho. He was in a beige silk Indian suit, and took my hand in welcome before sitting down. Frivolous talk of nonsense followed, with me sitting in awe of such a rare privilege. Are there going to be other guests? I asked myself. How do I manage this alone? What should I talk about? The questions whizzed around in my head, making me more and more nervous. But as I brought myself up to let nature take her course, I shut up and let her get on with it.

The lone photographer I had seen earlier was admitted after a servant came in to announce that he was seeking photographs. Photos were taken. 'He's the only photographer I allow in here,' said Nehru. Then dinner was announced. The three of us walked the marble corridor to the dining room where six to ten servants were waiting ready at the beck and call. My mouth salivated at the thought of the real Indian dinner to come; I imagined the taste of each dish, each different from the other, each a new and wonderful taste. How can I ask for a doggy bag to take back to my hotel? I waited with baited breath to be wonderfully, beautifully surprised. Three or four servants paraded through the swinging kitchen door bearing trays of silver containers that were placed in different areas; plates were placed on the silver platter bases, a servant stood behind each of us, a few more stood nearby in attendance. A transistor was placed to Nehru's left; it sounded like the news was being transmitted. My hands hugged each other in my lap, my eyes tried to remove the lids from the silver containers in my anxiousness to taste the real Indian dishes that were hidden beneath. The transistor radio held Nehru's attention, Lady Mountbatten was mumbling something frivolous.

Nehru gave some command, and the servants removed the silver lids to reveal Chicken-à-la-King. No more wringing of the hands or wild imaginings for me, I'm afraid. I wondered why Nehru was putting the little transistor radio closer and closer to his ear, trying to hear every word.

'He's listening to the news about Persia,' said Lady Mountbatten.

'Oh, the Aga Khan,' I said stupidly. 'Ali and Sadri are friends of mine.' (I had met them when they came to see me at Le Perroquet in Paris.) As the words left my mouth I bit my tongue in the sudden tenseness that surrounded us.

'He's having a problem with Persia at the moment,' Lady Mountbatten said tersely, making her words resound like Rank's genie hitting the gong.

There was little else to the dinner except fruit and coffee. Lady Mountbatten kept on with the small talk, Nehru went on trying to listen to the news of Persia, and I nervously went on trying to figure out this strange combination. The radio began to have a problem transmitting, making Nehru rather irritated. Finally he gave up, finished with his almost untouched Chicken-à-la-King, and waved to the servants to take it away. Lady Mountbatten looked at him with concern as she said, 'And that's his favourite. . . .'

The dinner ended and we returned to the room where we had met. Nehru explained some of the gifts on display around the room. I felt my stay was edging on the border of enough, so I made a move to dismiss myself. As Nehru and Lady Mountbatten walked me down the marbled corridor I found myself walking slightly ahead to look at the paintings and statues along the way. I felt there was more to their relationship than met the eye; I guess it's that female instinct. From the corner of my eye I saw they were holding hands in the long walk to the front door.

After saying my goodbye, I returned to my hotel in the waiting limousine. The hotel lobby was swarming like a beehive: photographers and reporters, English and Indian, grabbed me, placed me in a corner, and began a third degree.

'You had dinner with Nehru, was Lady Mountbatten there?' was the first question. Since I was more curious about the question than the answer, I thought I would be still and think before I put my foot in it. If you have something to say and don't know how to say it, be still, they will say it for you. Let them answer their own questions.

'Why are you asking me this question?' I asked gingerly. They all looked at each other in that knowing way.

'Well, was she there?' a voice from the crowd demanded.

I knew they knew she was there.

'You probably know the answer to that question, so why are you asking me?' I fumbled.

A young lady reporter squatting on her knees next to me said, 'We know Lady Mountbatten came to New Delhi some time ago and went straight to Nehru's house, but we have not seen her since. We think she is still there.'

'We know she is there,' a male voice said.

'If you know it, then why are you questioning me about her?'

I was getting a bit bolder. They all started talking to each other, arguing about the freedom of India. The controversy was that if Lord Mountbatten was supposedly the key figure in freeing India from British rule, and Lady Mountbatten was in Nehru's bed, then how free was India? I never had to commit myself to an answer as they all answered their own questions – of which there were many – taking the discussion into the early hours of the morning over beers and gin and tonics.

I sat in silence with my ears pricked up and acutely tuned to every word and phrase. Listening has often been more educational for me than getting involved in a conversation I know little or nothing about. Even when you think you know, listening can bring you another edge, another point of view.

Sleep to me is a waste of time. I often wonder why we need as much as six to eight hours of it to rejuvenate our energies. There is too much to do to sleep so long. I did not want to waste time sleeping, I wanted to do things, so I arranged for the hotel to order a car to take me to Agra to see the Taj Mahal. I did not want to go alone but since it is difficult to find someone to play with in the wee hours of the morning I took my little movie camera and twenty rolls of film for company. The drive from New Delhi to Agra was fascinating, particularly as we started out before sunrise and saw India as she was waking up. I watched the scenes of village life flash by: the daughters being driven on carts to another village to be taken in marriage, dressed in the pale colours of an evening sun; the pigs being driven along the roadside. Though these were poor villages the people seemed happy as they went about their daily lives. It always seems to me that poor people have a way of being happy with the little they have while the rich always seem to be uptight. Perhaps it's because it's hard to hold on to so much, making life weary and heavy as the burden to maintain one's wealth grows.

I kept my camera busy along the way, and it was still rolling when we reached the Taj Mahal at sunset. How I wished a friend could be with me to share in this moment, someone to whom I could later say, 'Do you remember when we went to see the Taj Mahal?' My head was crazy with excitement as I recalled the romantic stories I had read about this monument – how it had been built and why. Seeing a dead body floating in the Ganges running in front of the monument made my heart shiver, and combined with the full moon floating in the sky above to make this an eerie as well as a romantic experience. A guide with a candle took me and a few others who were there at that late hour down a stairway to see the crypt.

I returned to New Delhi in the dark of the night. Since my stay was only a week I wanted to see as much as possible, and spent my days roaming the streets searching for a better understanding. One day a lady called me to invite me for lunch (she had read of my presence there in the papers). I had no idea who she was, but from the sight of the chauffeured car she sent to bring me to her house, I imagined she was pretty fancy. On seeing the house, I was flabbergasted: all marble, antique rugs everywhere, artefacts, furniture of the old world that a museum would envy. Servants appeared from every corner of the house, and there was an army of workers mending and restoring parts of it. The lady explained that she was an admirer of mine and had taken a chance on asking me to visit her. The newspapers had reported my disappointment in not getting a real Indian meal at Nehru's, and she wanted to make up for it. A real Indian meal that would satisfy a Maharajah was served by at least ten servants who never stopped coming and going, picking up and carrying out. We enjoyed good conversation with each other, and I filled myself to the brim.

After the meal I asked to go to the ladies' room. The one nearby was being cleaned by a young girl and an older lady. As my hostess took me to one upstairs she explained that the young girl and her mother were untouchables; they were born into cleaning bathrooms and this position would be passed on for generations to come. This made me extremely uncomfortable in relieving myself as a sense of guilt came over me. I left the bathroom immaculately clean, but I still live with that guilt.

26 Around the World and Back to Slander

Soon after this I left New Delhi, stopping over in Burma. My hotels were planned by the airlines, so I always knew where to go. The Ford Foundation had a branch there and they called me shortly after my arrival to invite me to a cocktail party, which I was glad to accept. The party was given in a house that could have been a Hollywood movie set from a period film – it had been taken over by the American consulate, I believe. Beluga caviar, French champagne, Scotch whisky, and everything one could wish for was there in abundance. Members of the Peace Corps and other such groups were having the time of their lives. As I looked around watching the play of the evening, I thought of the American and British tax money being squandered, but then I guess all work and no play makes Jack a dull boy, as they say.

A lady, obviously affluent, kept following me around all evening. She was either American or British, I don't quite recall. When I finally had a chance to place myself on a sofa, trying to find peace of a kind, the lady wiggled herself next to me to say, 'Miss Kitt, I am a great admirer of yours. We hear your records all over Burma. I must say they are everywhere, and so enjoyable.' Then came the crunch: 'I am having a small dinner affair, and I would love to invite you. It would be such a pleasure for all of us if you would accept. I have had Louis Armstrong, Duke Ellington, Sammy Davis Junior, Lena Horne . . .' She went on naming proudly.

'Don't you ever invite any white people to your house?' I asked. Perhaps in her way she was trying to tell me she was not prejudiced, but I felt she was the kind of person who thinks that not serving black coffee to a black person was the kosher way to behave. As far as I am concerned, that does nothing to eradicate the attitude problem people have towards coloureds. Also, being too anxious to prove one's innocence can leave a bad impression. This lady meant no harm, she just didn't know. She wanted me to feel that I would be welcomed in her house. Her whole monologue of self-justification was just funny to me; I had to laugh at the nonsense, which made her realize that it was all nonsense too.

I was asked back to visit the consulate after meeting some of the staff at this party. A little boy with bent legs was on a trolley sitting next to the entrance, begging for money. During a conversation with some of the girls in the consulate I mentioned this little boy. The girls told me they had pitched in to buy the little boy the trolley because they felt sorry for him crawling along on the hard cement. They found him without it one day and asked where it was. The little boy told them his mother took it away because he was not making as much money as he did without it. So the girls had another one made for him and pitched in again to make up the amount he was supposedly losing.

On my walks one day (never without a loaded camera), I came across a ceremony. Being curious, I stopped to investigate; a contest was going on which made it very difficult for me to hold my camera steady: young teenage boys had hooks stuck into their back muscles and were pulling carts. This was an initiation ceremony; no blood, no tears, no whimpers. If any of these were evident, the verdict was cowardice. I certainly felt a coward as my knees buckled at the sight of this ceremony. My film came out rather hysterical from my trembling.

A few days later, I was asked to visit a school to talk to the students. It was felt that a person of their own colour from a free democratic country might have some influence against the communist sentiments that were infiltrating the schools via students who were educated in the Soviet Union and placed in the schools of Burma to stir up student rebellion. I sang a few of my songs to introduce myself; the piano was not only out of tune but the pianist whom I had rehearsed with played everything in chopsticks. Imagine 'Old Fashioned Girl' in chopsticks! But somehow I managed, probably because my voice is of the same vibrato as a middle eastern voice, so they could relate to my singing. After this, we settled down to an afternoon of questions and answers. Even though the communist students tried to disrupt the afternoon, they did not succeed and all went well. To most of them I became a person of the same colour relaying promissory dreams of a free democratic world, even though they knew that promise of dreams being fulfilled was beset by problems.

One evening I went to the home of a Mr Kwong, supposedly the fourth richest Chinese person in the world. Mr Kwong's was a dream house with all the luxuries. All the rooms were decorated in different-coloured teak wood; even the bath-house around the pool was made of teak. The dining table (teak) had a built-in lazy-Susan which, at the touch of a finger, twirled around so many types of Chinese food one was filled with the sight alone. I was leaving the next day, so as a farewell present Mr Kwong gave me a watercolour painting of a dancing Burmese which now hangs in my house in Connecticut – a painting I treasure, as well as the memory of him and his family (and, I think, the best Chinese meal I have ever eaten).

Then followed my first visit to Hong Kong: the Repulse Bay Hotel and beach; the hustle and bustle, exciting but a bit unnerving; too many people in one place; not enough flat land to support enough houses for so many; the British, the Americans, the Chinese, and God knows who else, vying over the money market; the talk of Chinese coming in by the thousands, fleeing daily from Communist China. Since the Repulse Bay Hotel was on the Hong Kong side I could not see too many matchstick areas, but to know more and see more I took my camera to the Kowloon side where I had been told there was a settlement on a hill. I was told if you walked along the 'street' there at dawn you could see whole families picking the trash for anything edible or for pieces of wearable clothing. I followed a mother who had a baby strapped to her back and a young girl of about four or five who was walking alongside her. I tried not to attract their attention to me or my camera. I had had sense enough to dress shabbily so as to not be noticed, and with my face almost covered with a hat I managed to follow them back to the settlement.

There, the edible bits of food were laid out with the rest of the findings from the others, sorted out, put into a community pot or pan, re-prepared and made ready for all to share. Young girls were bringing up water by the bucketful. Matchstick shelter was built from anything – cardboard boxes, plywood planks – and wedged into holes dug in the side of the hill. This mother had one of these for a home: a tiny cave with just enough room for her to crawl in with her baby still strapped to her back, the little girl squeezing in alongside her. There was a padlock hanging from a piece of tin pretending to be a door; a small black pot was sitting over three bricks holding the ashes of a burnt-out fire. It was a symbol of ownership, a semblance of a home – a semblance of me as a child. The little girl had had a hand blown off in the escape from mainland China.

From this hill of 'freedom seekers' I could see the comforts of the 'civilized' world in the distance: a world of plenty with all these matchstick shelters hovering above like flies on a jar of honey. The British were constantly being pressed into building proper homes for the 'freedom seekers', but the surge was too big to cope with. Not only could the British not build fast enough, but there was also the problem of finding space to build on. The main solution was to build up, not out: up and up and up. That was part of the answer; the other part was to find a way to stop the refugees from coming in such large numbers. There had to be other countries who would host these people – Australia, for example. But Australia was waspish in that no orientals or non-Europeans could obtain citizenship there (could this have something to do with the fact that she is surrounded by oriental territory?). I knew a Chinese restaurant owner who circulated his family every so often in and out of Australia to keep his business there running. Where there's a will there's a way, I guess. Even today, though I love Australia, I wonder about why such a vast country only has about fifteen million people. In many ways I agree with keeping the population small – more land yield, more all, etcetera – but is she taking her share of immigrants? Then again, perhaps she should think about taking care of the Aborigines first.

The boat people saddened me most, never being allowed to set foot on land, wandering like water-gypsies, docking only for food to be handed to them by vendors on land (with what do they trade for necessities?).

On my way back to the States I stopped in Hawaii, an American protectorate. This was a country one should have seen before she became an American state; then, she was beautiful and free from plastic and the extremism of the commercial world; the people still lived in a natural, unadulterated way. Then, you could only buy real cotton clothing, drink coconut or pineapple juice sold by the kiosk vendors at the airport, wear real straw or bamboo hats. It was a world *au naturel.* Once Hawaii became an American state the commercial world of Madison Avenue moved in, turning everything to plastic (at least I found it so on the main island of Honolulu last time I visited).

I'm told the Hawaiians want their islands back. Like me, they cannot understand why the natural beauty of things has to be 'improved'. It reminds me of how Shannon airport used to be. The planes to or from Europe always used to stop over in Shannon, where one was served real Irish coffee and could buy real Irish linen, real Irish everything. But since the 'improvement' of travel, no more. When will man learn that if it ain't broke don't fix it? These were also ways of getting a taste of other people's culture. Now it's rush here, rush there. Somewhere amongst this rushing something gets lost, like the apple carts on the streets of New York and the horse-drawn wagons of vegetables that used to stroll through the neighbourhoods. Everything was fresh and healthy then, and the vendors always attracted a cheerful gathering of neighbours who rushed out when they heard the sound of a particular cart. Now the vendors have all lost their jobs and have been replaced by fast mechanization. It's prevalent in the music business too, with the introduction of the synthesizer which has put musicians out of work and prostituted the artist.

I returned to America to get on with my career. My records were still popular so America had not forgotten me. I went straight into rehearsals for *Archy and Mehitabel*, with Eddy Bracken as Archy. The idea was based on a comic strip by Marquis, a writer for one of America's most popular newspapers; whatever Marquis felt about the social or political problems of the day, he put into the 'Archy and Mehitabel' strip. Eddy

Bracken learned all of Archy's speeches from the book that had been published as a result of the popularity of the series and was very enthusiastic about them to the extent that the show often ran overtime. One night the producer called me at home (I was living in my house on East 92nd Street) and told me he was running out of money and might not be able to open the show. I sent a telegram to the Aga Khan, who sent the money needed within twenty-four hours, no questions asked.

At this time I was also making frequent appearances on Ed Sullivan's television show. While RCA would want me to sing my latest record, Ed would often request that I sang from my Hebrew repertoire to appeal to the Jewish public. I knew a lot of Hebrew songs and it was obviously quite a novelty to have a black woman singing them. I was pleased to do it because the Jewish public was always faithful to me and I to them; having the same problems in overcoming oppression, the Jews were always sympathetic to the black American struggle.

Ed Sullivan also wanted me to wear trousers on his show because, he said, 'Every time you wear a dress we get letters from the Catholics saying you are too sexy.'

My sets for this show were always first class. I remember in particular the one they made for Victor Young's song, 'Mink Schmink, Money Schmoney': I entered on a staircase of plexi-glass, along the full length of which beautiful girls wearing millions of dollars of diamonds were lined up; I was choreographed to play with each piece as I descended the stairway. Two security guards stood at the bottom of the stairs as part of the act, to collect the jewellery (which was real) the moment the song was over. I must have been on Ed Sullivan's show for at least a month at one period. The show was fun, and the most popular of its kind at the time. Making an appearance on the Ed Sullivan show meant you were 'in', and it paid well too.

After a short run of *Archy and Mehitabel*, I continued to exercise my contracts in Las Vegas and other nightclubs across America, including at my steady base in the Plaza Hotel's Persian Room. My shows were always theatrical, with all my gowns made by Pierre Balmain.

'Eartha Kitt is the classiest show on the Strip,' said the Las Vegas critics. I was nominated for every area of the entertainment world: Best Nightclub Act, Best Recording Artist, Best Actress, and so on. So I got another offer to do a Broadway show, *Jolly's Progress*, an adaptation of *My Fair Lady*, with Wendel Corey and Ann Revier. The producer was Arthur Loew Senior, Loew's father.

It was not the greatest script in the world, but I thought it was very funny. The story takes place in the South: a runaway girl winds up in the house of a rich Southerner who takes her in as a helper then proceeds to teach her how to speak properly. No cost was spared for the production.

Rehearsals were chaotic, with Wendel Corey very often turning up late. The rumour was he spent his nights in Chinatown. When he did appear, he was often hungover from his previous night's cavortings. Ann Revier and he very often got into arguments over my lines as the character Jolly and, as a result, my dialogue was reduced. The play was becoming more and more a dialogue between the housekeeper (Ann Revier) and the master of the house (Wendel Carey). Whenever these 'discussions' took place I would go to my dressing room and wait until it was settled before returning.

Headlines appeared in Dorothy Kilgallen's column reading: 'It has been rumoured that Eartha Kitt and her director are constantly fighting and it is feared she may not show up.'

We were all shocked. The cast and the producers sent letters to Dorothy Kilgallen to say the opposite; they called her to plead for a retraction; but the more they argued in my favour, the more adamant Dorothy Kilgallen became about blackening my name. Being the one slandered, there was very little I could do. Dorothy Kilgallen was a gossip columnist of great power whom everyone was afraid of. She had no love, I was told, for anyone, especially women. If a pretty woman knew her husband (I had met him at his restaurant through a mutual friend), she was out for the jugular. Mr Langner, one of Mr Loew Senior's co-producers, told me of the many shows Dorothy Kilgallen was responsible for 'killing'. She must have been the most hated and most feared gossip columnist of her time. So much so that when she died mysteriously in her apartment, the whole of Broadway heaved a sigh of relief.

In those days, the fifties, columnists such as Dorothy Kilgallen could get away with anything as long as they said, 'It is rumoured that . . .' Rumours were rarely, if at all, checked out. Even if a rumour was contradicted with proof, a retraction would not be printed because they didn't want to ruin the original story; or, if it was retracted, it was done on a page no one read in such small print it could hardly be seen anyway. The theatres we were to tour began to cancel because of the rumour, so we opened in New York without a try-out. A closing notice was on the bulletin board the next day.

27 Loew Returns

Shortly after the show had folded, I was called by Mr Loew Senior to have Sunday brunch with him at his house. He came to pick me up from East 92nd Street, and we drove from Manhattan to his estate across the Sound (behind La Guardia airport) in silence. I had met Mr Loew Senior once, at Loew's house in Los Angeles. I had no idea how he felt about me and the relationship I had shared with his son. Did he produce *Archy and Mehitabel* to ease the pain I was still in over Loew Junior? Was there some guilt in him he wanted to eradicate? So much went through my mind, though I knew I would never have enough nerve to talk to him about it. What would be the point anyway? Let it go.

As we drove on and on, I found myself getting smaller and smaller on my side of the car. I was ashamed that my show had not been successful, but more embarrassed that the relationship between his son and me had failed. What did Loew Senior know about the break-up? Did he believe in the picture of me as a 'fast' person as was laid before him by RS? Did he have talks about me and Loew with his brother-in-law, the uncle who had told me that if Loew did not marry me he was crazy? Like a mouse waiting to be pounced on by a cat, I hovered in the corner of the car with my eyes always to the right, looking out of the window. We drove into his fifty-acre estate; the driveway was so long the house could not be seen. High trees lined this driveway and the lawns were immaculate. A scene from *Gone with the Wind* could not compare in beauty.

We drove up to a tiny house by the water – the boat house. A boat stretched in the water; bushes with blossoming flowers hugged the house. The housekeeper opened the door to usher us in. In the sitting room a blazing fire warmed the atmosphere. My coat was taken and I tried to make myself comfortable though I felt uneasy. This man was unpretentious despite all his wealth, like his son, but I wondered why he lived in such a small house?

As though he read my mind, Loew Senior asked, 'Would you like to see the place?' Without a word I followed as we walked the path leading to a huge mansion; though beautiful on the outside, it was like a ghost house. There was no life stirring. Mr Loew took a key and opened the front door. I was speechless at the sight. Walls had been stripped of paintings, the ceiling was crumbling, a marble staircase had signs of a carpet that had been removed. 'This is what I found on my return from London when I had gone to negotiate for the distribution of *Gone with the Wind*,' Mr Loew said, in answer to the consternation on my face.

He then led me to the swimming-pool area. It was empty, with traces of plants and shrubs that had once grown there; the mosaic walls of the bath hut were worn and damaged in places; the pool had the ghostly atmosphere of a grandiose past. 'I had no idea my wife wanted to leave me,' Mr Loew said. 'She ripped the house of everything she wanted and left.' He pointed to a lovely chandelier still hanging in the breakfast room overlooking the pool: 'That's where Arthur used to throw his breakfast when he did not want to eat it,' he laughed. There was a twang in my heart as I imagined the small boy being naughty. 'Arthur was a frail little boy,' Mr Loew continued. 'He always wanted to show his strength in boyish tussles with his sister, who looked stronger than him.'

I could not fathom the shock Mr Loew must have experienced on returning home to find all this. With his shoulders drooped he looked at me and said, 'If I had known how happy my son was with you, I would have forced the marriage.'

After his wife and children had gone, he moved into the boat house where he lived with his two servants until the day he died. I am sure the hurt that hovered over him when showing me his broken estate, which must have been his pride and joy, never eased. A hurt so great could never go away. Perhaps this had something to do with him saying to me 'If only I had known how happy my son was with you, I would have forced the marriage.' If I had played the game some do to trap a man, I could have had a child by Loew and forced the marriage myself. I really wanted a child by Loew, but only in the right way for the right reasons. Now I only have the feeling my daughter Kitt should have been Loew's child; but as Kitt has often said to me, 'Momie, it doesn't matter who my father was, I chose you to be my mother.' Sometimes I do feel that Kitt is really spiritually Loew's child, although the seed came from someone else.

Mr Loew showed me home movies of Loew and his sister when they were small, romping through the lawns in play. I felt hurt and sadness for both of us, Mr Loew and myself. As we both watched the movies the room swelled with our mutual feelings. I cared so much for Mr Loew I wanted to hold him, hug him, caress him, and tell him that what goes around comes around; that even though some people never seem to pay for what they have destroyed, God sorts it out in the end. Though we did not talk about our hurt, we had a silent understanding that was more powerful than words; our hurt was greater than either of us could articulate; a bridge we wanted to cross was broken, and neither of us had the tools to mend it. Even though Mr Loew is now gone, I still feel his hurt and mine mingled together when I think of that Sunday afternoon – just the two of us sharing our hurts in silence as we walked around a broken estate of sorrow. Mr Loew drove me back to my house and I spent the rest of the evening with the memory of all that had passed. There was no fixing the past, but in my heart I still felt Arthur would see the light one day.

It was Christmas of that year. I was in my house, alone as I usually was, and snow had covered New York. The little yard I had bricked in was covered in snow, and the two trees that I had planted were drooping with icicles that glistened in the spotlight I had trained on them. I was about to ready myself for bed when the phone rang. It must have been about midnight.

'Hello, this is Arthur, remember me?' the voice said. 'I want to wish you a merry Christmas.' My stunned silence must have made him realize how shocked I was to hear his voice. A happiness began to spread over me that the gods could not have described. Have my prayers been answered? 'May I come over for a while?' Loew asked.

'Why yes,' I said, trying not to show my excitement, 'But where are you?'

'I'm here visiting my grandfather for Christmas.'

This must be the grandfather who lived in the tower at the Waldorf Astoria, the one who was supposedly going to die if Loew married me.

'How long will you be?' I asked.

'About an hour,' said Loew, 'but you know what New York is like when it snows and it's Christmas.'

'I'll wait,' I said humbly.

I hung up the phone. In a trance of happiness I lit the wood in the fireplace; I took some Dom Pérignon champagne from the cellar and set it to chill in an ice bucket, together with silver champagne goblets. Since the house was filled with flowers my friends and fans had given me, I revamped them with fresh water, cleaned them up, put them in special places, lit candles to make a more romantic atmosphere, laid Beluga caviar on ice with the champagne and put the whole lot on the coffee table in front of the fireplace. I then took a bath, high on the spirit of love. My Hollywood-style bath and dressing room contained a small refrigerator in which I always kept Dom Pérignon. I could reach the fridge door from my bath tub. I also kept a silver goblet there. Lying in my tub, bubbles of bath gel surrounding me, I sipped my champagne and imagined how the night would be; how my body would feel around him; how he, in his awkward way, would not know how to handle it; how I would respond with my usual shyness before allowing myself to

give in to our mutual desire. I was bubbling with emotions like the
champagne in my goblet. Each sip made my desires stronger, more
sensitive, ready to be released.

I took myself from the tub, noticing the shape of my dancer's body as I
dried myself and smoothed my skin with oil; looking at every inch of it
to see if it was still the same as when we were last together. Were the
muscles still toned up? Was there an inch of excess anywhere? Was I as I
would like to be when his eyes looked upon me? Will he want me? Is he
coming back to me? Has he found enough strength to defy the obstacles?
Is he man enough? God help me hold the reins of my heart.

I stood for a moment and looked at myself in the mirror. I took the
brush to put my hair in place and saw Eartha Mae peeking through the
Eartha Kitt façade with that primitive savvy: 'Don't expect too much.
He is the only son, the family line can only be carried through him.
Didn't Jamie Dean tell you what his mother said? If Moma didn't want
you, nobody will. He gave you away just like Moma, and he'll give you
away again. Don't expect too much.'

I didn't want to see Eartha Mae, I didn't want to hear her. I've made
me into somebody, goddam it. I can be accepted now. I don't have to
hide any more; I've earned myself a place, I've a reason to be alive, I'm
worthwhile. I'm not an ugly duckling any more. Please God let him
want to keep me, don't let him give me away. But Moma gave me away.
'I don't want that yella gal in my house!' It all came back to haunt me as I
stood naked in front of the mirror.

The sounds of my imagination dimmed at the ring of the door bell. I
quickly threw on the silk *Vogue*-magazine negligée and robe I had laid
out as I ran up the stairs to the front door. The hallway of the lobby to
my apartment was gold-carpeted with black teak Japanese furniture and
an antique Japanese screen covered in peacocks and flowers that
separated the three-storey purpose-elevator from the main lobby.

Instead of ringing the bell to open the main door, I went barefoot to
let Loew in personally. There he stood, a hat covered with snow on his
head, a black coat trimmed with a mink collar, a white silk scarf and
gloves. I roared with laughter – I had never seen Loew dressed up in so
much finery. This was not at all the Loew I used to see in California; he
was all dolled up, looking very unlike himself and very uncomfortable.
He just stood there, almost like a statue, his hands by his side.

'So there you are,' he said, as the light hit his face. 'What's so funny?'
he asked, seeing me writhing in hysterics.

'Well, I never saw you so dolled up,' I said.

'I manage this once a year for the family reunion with my grandfather.
The party is still going on.'

Loew gave his usual cough, a nervous habit he had. I ushered him into the sitting room, taking his coat and accessories to be hung in the hall closet before he sat on the sofa beside the fire. I turned to sit in my usual fashion on the floor, where I am always more comfortable. I poured some champagne into the silver goblets. We toasted ourselves and the holidays.

'How are you?' he asked. I mumbled that I was fine, as I thought, 'My baby, a kind gentle man; a man I can trust, a man I can laugh with, grow with, communicate with, even in silence. A simple, uncomplicated kind of man who would not want to hurt anybody – but perhaps not strong enough to bend a bit when complications arose.' I watched the fire flames draw pictures for me of what he had really come for. The snow falling softly through the French windows which gave onto my back yard lent our little world a Hollywood air of romance. The conversation was of small nonsense to bridge the space of absence that had grown between us.

'I read you have been dating Joan Collins lately. Are you going to marry her?' I asked, knowing it was none of my business.

Loew gave his nervous little cough and cuttingly said, 'No, I don't really think she's my type.'

'I guess that means you don't love her,' I asked with a statement.

'If I ever loved anyone,' Loew said, 'I guess it was you.'

I bowed my head, not really knowing how to accept this, still remembering all the things Jamie Dean had told me on the phone.

'I don't know what the feeling of love is really like. I don't know if I have ever been in love, but if I have, it must have been with you because I never felt that feeling before you and I have never felt that feeling after you.'

Loew took a gulp of champagne. I remembered the time he had called me from somewhere in the prime of our relationship to say 'I love you' before hanging up the phone. I remember being so shocked by this that I had said when I next saw him, 'Loew, you said you loved me on the phone, do you remember?' 'Yes,' he had answered, 'But I had to have a drink to say it.'

Now here he was saying it again, in his semi-serious, awkward way. He could never be too serious – this was the most serious I had ever seen him. Maybe it was the serious clothes, the seriousness of his position, the seriousness of this moment which was forcing him to tell me something of how he felt. I was gazing at our past in the flames of the fire, not knowing what to say, hoping he would go on. I waited.

'Yes, I know I must have been in love with you. I must be still, but I don't know how to handle it yet.'

I looked at him, not daring to say anything, afraid to spoil the moment.

'I'm still trying to sort things out now and perhaps in two years I might be able to handle it.' He got it out in almost one breath.

Two years, I thought, two years of hope. As long as there was hope I would wait. A lifetime of hope, I would wait.

I don't remember Loew being a lover of champagne, but he finished his goblet. The fire burnt down to cinders, the candles dimmed as the dawn began to light the room with early morning. We curled ourselves around each other and just held on until I was awakened by the doorbell.

28 *On My Own Again*

My lawyer-accountant had arrived to talk business. I wanted to buy up the whole south side of 92nd Street, which was the reason for this meeting. When it was over, I returned to my bedroom to find Loew had left by the basement door leading to the street. No sign or note left. Naturally I lived in great hope of hearing from him again, but to no avail. My life went on with contracts for concerts all over, recordings for RCA and movies, including *Anna Lucasta* with Sammy Davis Junior.

The word was going around that I was to be nominated for my role in *Anna Lucasta*, but two thousand five hundred cinemas across America would not accept the film. I was told that the South – which was responsible for fourteen per cent of a film's revenues – was confused because I looked too white on the screen. This was not the right time for an integrated exercise, apparently.

Then I went on to do *St Louis Blues* with Nat King Cole, another great joy of a lifetime. Nat King Cole and I had such a rapport you'd think we had been together in another life; our spirits must have known each other many times before. Just a glance would bring a smile from both of us. A rare feeling like this doesn't come and go – once you have it it's there forever. Even now that Nat is gone, I still feel his presence around me, just as I feel Jamie Dean's. When I look at photographs of Nat, the feeling gets stronger; it is a feeling of love that has nothing to do with sex. It goes much further. I remember reading in Gandhi's biography that he said, when asked about his sex life with his wife, that when you have passed the desire for sex, then you will know love.

The desire for sex was never there between Nat King Cole and myself or Jamie Dean and myself. Nat and I had a feeling that had already surpassed all that; we had proved ourselves to each other many times in many lives. All the nonsense was over; we were kindred spirits. This can provoke jealousy in those who do not understand, as it did with Nat's wife Maria, who sent me the most vicious letter I have ever received after the film was finished.

I had to go on to Las Vegas to do my yearly engagement there, but Nat had also asked me to help him launch his new television show. The story we used was about a psychiatrist and his wise-cracking patient. Nat was the psychiatrist, I was the patient. Every day for two weeks I flew in from Las Vegas to Hollywood to help Nat with this show, praying that America would accept it. I never asked for payment and I even paid my own airfare. To thank me, Nat sent enough red roses to fill my bungalow for a month, with an accompanying note to say how sad it can be for those of us in show business who never get a chance to meet. But, Nat went on to say, he was grateful that we had not only had a chance to work together, but also to get to know each other as people who loved each other. He signed off with 'Handy misses Go-Go', which were our names in the film. I returned a note of thanks for the roses saying, in essence, that the feeling was mutual and that Go-Go also missed Handy. The note got into the hands of Maria, Nat's wife, who sent me a beaded cashmere sweater as a thank-you gift with a note pinned to it that must have poisoned the pen that wrote it. I was so shocked at this letter that I walked around in a daze for a few days until I decided to reciprocate. I still have her letter in my scrapbook.

'I don't know if you think of yourself as some kind of temptress siren, but the film is over and Go-Go is gone, let's leave it that way. . . .'

I reciprocated with: 'I feel sorry for someone who obviously has never had a relationship of love without sex, and I feel sorry for someone whose love of her husband is trustless. . . .'

I have both letters beside each other in my scrapbook. I had the beaded sweater put in mothballs and framed but, alas, time and moths finally got to it.

Life went on. Since most of my lucrative contracts were coming from the West Coast – California or Las Vegas – I decided to buy a house in Los Angeles and rent my apartment in New York. I was doing *The Skin Of Our Teeth* with James Whitmore, Cloris Leachman and Dennis Hopper in La Jolla Playhouse while this plan was in my head. I made stipulations that I wanted a house I could move into right away, not more than a five-minute walk from the Strip, not less than two acres of land, not more than one hundred thousand dollars, and I wanted to be able to see the Pacific Ocean.

'Impossible,' said everyone. I saw houses and I saw houses, all too expensive or lacking the right spirit. There was a house in Bel Air with good vibrations that I liked, though it did not meet all my requirements. I decided to take it anyway. My accountant-lawyer had left for London, and was to be gone ten days. He had left me ten thousand dollars to play with. Since Brian (the accountant) did not know me very well, I am sure he was expecting me to squander it. Typical show person, he probably thought, never thinks of the future. I put nine thousand dollars down for the Bel Air house, to be held until the accountant returned. If I changed my mind, I would not lose the deposit.

I was not completely happy with the amount of land that went with it, but the house itself was fine. At the time I was renting a house in La Jolla, a huge rambling house on the side of a cliff overlooking the ocean – a great place to kill yourself if you happen to fall from the balcony. I was happy there. Orange trees gave me orange juice for breakfast, there were avocados for lunch, lemons for whatever, and bougainvillaeas for beauty. The morning sunrise was glorious, the sunset more so, and the people made me feel wanted.

In *The Skin Of Our Teeth*, Dennis Hopper played a soldier coming home from the war. He had to run onto the stage tired out, something he could not do without running around the block several times just before his entrance. Sir Laurence Olivier once asked Dustin Hoffman, 'Why don't you try acting?' He should have said the same to Dennis Hopper. All that method training only works for a few. My training at the New York School of Performing Arts was not to act but to be. When Stella Adler, who ran a studio for actors, saw my show once she said, 'Eartha, you do in an hour what it takes me seven years to teach my students.'

Dennis Hopper was very amusing. He would break into the house where Joyce King, my secretary, and I lived. He'd run to her room and try to make love to her, then he'd run to my room and try to make love to me. Joyce and I spent many mornings laughing over this at breakfast, never figuring out how he got in without a key. I thought Dennis was cute, but not that cute.

The real estate people called me from Los Angeles one day to ask if I would have lunch with them. Something was wrong, I could smell it. They drove to La Jolla to tell me over lunch that the neighbours in Bel Air were nervous about a coloured person moving into the area. They told me my money would be returned, and asked if I wanted to press charges under the Discrimination Act. I told them I would think about it and would let them know in about two weeks.

The Skin Of our Teeth was a huge success. Cloris Leachman, James Whitmore and I had a great time and became good friends. I met many wonderful artists, including Aldous Huxley, with whom I used to have lengthy discussions over lunch. La Jolla was a great place for thinkers. After this I returned to Los Angeles, still on the look-out for a house to buy. One day, we were on location in Pasadena shooting the beginning of *Anna Lucasta*. I was standing on the sidewalk, waiting for my call, when a West Indian shouted to me from the watching bystanders: 'Miss Kitt, I think I found the house you want!' I turned to look in his direction. 'Miss Kitt, I'm here! I have your house!'

'That man must be crazy,' I said to Annie, my helper. 'Who wants to live in Pasadena?' Annie and I looked at each other and laughed. Pasadena is beautiful, but. . . .

'I'll call you at the studio!' yelled the West Indian man.

Some days later he did call, telling me a real estate lady in the Los Angeles area would be calling to show me *my* house. I was so tired of seeing houses by now I was becoming discouraged, but decided to give it a try just in case. The appointment was made for her to pick me up at lunchtime when she would drive me not more than ten minutes away from Paramount to see 'my' house. At the end of Sunset Strip where the Beverly Hills residential area starts, the car turned right. Into the hillside we drove, through a gate in a brick wall, up a narrow driveway leading to a rambling house covered with bougainvillaea vines. I could not see much of the house for the vines. I was taken through to the bedroom, which had a balcony overlooking a kidney-shaped swimming pool; a small garden house was on the other side; I could see nothing but trees and flowers surrounding the house. Downstairs there was a long narrow room with a fireplace and French windows looking onto an inside patio. There was a dining room on the other side. Though it was dark and dingy, I could see immediately that it *was* 'my' house. The kitchen was large and sunny, but the brick walls had been painted over with dark colours. I could still see it was 'my' house. Afraid to ask the price, I said nothing as I was taken outside to a front yard covered with geraniums. There was a huge bird-cage filled with pigeons, and a falcon cage which was empty. The street was called La Collina.

'Before you say anything, Miss Kitt, do you like it?' asked the real estate lady. 'Tell me honestly.'

'Yes,' I said, still holding my breath as I waited to hear the price, convinced that it would be out of my range.

'Good,' said the agent. 'If you want it, it's eighty-seven thousand dollars: fifty thousand down, the rest to pay as you wish.'

'How much land is there?' I asked.

'About two acres.'

My heart was going at a thousand beats a second.

'Can I move in right away?'

'In ten days,' said the agent. 'The doctor who has been living here for ten years wants to buy into a clinic. Thus the need for fifty thousand dollars straight away.'

I only had a thousand dollars left from the ten my accountant had left me with, so I made the deal: a thousand dollars to hold the house until Brian came back from Europe. The nine thousand was to be returned from the Bel Air house – I hoped – but in the meantime I had two houses on my hands. As the gods would have it, I was refused by Bel Air, but I got what I really wanted – La Collina.

I relayed all this to Beldon Kattleman, the owner of El Rancho in Vegas and, as a present in return for all the audiences I brought to his club, he had it decorated by Tom Douglas and Company when all was settled. I moved in before the decoration started, living alone with a Royal Standard poodle that Beldon had given me, called Snowball. We lived in one room with a bed I had bought; kitchen utensils were borrowed; Snowball and I were there in the empty house for about three months and had the time of our lives. I planted a vegetable garden after clearing off the grounds that had not been cared for in twenty years (or so the gardener told me). There, in an empty house that stood alone in two acres of land, I found myself rehearsing a television special with Roddy McDowall, laughing ourselves sick over the silliness of Hollywood.

One of the scenes called for Roddy and me to kiss and hug each other in the jungle of Africa. Roddy's character was in search of a penny that would reveal truth. It was the key to knowledge. Told that it was last seen in the hands of an African queen, he had to find her. In the love act he would obtain the penny, which she had hidden about her person. Roddy and I rehearsed this scene in my empty house, getting it as well learned as possible before the actual shooting, only to have it all ruined by the director who said the love scene had to be taken out. No white man could kiss a black woman on the screen. He could throw her around a bit, but not make love to her.

I had a similar experience with *Salomé*, a television special I made with Leo Genn, Patricia Neal and Sal Mineo. Sal played the younger brother of the guard whom Salomé takes by the throat and throws down the stairs of the cave where John the Baptist was held as she cries, 'Bring me the head of John the Baptist!' Then Salomé, a little bit insane by now, takes the head on a platter and dances her way to where her mother and father are sitting to present the head to them.

The director, Paul Faigey, told me he was trying to keep the head of the network out of the studio during dress rehearsals because he did not want any interference from him, but he was unsuccessful. The dress rehearsal should have been filmed because immediately after it was over, the whole soliloquy was cut in half, taking out the part where Salomé rams the guard down the stairs. No black person can strike a white person; a white can strike a black, but not the other way around, no matter what the script says. Mr Faigey explained this to me as gently as he could, knowing that I would understand his predicament. At least the special was being done with the first coloured Salomé ever (ironic, in view of the character's origins), and a young one at that. The part of Salomé had always been played by a full-grown woman – Rita Hayworth, Yvonne de Carlo, or someone of that ilk.

The music was by Leonard Bernstein, and the choreographer was the late Bob Fosse. It was shown on the very popular Sunday afternoon programme *Omnibus*, hosted by Alistair Cooke and sponsored by the Ford Foundation.

I had called my representative at the William Morris agency to say I wanted to do this show, I wanted to play Salomé, and I wanted to choose my own cast.

'Don't you know there are certain people who cannot play certain characters?' the agency said.

'I don't understand what you are trying to tell me,' I told them. 'Please get me the name of the person to call if you won't ask.'

A long time passed and nothing was done. I called several times asking if they had made a move but they always gave excuses. 'If you are not going to do anything, please get me the name to call, and I will do it myself,' I would argue.

Finally – to get rid of me, I suppose – they gave me the name of Paul Faigey. I called him and said, 'Mr Faigey, my name is Eartha Kitt. I'd like to have lunch with you.'

I could feel him trying to figure me out. Finally he laughed and said, 'Well, Miss Kitt, I'd love to have lunch with you. When shall it be?'

I was doing *Mrs Patterson* at the time, I think, so we met between shows on a Saturday and went to Sardi's. I told Mr Faigey my idea, named my cast, and the following week we went into rehearsals.

One of my other contract offers at that time was for the Hilton Hotel in Puerto Rico. I had become very popular there because of a song I had recorded with RCA, 'Angelitos Negros', which I sang in Spanish. I was glad to accept this engagement, not only because the language was familiar to me, but also because the Puerto Ricans are amongst my favourite people. They had helped me a great deal during my very young years in the neighbourhood of 1756 Madison Avenue, when I was being abused by Aunt Mamie; when I was running away from her these people often took me in, feeding me and keeping me from sleeping rough on the subways or rooftops of Manhattan.

The engagement at the Caribe Hilton was extremely successful. I received a call from the management one day asking if I would attend a cocktail party given by a Mr Charles Revson. I did not know who Mr Revson was, but since the management described him as a gentleman I decided to accept. I dolled myself up in my Parisian finery and went upstairs alone, to find that the whole of the top floor of the hotel was Mr Revson's. Orchids of various types and colours filled every nook and cranny – even the bathrooms were full of huge branches of orchids. Jack Benny and others were consuming great quantities of Beluga caviar and Dom Pérignon. I was introduced to Mr Revson who, seeing my fascination with such luxury, took me for a tour. When I saw a tree of orchids in the bathroom my stunned face made Mr Revson smile with delight. He must have been amused to see how something so simple to him could make the likes of me so excited.

I could not stay long because I had a show to do, so I bade farewell to all. As I was leaving, Mr Revson gave me his card, saying, 'I will be in New York soon. When you get there, will you give me a call?' I took his card without paying much attention, though Mr Revson's vibrations felt good to me. I really wouldn't mind seeing him again, but what would be the reason? Usually a man of this sort thinks every girl in the world wants to get to know him better because of his wealth. Why would he ever want to see me again? I had done my bit by showing up at his cocktail party. That is probably all he wanted anyway, I thought. I put the card in my wallet. Maybe one day I would get up enough nerve to chance a call.

My show went on at eight-thirty. When I got back to my suite, every nook and cranny, including the bathroom, was covered with the orchids I had seen in Mr Revson's apartment. Obviously the age of chivalry was not dead; this was a gentleman indeed, one who knew how to treat a lady.

I returned to Los Angeles in between contracts so I could rest at home. Virginia Wicks' ex-husband, Jack Dunaway, called to ask me out to dinner. I accepted. We were in a restaurant somewhere on Sunset Boulevard. During the conversation Jack said, 'Oh, you know Arthur Loew Junior got married?' Not knowing what to say or how to react to this news, I just looked at him, dazed. Hold on girl, don't let him see how this news has hit you.

I could have been hit by a ton of bricks and not know it. Jack did not know how to take the words back after he saw how deep the hurt was. He had no idea I did not know. He watched as I slowly got up from the table and headed for the ladies' room, where I fell apart. I was so broken up the ladies' room attendant was going to call a doctor. She thought someone close to me had died. When she heard me say Loew's name, she said, 'Oh my dear, he married Tyrone Power's widow. Of course she was three months pregnant, so he did the right thing. What a nice man.'

I could have picked up the toilet bowl and crowned her with it, but I was too hurt. The hurt was so deep I could not even get to the core of it; all hope was lost. I was empty, useless, without reason, without place, without love, given away, yella gal, ugly, rejected bastard child. You don't know where you come from, and now more than ever you don't know where you're going, and you have no one to go there with.

I tried to pull myself together, looking in the mirror at red eyes, uncombed hair and a fancy Parisian cocktail dress spotted with tears. The dress and make-up made Eartha Mae feel out of place. The ladies' room attendant tried to help me re-do myself, but with Eartha Kitt and Eartha Mae struggling for their part in it, I had a hard time figuring out which one was going back to the table. Neither one of us wanted to be seen at this moment, and both were in sorrow for the other one. Eartha Kitt could stand against the world, but Eartha Mae was too abused and could easily be broken. Eartha Kitt had to protect her, hide her, soothe her, until the pain subsided. Eartha Kitt put the pieces of their broken hearts together as best she could for the moment, with the help of the attendant, and went back to the waiting Jack Dunaway. Jack had paid the bill, anticipating my desire to return home immediately.

I walked into my beautifully decorated fifteen-room rambling converted stables alone. I walked from one room to the other, wondering what I was doing there with all that success and no one to share it with. I spent the rest of the night sitting on the balcony overlooking the swimming pool. The smell of midnight jasmine that combed the panes of my bedroom window drowsed me to sleep. I woke up to the sound of birds. The magnolia tree was in full bloom, standing tall and straight alongside the balcony that at times was almost strangled by the copa-de-oro and the bougainvillaea vines which greedily sapped the sunlight. Still in my Parisian finery, I took the cutting sheers and started freeing the magnolia tree from its imprisonment amidst the vines as if I was freeing my own soul from bondage. With each clipping I clipped away the hurts and realized there was nothing for me to do now but enjoy the beauty the gods had allowed me to see around me; a world the gods had allowed me to obtain, if only for a moment. All that I could see around me served as an example of the potential to start again. I must use the manure that has been thrown on me to fertilize myself and grow from seed again.

As the dawn grew into full day I looked over my little world and prayed that I would never be so hurt again; that I would be given enough strength to use these hurts constructively, not only in my work but also as a person. I prayed to my mother to help me forgive her for giving me away, to help me understand her reason, and to forgive those who trespassed against me. Let me not give in to weakness, but rather strengthen myself in its path. But God, how many times must I cross the River Styx? My oars are wearing out.

Suddenly Paul, the pool man, arrived to clean the pool (he had been introduced to me through Mr Newhouse, the man who cleared off my acreage and stayed on until I sold La Collina in 1988). I don't know what he thought of me all dressed up at this hour of the morning, but being a man of discretion he never mentioned it. We exchanged our usual cordial greeting, and he never knew what I was feeling.

Some time later, during one of my scheduled engagements in Las

Vegas, I met Bob Dix and his friend Bill McDonald. Bob was an extremely handsome guy, who attracted girls like flies to honey, and it seemed Bill caught the overflow. I didn't pay too much attention to either of them, but Bob kept coming around to El Rancho with Bill in tow. I went out on a few dates with both of them after my shows, and always had a lot of laughs. They helped me hide my feelings for Loew by keeping me amused (though I am sure they never knew what I was going through). I had made up my mind that Loew and I now had little or no chance of ever being together, though I always kept a candle of hope burning.

Bill McDonald started coming round to La Collina more often, stopping by after school to tell me about his girlfriend (whom I eventually met and liked). Then Bill and his girlfriend broke up, and he began to spend even more time at my house. His stories were always very amusing, although sometimes totally far-fetched. He told me one story about his time in the Korean war: he went out on night patrols in the jungle with a partner whom he hated so much that he shot him in the back and claimed it was done by a sniper. This was one of his less amusing stories, though I never believed it. Bill told me that his index finger was blown off by a shell that exploded near him and that he was still carrying shrapnel in his back; that with his wounds he half-walked, half-crawled across a field towards the only light he could see in the distance. As he came closer to the light he saw soldiers waving at him but they would not come out to get him. Bill said he cursed every word he knew at them – 'Why don't you come and get me, you –––––––!' When he reached the waving soldiers, they told him he had been crawling and stumbling through a minefield. Seeing what they thought was a head wound, the soldiers threw him over their shoulders; but the wound was in his stomach. The pain of the shrapnel that was embedded in his stomach made him pass out.· He was kept in hospital for a year or so with the doctors trying to put him back together again, even trying to replace his index finger. Bill's mother kept fighting for his release but, said Bill, they like to experiment with war wounds. His mother was finally able to get him home by calling some general and asking him to use his influence. Bill told me how he feigned pain to get the nurses to give him a morphine injection, which he became addicted to in the course of his treatment and had to be weaned off when he got back.

These stories fascinated me, making me feel sorry that he had gone through so much, like so many of our boys. The boys are brought home after a war and thrown back into society without a thought of rehabilitation. Whenever I was home at La Collina, there was Bill standing around my swimming pool area with books in hand, telling me his stories. He would go home for dinner at about six-thirty and return to my house in time for a repeat performance. Dinner at my table was usually steak and salad, champagne and fruit salad for dessert. Since Bill's stepfather was a meat and potato man, dinner at home was usually boring. Bill was all right to have around for a few laughs but he was nothing to fall in love with. A good sense of humour was what I needed most at that time, so I accepted his visits, as long as they did not last too long.

I had rented my apartment in New York, so on my return there I took a suite at a hotel. Looking out of my window I could see the 666 building. The number looked familiar. Mr Revson, I remembered.

29 Revson and Revlon

Finally I mustered up enough nerve to pick up the phone and ask for Mr Revson. When I mentioned my name, I was put through immediately. He sounded as though he was happy to hear my voice. We exchanged greetings and made an appointment for lunch in his office the next day. I became quite excited about this meeting, though I did not know what to expect. The vibrations I had received from him made me feel good, so I knew at least my afternoon would not be wasted. Nothing is more exhausting to me than wasted energy.

I dolled myself up in a cerise silk Pierre Balmain suit and hat to match – I hate hats, but I wanted to look neat and tidy in a tasteful way. I still did not know Mr Revson *was* Revlon. I looked in the mirror as I left my motel suite and was pleased to see that I could have passed for a *Vogue* model on her way to meet a gentleman. When I got off the elevator on the Revlon floor, I was shocked by what I saw: the receptionist who met me led me down a replica of Fifth Avenue, then down Paris's Rue St Honoré, then the Via Condotti of Rome, and finally into Mr Revson's office, where he dismissed the man he was having a meeting with. He took me by the hand and led me to a chair in a corner of the office. I sat there until the table, which was set for two with very fine china and silver, was made ready. Dom Pérignon and caviar were already on ice in the centre. A large vase contained the kind of orchids that had been in his suite in the Caribe Hilton.

Mr Revson and I were both shy with each other initially but we instinctively knew that this would be overcome with the joys of a deeper friendship. Is he married? I asked myself. What does he want of me, from me, with me? Eartha Mae, hide yourself, we'll see what he wants from Eartha Kitt first, then we'll decide how to play this game. If he's honest with Eartha Kitt, then Eartha Mae can come out of hiding and show herself. Behind Mr Revson's façade there's probably an urchin like yourself. There is a spirit that is beyond all this that I see, beyond these mahogany walls, these panels with different faces.

As I looked around Revson's office, I could feel the hype of nonsense being sold to us women who spend seventeen billion dollars a year on make-up (I read the figure somewhere but it's probably more now). For what? To turn us against the natural process of aging? A cream for this, a mascara for that, a rouge to blush the age to hush? Revson showed me the view from his fortieth-floor window, as if to indicate how high he had risen. The height and the sight of rushing traffic below made me sick to the stomach as I wondered how one would get out in case of fire. Then Revson showed me the one-man gymnasium where he worked out daily. The office was so impressive I almost felt guilty to be there. Eartha Mae began to feel guilty, that is, whilst Eartha Kitt was enjoying every moment of the fun.

We sat down to a lunch of steak and salad, served by Revson's personal chef. It was not too long into the lunch that he explained that he was separated from his wife, that he was seeking a divorce but they were arguing over the two boys. He did not go into details, but I am sure he could sense that I was more at ease knowing he was no longer married. I had a wonderful afternoon laughing at his stories and enjoying his company. I left hoping to see him again.

The next morning I received a call from a man telling me Mr Revson had asked him to call to see if I needed anything. I thought this was a joke, so I said, 'Yes, a toy poodle.' My doctor, Pat Harrow, had told me to keep a dog because it would force me to go out for walks as I was too much of a recluse; I never went anywhere except to work or do interviews. Tony, our go-between that afternoon, came with a box all wrapped up with ribbons and bows. Strange, I thought, no one gives a toy poodle wrapped up in a box. When I opened it there was a toy poodle – a stuffed one. When I picked myself up from the floor laughing, I explained I wanted a non-stuffed, blood-running toy poodle. Tony laughed and said, 'Okay, I didn't understand, but if you look in the box again, you might find something else.' There was a gold bracelet under a layer of paper wrapped in a black velvet pouch, with a note saying, 'Thank you for a happy afternoon.'

I gave this a lot of thought. Was this going to be another John Barry Ryan who could only show affection through gifts? Gifts are fine, and greatly appreciated, but what I needed most was loving, real loving, personal holding, caring, loving. Men – except for Loew – always appeared to be 'buying' me. Mr Revson was mature, he was old enough to have passed all the nonsense of youth's foolish desires, I argued with myself. Now he would need a woman he could trust; a woman who was responsible for herself; a woman who needed him, but did not want to possess him, who would want him but not chain him. Or did he, at his age and level of success, just want something to play with? I was tired of being played with. Yes, I thought it was fun being considered a sex symbol, a 'beautiful creature' as I was called at the William Morris agency; I could laugh at this, tease with it, play with it, but all along I was still looking for someone who really cared. Someone who wanted that little cotton-picking urchin who just wanted to be wanted and needed.

I told Tony how wonderful the bracelet and stuffed poodle were, but now, if you don't mind, I'd like a real one. I took him to the pet shop where I had seen little toy poodles. We bought one just large enough not to be sat on, but small enough for my handbag. Every morning thereafter, Tony would meet me at ten – or call me – to ask if I needed anything. Most of the time I said I didn't need anything. I wanted Mr Revson to know I wanted him, not his material things. I did not speak to Charlie personally on the phone: Tony would call me to relay messages – that Charlie would like to take me to dinner or would see me at my house on Sunday afternoon. I had moved back into my apartment on East 92nd Street at this time. Charlie would go to play golf every Sunday, see his children, and come to me after.

We never saw much of each other in public, only rarely at his favourite restaurant. When we walked in, a table was always ready. I was taken home by Tony, who saw to it that I was well inside the door before leaving. At this time Charlie had a very popular television show sponsored by Revlon, *The Sixty-Four Thousand Dollar Question*. There were meetings from time to time at the Pierre Hotel on Fifth Avenue (where Charlie had his base), which I would sometimes attend. Charlie and his business colleagues would talk, conversation I never really listened to. Tony and I had our little private conversations with jokes and laughter until the meeting was over and Tony would take me home.

Charlie sent Tony to pick me up one night and bring me to the Gotham Hotel where he and some friends were watching a big boxing match on television. I had dressed up in a Balmain broadtail two-piece suit, black silk shoes and bag, and was still made-up from my show. It was after midnight. I was not interested in the fight as I hate boxing, so I sat in a corner and tried to read a magazine to distract myself from it all. The men were having a great time with each blow. Charlie must have seen my discomfort. He took me by the arm saying, 'Come here.' He led me to the bedroom and sat me down on the side of the bed. Then he threw a package at me. I opened it to find an Audemars Piquet watch inside; very simple in style and thin as a gold dollar piece.

'I noticed you don't have a watch, so I bought you one,' Charlie said.

Not knowing how to thank him I stupidly said, 'Oh Charlie!'

'Do you like it?' he asked.

'Do I!'

'Then here's another one.'

He threw another box next to me. It contained another watch.

'Twenty-eight carats,' he said. 'That one's for evenings.'

Getting married to Bill, 9 June 1960. The little flower girl is my god-daughter, Christine Engel. *(Associated Press)*

With Bill during my pregnancy.

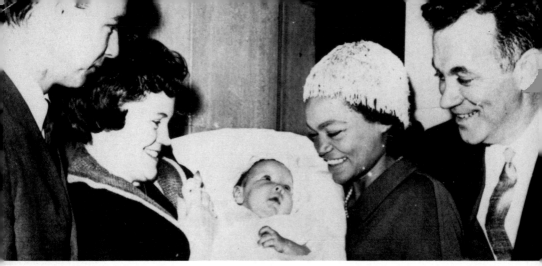

Above: Kitt's baptism, 20 January 1962. Left to right: Bill; Mother McDonald, the godmother; Kitt and me; Mike Connolly, Hollywood columnist and godfather. *(Associated Press)*

Left: Kitt, aged four months.

Below left: Two years old.

Below right: Kiss time after bath.

Above left: Three years old – on stage with me at the Plaza Hotel closing night.

Above right: About four.

Centre left: In Sweden with me, aged about seven.

Centre right: Aged seven, in the garden.

Right: At the Acropolis in Athens – Kitt was seven.

Teaching kids from the Watts area of Los Angeles.

Talking with the Poverty Programme people in New York.

Talking to Lady Bird Johnson at the White House. *(Associated Press)*

Arriving back in LA after the White House lunch, I was met by Doug Best (left) and scores of reporters and TV cameras. I didn't know what all the fuss was about. *(Associated Press).*

La Collina, my beautiful
home in Beverly Hills.

The house in Connecticut
where I live now.

A modelling shot of my beautiful daughter Kitt, aged eighteen.

The wedding of Kitt and Charles Shapiro.

I *loved* playing Catwoman.

My one-woman show.
(Photo by Francis Loney)

'I don't know what to say,' was the dumb remark that left my mouth.

'Don't say anything,' said Charlie. 'You deserve the best and I'm going to give you the best. I have plans for you and me.'

Naturally I wondered what these plans were, but it did not feel right to ask at this moment. I decided to let it go until he felt the time was right.

Sometimes Charlie would come to my apartment after his Sunday in the country, very angry after arguing with his estranged wife about his two sons. Charlie said he told her she could have all the money she wanted but not the custody of the boys.

Charlie and I would usually sit by the fireplace sipping champagne (that Tony always kept a stock of in my cellar) as he talked about his personal problems; how his wife always wanted him to wear what he described as a 'monkey suit' with a bow tie. He said he hated this monkey suit evening wear and refused to put it on unless it was absolutely compulsory. His wife saw a photograph of him in a monkey suit and bow tie with one of his models in some fashion magazine. She walked into his office one day, threw the magazine on the desk and said, 'I want a divorce,' and walked out again. Charlie said perhaps there was no real love on her part from the beginning. They had met at Schorffes, where she was working as a waitress after migrating from Holland.

There were many Sundays with Charlie just telling me about himself: how when he was young he had no ambition and was an extremely heavy drinker. 'One day, when I was about twenty-seven,' he told me, 'I woke up in a motel room, heavy-headed from drink. I looked at myself in the mirror. I was so disgusted with myself I couldn't stand it. I took a bath, went for a walk to find a cup of coffee. . . .' The story was that Charlie saw an old lady selling a small jar of cold cream on the corner for a dime. With only a quarter in his pocket, he bought the cream for a dime and a cup of coffee for a nickel. He examined the little jar of cold cream and started thinking. He said he had a friend who was a chemist; he took the little jar to his friend, who analyzed it and found out what was in it. Charlie went to a bank, talked them into lending him three hundred dollars, and he and his friend set up a cream-making machine in the side of a garage. They manufactured the cream, packaged it in small jars, and peddled it on corners for a quarter, making a profit of at least fifteen to twenty cents per jar. And on they went, to build themselves into what is now one of the most popular make-up businesses in the world.

'They say I am rich, but I am only worth fifty million dollars personally. If that's what they call rich, I wonder what they call Rockefeller or the Aga Khan?' Charlie laughed.

I returned to La Collina in Los Angeles for something I had to do there. Charlie called me a while later to say he was in town to contract stars for a new television series he was about to launch. I invited him over to talk about it.

'I don't understand,' he began. 'Of all the stars in this country, only six out of ten can hold the public's attention for an hour and they are all black.'

'So?' I said, laughing.

'I can't have a black leading my show,' Charlie protested.

'Why not?' I asked, still laughing.

'Well,' said Charlie, 'my stockholders wouldn't accept it.'

'Mr Revson, aren't you the one who dictates to America what we should be putting on our faces? You are a very powerful person in this country. Don't you realize blacks use make-up just as whites do?' Charlie was still. 'As powerful as you are, Charlie, you should be able to do what you want. With one gesture, you can relay to the black people that they too are being considered.'

Charlie was still, but he moved to a chair more in the shade.

'I know you can't use me for obvious reasons,' I went on, 'but a black personality whom the public recognizes as a person of prestige and intelligence could be a first for such a programme. What is the format, Charlie?'

'A luxurious Hollywood-type penthouse apartment; a large acrylic staircase for entry into a lower section of the apartment; a party is being given, attended by other artists; they gather round the piano and entertain each other. They have offered me Esther Williams, but after I get her out of the penthouse swimming pool, then what do I do with her?' We both laughed.

I was laughing because a friend of mine, Gerry, who was a writer for MGM, had told me of his difficulty in figuring out, story-wise, how to get Esther Williams in and out of the water. I adored Esther Williams, but I could see Charlie's dilemma.

'Also,' Charlie went on, 'they want one hundred and seventy-five thousand dollars a segment for her. They must be crazy.'

'How many stars do you need, Charlie?' I asked.

'Thirteen stars, thirteen weeks. Some will be repeated.'

'Why not use Lena Horne? She's beautiful, glamorous, and represents prestige. If not a woman, then Harry Belafonte. That will show make-up has no prejudice. Oh, by the way, Charlie, do you know you have no colours for my complexion, especially in lipsticks? The only colour lipstick I have found that I like was in Paris.'

'What colour is that?' Charlie asked.

I ran to my dressing room and brought it to him. Fortunately I had more than one tube as Charlie put it in his pocket, never to be seen again. Some time later, the exact same colour lipstick was on the Revlon market.

When Charlie's television show was launched, Harry Belafonte was the star. I was in my apartment watching it. The moment I heard the first song, I cringed. Oh my God! I cried in silence. The second song I heard made me cringe again. The phone rang. I knew it was Charlie: 'Kitt, I will never hire a black star again. Do you know how many phone calls I have received in the first five minutes of this programme?' I was scared to death to hear what was coming next: 'How dare he insult us with a chain gang song?'

I had to admit Charlie was right. I would have thought Harry and his people would have understood the position they were in; they had an ideal opportunity just to say they were here, without rubbing salt in an open wound.

'I signed this man for two segments,' Charlie went on. 'I will fulfil that contract, Kitt, but I will never hire a black star again.'

When Charlie hung up the phone I thought, 'What have I done?' A beautiful chance was given to one of us, and it was screwed up in less than five minutes. Perhaps those on Belafonte's side did not think of the repercussions of what they were doing; they were only thinking of the moment. Non-thinkers follow advice; thinkers follow their soul after analyzing the effects their thinking might have. Thinkers do not only think of themselves, but of the effect they might have on others. There was nothing I could do but let it go, yet again.

The show went on for a while with white stars, before it was cancelled altogether. As was the *Sixty-Four Thousand Dollar Question*, mainly, I believe, because a contestant publicly claimed that the show was rigged. The contestant was very popular with the public, and was winning week after week, but he never reached the sixty-four thousand dollars, got angry, and decided to get even. Charlie, in answering all the adverse publicity, became a television personality himself, fighting for the survival of his shows.

Charlie now had trouble from all sides, as a gossip columnist had written that Charlie's ex-wife-to-be had threatened to expose his black mistress if she did not get what she was demanding. Charlie, concerned about the effect of this on his stockholders, called me to a meeting on 'urgent business'. I went to his apartment at the Pierre Hotel, along with several of his men friends. The friends, along with Tony who had come to collect me, stayed in the sitting room while Charlie and I had a private meeting in the bedroom.

'We have to separate for a while,' said Charlie.

I squirmed as I realized that I was going to lose him. In the back of my mind I had been beginning to hope that he would be the man with whom I could have the family I wanted so much. John Barry Ryan was gone. Loew was gone. Now I had a new hope in Charlie. I adored him; he was like the father-figure I was perhaps imagining would take care of me – the lover, the friend, the caring, warm, humorous all-in-one. A strong, no-nonsense man. He knew from whence he came, approximately where he was, and definitely where he wanted to go. And he wanted his sons to help him continue the journey with him and eventually for him.

'I am looking for a house for you in Connecticut,' he said. 'There is one I have seen that I am sure you will like.'

My heart pounded, waiting for the rest to be said. I wanted desperately to ask 'Are you going to marry me, Charlie?'

'I will take care of everything for you. You will have a home of your own. I think the place I have in mind has about fifty acres. I know you like land.' I waited for his words. 'You will have servants, a chauffeured car, anything you want. Charge accounts anywhere, everywhere. Tony will be there to see to your needs. I will not be able to see you for a while, until this stupid nonsense has passed.'

I wondered if we could ever have a child between us; I wanted a child by Charlie, a child through marriage. 'We will be together again as soon as this mess is over. My wife is threatening to expose you. I have to destroy all the paid receipts at Cartier and any proof of the gifts I have given you, so keep everything hushed until the time comes.' I was put on hold, but the time never came.

In the meantime, I noticed many changes on the Revlon market: a new lipstick came out named 'Fire 'n Ice', the nickname Rubirosa had given me; shades of make-up for coloured people were going to be introduced; and all of my other suggestions gradually began to appear. Tony was still at my beck and call, and would phone to let me know how Charlie was, how the case of *The Sixty Four Thousand Dollar Question* was affecting him, and how his private tussles were continuing.

'He has to take it easy,' Tony told me. 'Doc says he should not exert himself.'

I could see Charlie weakening physically when I watched him on news programmes discussing the accusations being levelled at him. I could see this was not the kind of pressure he could deal with easily without it affecting his health. There was nothing I could do; I could not call or see him, I could only send messages through Tony. Now Charlie was caught between his wife and *The Sixty Four Thousand Dollar Question*.

In the end we all lost. The case went on for some time and was finally settled out of court, I believe. The almost-ex-wife got her settlement. Meanwhile Charlie, I found out later, had received an anonymous telephone call saying that a certain Bill McDonald was with me around town.

I had told Charlie about Bob and Bill, that I had been escorted by them from time to time. Charlie had said he preferred me not to have them escorting me anywhere. If I needed an escort for any reason, Tony was always available. True, Bob and Bill did suddenly start showing up in New York and checking into the same hotel I was in or even staying in my apartment. But I never thought Charlie would feel the need to check up on me. An anonymous phone call is enough to make anyone suspicious though. My relationship with Charlie dwindled into silence as Bill McDonald moved closer and closer.

I was extremely unhappy about Charlie's silence. It seemed like every time I found a man with whom I wanted to have a family, he would always run away. What have I done wrong now? I was constantly thinking. Was I doing something unconsciously? Was I relaying a message saying 'I know you're going to give me away so I will give you a reason to give me away?' Why did I allow Bob and Bill to be in my house when I was waiting for Charlie? Though I was never guilty of any wrong-doing, I suppose it looked suspicious, especially considering the songs I was singing.

I had once been asked by a disc jockey in Philadelphia, 'Is it true that when you wake up in the morning you put your feet into mink-lined slippers, step over seven men, and brush your teeth with Dom Pérignon champagne?'

'Yes, doesn't everybody?' had been my answer.

The audience may laugh, but your stage personality is taken by some to be your real personality. People are scared to meet me sometimes, after I've sung songs like 'I Wanna Be Evil' so convincingly.

'That's the way she really is, you know,' I've heard said of me. My musicians tell me they are constantly being asked what it's like to work with Eartha Kitt.

'Does she have a lot of men?'

'No, she's a one-man woman.'

'Does she drink a lot?'

'No, she drinks socially, once in a while.'

'Does she take narcotics?'

'No, she lives a very normal life.'

'I don't believe that! No one can do what she does on stage and not be on something.'

They jump to conclusions about what they don't see, especially if it makes a good story.

I adored Charlie, but I knew I could never have the family I had always wanted with him, legally at least. I could live in luxury, but there was no one legally to share it with. I had to juggle luxury against real wealth – to be fulfilled as a woman; to feel and know what that fulfilment really meant. Money can make you rich but it does not make you wealthy and fulfilled. Richness and success is not what is on the marquee or in the bank, but what you have inside you; what you have accomplished; what you can look back on with pride and say 'I did that'. My desire for a family was much stronger than my desire to live in luxury, and I suppose this is what my subconscious had been telling me all along.

30 *The Birth of Kitt*

I was not in love with Bill McDonald. I didn't even desire him, but I did
have a liking for him which is why I allowed him to get closer. Bill was
physically strong, not bad to look at, and seemingly intelligent. He had
a certain amount of charm, and he used this to good effect both on me
and on his later partners. Added to that, he had a mother whom I felt
very comfortable with; who gave me a sense that I could be accepted and
treated as part of a family unit. I had never had this feeling from any of
my previous boyfriends' mothers – most of them had actively tried to
destroy the relationship. Mother McDonald was just that, for me –
Mother. So Bill moved in and, catching me on the rebound, offered me
a security that I had just been deprived of. I did not want to go it alone
any more. Bill would be my partner and, for all my misgivings, I was
glad.

After Charlie, who could not give me a family, I started planning.
The fun of being Eartha Kitt was one thing, but what did Eartha Mae
want? A someone to call her own, a someone to share with, to love
with, to like with, to be with, to be a part of. Eartha Mae wanted a child,
a child she could be proud of. I was proud of Charlie, with what he had
achieved, and in his realization that one's value is in what one creates.
The mind and being is to wonder, not to plunder. Thus, every move I
make is in wonder of what I create and the effect it has on all around me.
I was not interested in what Charlie had to offer materially but in his
valuable mind. I wanted to share my offspring with someone who had
walked the same path as me. Charlie and I had more than that: we had
the same footprints.

I decided to take my chances with Bill McDonald, despite the fact
that some aspects of his character worried me. I was in Las Vegas
working at El Rancho: Bill kept threatening to kill himself if I didn't
marry him, writhing on the floor of my dressing room, my hotel
bungalow, and so on. 'I'll kill myself if you don't marry me,' he kept
saying, even to the management. Beldon Kattleman came to me saying,
'What is this all about, Eartha?' Even though I was not in love with Bill
– and I told him so repeatedly – the idea of marrying him, of having a
partner to care for my child and look after the business side, became
more reasonable. All Bill had to do was play the game fairly. His father

was Jewish, though he was never referred to I was aware that I had a mixture of ancestral bloods. In my mind's eye I took all the bloods and cultures of this partnership and saw them being reproduced in my child.

So I married Bill in June 1960 and began to concentrate on getting pregnant. We had been married for some time before this happened. I knew the very instant that my egg was fertilized, decided which gender, then decided to become Kitt. It was in the maid's room in my house in Beverly Hills, in the converted stables. I knew the instant of conception – but only I knew. Now the doctors must know so I can be on my guard to protect my child, I thought. I knew I was pregnant.

'Negative,' they said, when I went for confirmation.

'But I know I'm pregnant.'

'Mrs McDonald, you are not pregnant. You have had your regulars, have you not?'

'Yes I have, but I know I am pregnant,' said this stupid sex-symbol mother-to-be.

'How can you be pregnant when you are regular?' asked the intelligent, know-it-all doctors.

'I don't know what your nonsense is about,' I protested, 'All I know is I am pregnant.'

'Sorry, negative,' insisted the doctors. The rabbit test (where they extract the rabbit's ovaries and use them to determine human pregnancy) said I wasn't when I knew I was. Unfortunately, doctors sometimes listen to a rabbit before a mother-to-be. For two months I was telling them I was pregnant, and the rabbit was telling them I was not.

I went to New York to do *Wingless Victory*, with Hugh O'Brien and Cathleen Nesbitt. The script was given to me by Guthrie McClintic and his wife Catherine Cornell, who said to me, 'Eartha, you must play this part.' It was the story of the son of a Bostonian family who went off and found wealth in the islands of Indonesia by pearl hunting, returning home to find the family fortune had been lost in greed and lust. But he was now wealthy in his own right, and had an Indonesian wife and two children. As the play charted his problems, I was busy dealing with my own.

While I was in rehearsal for *Wingless Victory*, Maurice Levine (my musical director) said, 'Eartha, if you think you're pregnant, why don't you go to the Presbyterian Doctors' Hospital for a thorough examination?' I went, and when the doctor there said, 'I hope you are happy about this, you are two and a half months pregnant.' I was fulfilled, I felt rich, wealthy, complete; I felt a reason for being. It was now I began to realize my full value and I started to look forward to a warm partnership between Bill and myself.

So there I was, in the Presbyterian Doctors' Hospital, with Dr

Gusberg sitting at his desk saying emphatically, 'You are two and half months pregnant, Eartha.' I got up from the chair, went into the toilet and did not come out. The nurse came in to find out what I was doing for so long. I was bent over the sink with a thousand sheets of Kleenex. She looked at me and disappeared, returning with a whole fresh box. When I returned to the doctor's office, he said, 'Eartha, I hope you want this baby?'

'Want it?! It's all I want in this world!' I cried in glorious happiness.

Dr Gusberg laughed as he said, 'I've seen happy mothers-to-be, but this is ridiculous!'

Kitt's first word was 'Dada'. I was sick – how dare she say 'Dada' when I went through the pains of carrying and bearing her. It was me who nearly cracked my cranium against the walls of the little cage the doctors put me in after they realized my frame was too small to bear a seven-pound-eight-ounce baby.

'I have to give you a Caesarian, Eartha,' said Dr Golenternek.

'No, please, doctor, I don't want a Caesarian. I'll do it myself. I want to feel the pain, to know. Please, just tell me what to do.'

'You must help me, Eartha, you must help me.'

'Yes doctor, just tell me what to do.'

The memories started to flow through my head: Sunday night at the Palladium; I was seven-and-a-half months pregnant, wearing an Empire-style dress. I had had the producer build a bar with stools that I could sit on if I needed to; I had written music and words put on the bar so that I could glance at them. At the moment I was about to place myself gracefully on the stool, Kitt kicked me. I was shocked by her behaviour: the child is not supposed to make you aware of her presence while you are working, or so I thought. But Kitt had decided to say, 'I'm here, I'm here. Remember me?' She still says it to this day, 'Hi Ma, it's me. Remember me?' I put my hand to my stomach and said, 'It's okay, Junior, this is the last job Momie will take until you are born.' The audience started laughing. I started laughing. The orchestra started laughing. The stage hands and everyone else started laughing and we all laughed our way into me not working until Kitt was born.

The doctors had told me Kitt would be born on the twenty-eighth of November. I said, 'No, she will be born on the twenty-sixth.' I talked to her all the time: 'Momie knows when you are coming, so listen to me: I have a contract to be fulfilled for the both of us. Momie has to work to help us both survive, so let's do what we have to do. We are working this programme together.'

'Do everything you do normally,' the doctors had told me. 'No smoking, no drinking, anything to give the baby the best chance possible.'

When Kitt and I knew the time was right for her and I to handle the situation, on Sunday the twenty-sixth of November 1961, at eight-twenty in the morning, she said, 'Ready when you are, Mamie,' and the waters broke.

'Bill!' I called to him from my bedroom. (I had moved him into the room below me, as I couldn't bear to have sex with him any more.) 'Bill,' I called calmly, 'the water bag has broken. Do you think you should call Dr Golenternek?'

'What, what, who, wha, wha, wha?'

'Bill, call the hospital please.'

'Wha, wha, wha, wha, wha . . .' The sounds of Bill.

'My necessity bag is packed. I'm ready from yesterday night,' I said softly, not wanting to harm the baby with unnecessary commotion. I heard the phone being picked up. Some words were sounding in my ears, and I realized all was well. I brushed my teeth, bathed myself, and galvanized myself for the great production. As we drove down my driveway (which is one-way), I called to Stan, the man who was helping around the house, from the window of my Cadillac: 'I'm having my baby!'

'Wha, wha, wha, wha, wha . . .'

Stan was jumping up and down as Bill drove my car through the brick wall gate. Stan was having more fun at the idea than Bill was. It was Sunday, nine-thirty in the morning, all was quiet; still like the stillness of the monsoon winds before they hit; no traffic, no sounds of horns, no noisy -isms of civilization.

A parking place was at hand when we arrived at the hospital, and a chair was brought out to carry me to reception. 'Watcha name, lady?' was my greeting. Bill was running around helter-skelter. 'How ya gonna pay, lady?'

The minutes were getting closer and closer. 'How much insurance do ya have, lady?' The minutes were closing in on Kitt and me; I was about to throw the wheelchair at the receptionist's 'pay or you don't have your baby' attitude when suddenly Dr Golenternek came through the doors of heaven to drag me and the chair into a womb prison.

The pains had obviously come on so strong that when the nurse touched my stomach she said, 'Eartha, you need something to help relieve the pain.'

'No, I want to know the pains of bearing a child. Just tell me what to do' I said, through gritted teeth.

The nurse left me in my prison womb, with a fence around me, a cushioned wall, like a baby's crib. But I stood up and banged my head against the walls without cushioning. Kitt had decided she was tired of this womb service, and wanted to see what it was like 'out there'. While

I was hitting my cranium against the wall, Kitt was saying, 'All right, I'm ready; I'm folded, I'm moulded, my fingers, my eyes, my hair, my toes, my brain, I'm ready. Now get me out of here. Momie, you told me to be ready — well I'm ready, I'm ready!'

In came Dr Golenternek with the nurse, who said, 'Eartha, you need something to kill the pain.'

'I'll do it, I'll do it . . .'

By this time I was crazy with pain, refusing to have painkillers because I didn't want to hurt my child. I remember them taking me to the childbirth room with the sound of Dr Golenternek's voice saying, 'I know Eartha, she'll do it.' Then leaning over me saying, 'Eartha, you told us you would help us. It's time, please help us.' Dr Glenternek was standing at my feet with gloves on his hands while the others mingled around. 'She's too small,' I heard. Then I remembered my girlfriends saying to me, 'Ah, Eartha, you're an athlete, you'll drop the baby easily.' Ha, ha. 'An athlete,' Dr Golenternek had told me, 'can have more of a problem in birth because the muscles are so well trained they will not give in so easily.' But with the threat of a Caesarian, I pulled my head up and said, 'Please don't cut me open! I'll do it!'

'Eartha, her head is turned wrongly. We will have to use forceps to pull her from you. Her head is a bit larger than we anticipated.'

'Are those forceps going to make her crazy?'

'No, we are using soft padding on the forceps,' came the answer.

'Please don't harm my child!'

'No, Eartha, we won't harm your child.'

When she came upon the scene, bloody and with eyes closed, Dr Golenternek said, 'Eartha, she's here.' I had done it, and had tears of joy and pain in my eyes. 'She's here, Eartha,' Dr Golenternek said again, as the image of the tiny thing he held in his hands appeared before me.

'Is she healthy?' I asked.

'Yes,' said Dr Golenternek.

'Is she pretty?'

'Yes Eartha, she's beautiful.'

I reached out to touch her, then put my head and body to rest. I saw my mother-in-law somewhere beside the trolley bed that took me from the birth room.

'Mom, you didn't tell me how painful it would be,' I sort of joked with her.

'You didn't ask,' she replied, as her hand touched my forehead in comfort.

Coming out of the hospital with so many photographers and the etceteras of the show business world made me nervous, but having a baby did not put me out of business as the William Morris agency had predicted. 'How can you tell the public you're pregnant? You'll never be able to sing "Santa Baby" or "Old Fashioned Girl" again. No one respects a sex symbol who got pregnant. You're out of business, kid,' they had said. So when I was rolled out of the hospital in the face of all those reporters, I had tears in my eyes thanking them for helping me to feel I was still here. To this day I feel the same gratitude.

I had asked Dr Golenternek about breast feeding – whether it was better to or not. 'It's best to,' he answered. 'It helps the baby and it helps you physically by helping your body come back to its normal self faster. The first three or four days of nursing can be very painful, but it cleans out the body. The cholesterol is all that will come in this time, then comes the milk to feed her.'

So, six weeks later I was on stage at the Chi Chi in Palm Springs with milk coming through my gown. It was so obvious I started laughing as I said to the audience, 'Excuse me, but Kitt wants to be fed.' I excused myself, went to my dressing room, and fed Kitt, who laughed with me. Thank God for an understanding audience.

The Chi Chi also happens to be where I made my favourite album, *Eartha Kitt at the Plaza*. The album is called this because RCA thought the public would not know the name 'Chi Chi', whilst the Plaza and the Persian Room are household names. The dress I am wearing on the album cover is the milk-dripping one, hand-crocheted and hand-beaded, thread by thread. It has since been spirited away, but the memory of it lives on forever.

31   Breaking with Bill

After Kitt's birth, the warm caring relationship that I had hoped would develop between me and Bill did not happen. He seemed to resent me working and having independence and strong opinions. Why had he begged to come into my life in the first place? To punish? To put down? To deplete my ability to do things for myself? I bided my time, waiting to see what would happen, wishing that things could be stable for Kitt's sake and also for the sake of Mother McDonald who I was now very close to.

Finally, I knew there was no longer any point in trying to make things work out when I found out that Bill had sold my New York apartment buildings without my knowledge. In his role as my accountant he had the legal right to do this but I was shocked that he would do so and not tell me, knowing how much they meant to me and how long it had taken me to buy them all. If only the tenants had come to me and told me what was going on, I might have been able to save them. I was so upset when I found out about this that I knew I would never be able to forgive Bill. A contract came in from Australia with an offer for the Chevron Hilton Hotel through Nat King Cole's manager. This was the moment I had been waiting for.

I decided to try to convince Bill's mother to come to Australia with me, so that she would not be in America to learn the news that I was filing for divorce from the newspapers. I would wait for the right moment to tell her myself, and I hoped that we would be able to remain friends. But would she accept? Would her husband let her go? I always asked for enough aeroplane tickets to take Kitt, my pianist and one of my students from the Watts area of Los Angeles – the most deserving and dedicated of the neighbourhood kids. If Mama McDonald could come, she could use this ticket and it would not cost her husband any money. When the best moment came, I would sit Mama McDonald down to tell her I was divorcing her son. It was all planned in my mind; the day I faced the judge who would give me my divorce would be the day before we left for Australia, so it would not hit the newspapers until we were gone.

Mama McDonald did come. All went well until we got to Australia. I did not say anything to her on the plane, as she was having such an enjoyable time on her first trip to such a faraway place. Kitt was her favourite grandchild, though she would always say, 'Oh, I'm not supposed to say that; my other grandchildren wouldn't like it!' We'd laugh and let it go. I did not want to disrupt her enjoyment. We landed in Sydney, where I had to give a press conference immediately, so there was no chance there. When the press conference was over, we were put on a plane to Melbourne. I did not take the opportunity at this time either; I was still waiting for the 'right moment'.

On landing in Melbourne I only had time to bathe and dress for a ladies' luncheon appearance. No chance there. The luncheon was filled with reporters and photographers, who kept me very busy. Mother was kept very busy taking care of Kitt (who was about two and a half now, an extremely beautiful child with blonde hair, greenish-brown eyes and a complexion the colour of unripened wheat: she was getting a lot of attention). None of the reporters said anything to me about my divorce at the luncheon, so I was comforted that the news had not reached Australia yet. I still had time to sit Mama McDonald down and tell her in my own way.

When I got back to the hotel I found our suite now filled with cases of baby foods, and toys were everywhere. Little Kitt was testing out her walking ability when suddenly Mama McDonald screamed, 'How can you possibly be carrying me around the world with you and divorcing my son at the same time?' She ran into her room and slammed the door. Oh my God, I thought, how did she get the information? Out she came from her room.

'Why didn't you tell me before that reporter did?' she screamed.

'Mama, please don't yell in front of the child, it will make her nervous,' I requested, as softly as possible.

'I don't care about making her nervous! How do you think I feel? I feel like a fool, travelling with you and you divorcing my son.'

'Mama, I was thinking about you. I wanted to save you as much hurt as I could by taking you away from your phone with "friends" calling you to say "I told you so",' I said, when I could get a word in.

'I don't care what you were thinking. I'm thinking of what a fool I am being here and you divorcing my son. Why are you divorcing my son?'

She finally sat down on the sofa next to me in a very belligerent attitude. I watched Kitt roll her little baby carriage up and down and around the room. I did not want to have to tell Mama McDonald about the atrocities of her son.

'Mama, don't yell in front of the baby please,' I said as calmly as I could.

'I'll yell if I want to. Why are you divorcing my son?'

'Mama, the man doesn't talk to me!' the words came out.

'That's no excuse!' she yelled, 'I've been married to a man who doesn't talk to me for twenty-seven years!'

She picked herself up and jetted off into her room, slamming the door behind her. I sat on the edge of the sofa, my hand holding my cheek, wondering what I had done. I felt cruel and ugly as I watched my beautiful child in her peaceful innocence, trying out her wings of freedom, pushing, pulling, in her little world of hope, to be accepted in this world of organized-unorganized confusion called 'civilization'.

Mama McDonald suddenly came flying from her room. She pointed at Kitt: 'You tell your mother I understand. She was thinking of me and I thank her. But don't tell her I said so.' She was a bit calmer by now. She was thinking about her own experience, of being married to someone she loved but because he was Jewish and she was Catholic, never the twain did meet. Her family had forced her to divorce the Jewish father of her two children, Noreen and Bill, and she had had to put them into a foster home until she found someone (a Catholic) whom her parents accepted. She married him on the condition that he would adopt her two half-Jewish children.

Mother McDonald and I became very close. She used to say, 'Eartha, you are my real daughter because you've earned me.' I never forgot those words because they struck me to be as true as a truth can be: we have to earn each other no matter what the relationship, just as we earn our daily bread.

From a successful engagement in Australia, we went on to Manila. The Philippines were ruled by a military government at this time, so we were confined to a prison-like compound called the Araneta Colisseum. We had to stay within the walls. An apartment was made up very nicely for the three of us and there was a swimming pool which had only enough water for ants to swim in, which infuriated my mother-in-law. Her suitcases had been sent to another part of the world – God knows where. I had given her a mu-mu in Hawaii when our plane stopped there for refuelling; the shawl was one hundred per cent cotton, enabling her to be comfortable in the humid heat of the Philippines. She expected to be in this mu-mu for only a few hours, so to find herself in it for days made her that much more furious. There was a kind of food station near the pool serving food that even the military must have found unpalatable. Mother McDonald would sit by the pool and play with Kitt, watching the ants running like soldiers in a war; whenever they came near she would leap away with an 'eek' and an 'argh', instilling fear in little Kitt for something she would never have feared otherwise. And so it is that Kitt, to this day, still calls me to brush insects away.

I was about to ready myself for bed one night after my show when one of the Colisseum personnel knocked on the door of our apartment to announce an American friend who wanted to see me. It was Rod Serling of the TV show *The Twilight Zone*. 'I've come to take you to the twilight zone, Eartha,' he said, by way of greeting. We were escorted out of the compound by two guards with guns over their shoulders. Once out of the gates we hailed a cab which took us to a jostling area of town. Rod, seeing an empty taxi pulling up next to us, quickly paid our driver off, pulled me by the arm, and jumped into the neighbouring cab saying, 'Let's see if they find us now.' This was fun. Rod was fun. But will I ever see my baby and mother-in-law again?

Rod took me to an after-hours place. There was a sign over the desk at the entrance which read: 'Please check your guns before entering.' Our wraps were taken, we were checked over, and admitted. The show was so bad neither of us wanted to remember it, but Rod and I had a wonderful time laughing and giggling over what we could be getting ourselves into. With Rod's know-how we managed to get back to the Colisseum under the escort of the military police, who had obviously known where we were all the time. The gates of the compound were opened for me in the wee hours of dawn by a military macho soldier with a gun strapped over his back; a young handsome son of a mother, who perhaps had no choice but to earn a living through a government's gun. Rod left me at the gates. I went to my apartment, looked into Mama McDonald's room where she and Kitt were, and all was well. But I thought about my night on the town, and the situation of the people I had mingled with. I thought about myself as a child in South Carolina; the enslavement for cheap labour, making one feel ugly, unintelligent, incapable of thinking for one's self. We will think for you; as long as you obey, all will be okay.

I was reminded of Dr Seuss's *Yurtle the Turtle*, which I was then reading to my baby: Yurtle was chosen as the king of the turtle village; as king turtle, he thought all that he could see around him was his, but he could only see what was at his own eye level. By chance, one day, he happened upon a rock in the mud pond: 'Ahhhh,' said he to himself, 'All that I see is mine.' Then he thought, 'If all that I can see from that rock is mine, then if the rock was higher, then all I could see from there would also be mine, as far as I could see. The rock is only so high; how do I build the rock higher and higher to see more and then get more and then call it mine?' Yurtle the Turtle placed the citizens of his world one on top of the other in order to see more and more and more, and therefore take more and more and more, and therefore feel more and more and more machoistically important. But then one citizen of the mud civilization said 'Ouch!', sneezed, and the whole world came tumbling down.

I went to see Mr Araneta, a rich sugar cane magnate who was trading cane between Manila and the United States. I was very fond of him and his family, but I felt uncomfortable in their world. They took me on a canoe ride up the river of whatchamacallit. The young and the old were pushing us tourists up the river in their canoes of survival; pushing and pushing, me and a fat, fat, fat man. Up, up, up, up; I felt so guilty; with every push I felt every finger on my hand pulling the cotton from cotton bushes that were taller than me. No one knows how much I see of these things through the corner of my eyelashes. My eyelashes may be false, as the wigs may be, but the thinking person survives the truth. I also felt all the nonsense of the situation when I went to the Marcos's house for dinner, a dinner to show off how successful the power game was.

By the time we arrived back in America (via Formosa, where I entertained our soldiers who were still on service there), the noise of my divorce proceedings against Bill had calmed down. I was told it would be two years before the divorce would be finalized. 'You may have divorced my son, but you will never divorce this family,' my mother-in-law would say to me. Despite my proceedings against him, I had kept Bill on as my accountant. Since I had no family, and he was after all the father of my child, I hoped he would at least think of her future and help me for her sake.

Kitt and I went on with our lives. When she came of school age (about three and a half), I put her in the Sloane Garden School in London since it had a good reputation for very young children. Kitt being an only child, I thought it best for her to learn how to get along with other children, especially children of other cultures; and to learn a foreign language, especially French. I would sit in the classroom until she became comfortable before leaving her on her own. My engagements were becoming more frequent in London – thirteen weeks a year at the Talk of the Town – so eventually I put Kitt in the Lycée Française, a school that was well equipped for travelling children. I could carry her with me to any major city in the world and, giving the relevant Lycée enough notice, install Kitt there and know that she would find herself on the same page as the rest of the children in the class. So we travelled together until Kitt was about fourteen, when she decided she wanted to stay at home with her peers.

I did not take to this too well. This is when I began to get that twang in my stomach that she was pulling away, looking for independence. Now she was getting interested in boys; now she was becoming a woman; now I was beginning to realize I was going to be alone again, I was going to be given away again. It's funny, no matter how much fame and fortune you achieve, no matter how much a public may want you, you start feeling the pains of loneliness and inadequacy the moment the child starts pulling away. The child is the only thing we have of any real value. Now you start living in fear of the day when someone will come and take her away from you. As Kitt grew in years, I grew more and more afraid of when this day would come. She was my playmate, she was my pal, we laughed and joked together, we grew together. My whole world was Kitt and my work was for Kitt, and the public made me happy that I could take care of her as well.

Bill McDonald was refusing to pay even small amounts of child support, and when I took him to court to enforce his obligations he told the judge he saw no reason to help us. Not that I needed it, thank God, but it was a matter of principle. When Mother McDonald died, leaving Bill some two million dollars, and he could easily afford to help us, he told the judge I was worth more than him, therefore he saw no reason to help. The judge told him that was not the point – 'A child is by two people, therefore the two people are responsible for the support of the child' – and he increased the amounts Bill had to pay. Bill took me back to court and had it reduced again but even then, after initial compliance, the money dried up. I even had to take him to court to get him, as executor of Mother McDonald's will, to release the inheritance she had left for Kitt.

Bill McDonald married again – a beautiful, wonderful girl – but this second wife died tragically, leaving a son. Bill's third wife, another beautiful woman, had the marriage annulled.

Without holding bitterness (at least I tried not to), I went on with my life with Kitt at my side at all times. I worried about her safety when I couldn't be with her, since there are a lot of madmen around who might try to harm the daughter of someone famous. I even had my house put on police patrol on the rare occasions when I had to leave Kitt at home with my caretakers, to go off on a short contract offer. My caretakers never knew the house was being scrutinized, except by the Bel Air patrol in case of emergencies. Without my buildings in New York – even though, thank God, I had other properties – life was not so easy since I had very little cash in hand. Properties are all very well, but difficult to liquidate into cash at short notice. I was still okay; I was working constantly so money was coming in, but a woman alone on an income that might *seem* great can find it extremely frustrating and difficult to keep a hold of it; the government always has a hand in your pocket, and accountants can be careless, especially when you are not always on hand to try to oversee your own affairs.

32 Lunch at the White House

As long as I was still in popular demand, all went well – until Lady Bird Johnson. Kitt and I were on tour with *The Owl and the Pussycat* in Washington. I was asked by a group of young kids who came to my dressing room to attend a talk on the problems of certain areas in Washington. Their group was called 'Rebels With A Cause', and they wanted me to be their spokesperson. They were asking for one hundred and seventy-five thousand dollars to obtain a building whereby they could get kids off the streets, bring them into the fold, train them in jobs, and thus enable them to become self-sufficient and constructive members of society. These kids took me to areas of Washington where the streets were unpaved and covered in mud, looking like something from the horse and buggy times. Some houses had no hot water, and little if any electricity; most were without inside sanitation. Jobless people were hanging about on tenement stoops; it could have been a scene from my South Carolina cotton-picking days.

I was taken to see the offices where monies were organized to be distributed to the poor all over the country. This is where I learned that the system didn't seem to be working very efficiently and that the money wasn't always reaching those who were most needy. The kids told me whom they wanted to confront publicly to ask them face to face what was happening with the poverty money and other areas of welfare organization.

People can be made fools of when government thinks them stupid, when all we want in fact is a job to hold our heads up with dignity and keep what is needed to maintain that dignity. Give-away programmes are not what we want, except in cases of those who really cannot take care of themselves. The unions don't seem to be helping us either. They put us out of work more than they help us get and keep it. Seeing all this for myself, and remembering my childhood in the South, I asked the kids, 'What can I do?' The 'Rebels With A Cause' told me the names of those they wanted to see face to face. We planned a meeting in a school at a chosen location, where the people, young and old, could confront those names face to face. I called Adam Clayton Powell, a black congressman, and asked him for advice. He suggested I call Mr

Puchinski, who I had met on one occasion with Adam, and he gave me his number.

'Mr Puchinski,' I said when I got him on the line. 'It's Eartha Kitt here. Can you meet me tomorrow night to see the "Rebels With A Cause"?'

'I think I've seen that film, Eartha. Isn't it the one with James Dean?' he answered, misunderstanding my question.

I had to laugh at the confusion, and remembering Mr Puchinski had a sense of humour I teased him a bit before explaining which 'Rebels With A Cause' I was referring to. He agreed to arrange a meeting with the people the kids had asked to meet. The meeting was scheduled to take place at midnight, after my show. The auditorium was filled to standing room only with a crowd of teenagers and grown-ups. Mr Puchinski had come through with the list of names the kids had requested. Food and entertainment had also been arranged by the community, but the police had not: they were uninvited guests who probably came expecting trouble, of which there was none. All the community wanted to do was see the faces of those responsible for the lack of attention they were getting. The young ones did their entertainment at the beginning, then they and the adults got down to business.

It was amazing how much the community was aware of; how astute and knowledgeable it was as to what actually goes on and how you can fool some of the people some of the time, but not all of the people all of the time. The questions were put, but no answers were given. Mr Puchinski, his wife, and I had a very early breakfast at the Shoreham Hotel when the meeting was over. Over the breakfast Mr Puchinski said, 'I had no idea.' As a fair man who wanted to do the right thing by and for the people, he could do nothing if the problems were not brought to him and those such as him. After this meeting, he realized the magnitude of these people's problems for the first time. If problems are not articulated, they are never solved; they just feed upon themselves.

With the help of Congressman Puchinski, 'Rebels With A Cause' was able to get financial help from the government to fund themselves properly into an organization which is now called 'Pride', I believe, whereby they get the kids off the streets, train them for jobs, find them employment, and thus make them prouder of themselves and the community, and better citizens for the country.

The Vice-President, Hubert Humphrey, heard of my efforts in this and other similar projects all over the country. He brought it to the attention of Mrs Johnson, who then invited me to the White House as a part of a luncheon for fifty women. The question to be discussed at the luncheon was: 'Why is there so much juvenile delinquency in the streets of America?' When the invitation arrived at my house in Beverly Hills I didn't want to go because I thought it would be a lot of nonsense – flowers, champagne, a chance to show off. I felt a con coming on. I am not a show-off and I do not seek publicity for publicity's sake. I had no intention of going to the luncheon, but since Mrs Johnson's secretary was so adamant that I should, constantly calling and imploring me to come, I thought perhaps the White House was serious after all.

So I packed my overnight case and went. A reservation was made at the Shoreham Hotel where I spent the night before being taken to the White House the following morning in a waiting limousine. The security doors opened and my limo passed through. I was nervous as I walked through the doors of the White House, greeted as I was by black faces with furrows of slavery still marking their brows. White gloved hands reached out to welcome me; the smiles on their faces showed a restrained kind of pride – at least we can come through the front door now. Portraits of various presidents on the walls made me shudder as I wondered how many of them thought of the American Indians and negroes as American, as being included by the Declaration of Independence and the Bill of Rights. Were we ever really included, or was it all decreed and declared only for whites? Did Abraham Lincoln really free the slaves because no man has the right to own another man or woman? Or were they freed because the gin mill had been invented and they were not needed any more? And if all people are to be treated equally, why were the slaves not educated before being thrown into the world? Why was it women were never allowed education either? Black or white, subservience is for the uneducated; educate the servants and they will no longer want to serve you. So, divide and conquer, the educated and the uneducated.

Many things went through my mind as I walked through the corridors thinking of those who had been resident there before, who had made the laws 'by the people and for the people'. The saddest and most memorable portrait I saw that day was of John F. Kennedy – arms folded, head bent down, shoulders resting in hopelessness: 'How can I get through?' he seemed to be saying. This portrait alone made me feel the nonsense, the con, the razzmatazz of what he as president felt. But perhaps the luncheon today could lead to an awareness of what is on the minds of the people and their children; perhaps today is an honest effort to become aware of the possible ways of helping the people to help themselves, help the government and help us all.

Photographs and filming were done at the drinking trough before the actual luncheon, then we were all ushered into the room where we were to eat. 'There is a rumour that President Johnson might pop in . . .' I heard someone say. 'I wonder if he will? After all, this is a day for us

ladies only; you know, there aren't supposed to be any men here . . .'
And so on and so on. 'Oh dear, I do hope he does. Sure will be
something to tell my grandchildren about . . .' And so on and so on.
'Do you think it might be possible to get his autograph?'

It was Hollywood time in Washington. The atmosphere began to hit
me, but still I hoped it might become a constructive opportunity to air
the problems we had supposedly come to talk about. I thought about all
those boys who had come to my dressing room, not only in the States
but all over: Canada, Sweden, Denmark, Germany, God knows how
many dressing rooms all over the world, where we shared our thoughts
about the US involvement in Vietnam. They, the young fleeing boys of
America, told me about their feelings: about their love for America;
about the reasons for their flight; how they refused to be forced into
killing for reasons they did not agree with. They would rather have a
small stigma on their personalities to render them undesirable as soldiers
in the eyes of the government. That is why many of these boys fell to
petty crime, just to get the criminal record needed to make them
'dishonourable', and therefore struck off the conscription lists.

When we reached our given tables, the ladies were turning the plates
upside down looking for the markings on the bottom. I could understand that: when I look for antiques I do the same. I love the old world
things; I love handicrafts; I love the beauty of the old world self-made
styles; and naturally the White House of all places was rich in old world
history. But the sounds I was hearing as we were being seated were more
suited to Hollywood's 'Can I have your autograph, Mr Grant?' Were
these women really commited? Were these women really willing to
speak the truth of their own feelings, or just there to add to the bullshit?

Suddenly, through the walls of Jericho, came President Johnson
himself, cameras following behind to add to the Hollywood excitement
of the fifty chosen women of America. Through the tables came the
grandiose Texan to the centre of the room where a pulpit-type stand was
produced out of nowhere. Onto the pulpit went the Texan, tall and
strong and fearless; no hat, no lasso, just the intention of lassoing us all
into a commitment to promise to tell our communities what a wonderful
family we had in the White House. I could not believe the words I was
hearing.

'I want you to go back to your communities and tell them what a great
family you have in the White House.'

The speech he made to us fifty ladies was so banal I doubt if any one of
us can recall what was actually said, except for that one statement,
which hit my ears like a boomerang. Out of the nonsense of his speech
came something about making funds available through social security
for elders to do something or other at the age of something or other. I

raised my hand to ask about the *now* of the something or other. I said that if parents had to hold down two or three jobs to make ends meet they had to leave their children in a latch-key situation, a wandering world of undisciplined freedom, as they were unable to be at home with them. What would the President's solution be to this kind of problem?

'Well, we are building a better social security system for older people . . .' and the nonsensical words drifted off into more nonsense before he was suddenly snatched away by security people. He was obviously not prepared for an unexpected question. Back through the Walls of Jericho he went, not to be seen again for the rest of the luncheon.

The luncheon. I don't remember the menu, I only remember the hue, the atmosphere, the desires, the wishes, the excitement of the fifty ladies at being part of an afternoon with the First Lady of America. And there we all were, to be suckered into helping Mrs Johnson beautify America. I thought we were meant to be there to answer the question on the invitation – 'Why is there so much juvenile delinquency in the streets of America?' So why didn't we stay with the subject? We kept going off into what everyone thought of Mrs Johnson's beautification of America; flower pots on the window sills of poverty, trees that needed watering on the embankments of the Seventh Avenues of the world, whilst the people were being told to count each drop from the sprinklers of their lives. Beautify America, and let the potatoes and corn and cheese and wheat and God-knows-what-else be turned over by farmers who are paid not to distribute their crops; they are all kept in a warehouse to rot while the people go hungry. Beautify America to me means take it all out of the warehouses and let the people pay whatever they can afford for whatever is being boarded up, and leave the farmers alone to do their own thing according to their ability and needs. Taxes should be ten per cent for all, rich or poor – you make a dollar, ten cents go to the government. What's so complicated about that? If I grow potatoes, for example, I sell my batch of potatoes for a dollar; I pay 10 cents to the government, I put ten per cent in the bank and the rest goes back into growing potatoes. What's so complicated?

It's not that I, the citizen, don't want my government; it's just that I resent paying it to protect me from an enemy ten thousand miles away that I know nothing about. Are we being taught to hate and then forced to pay for the hatred we have been taught? Are we paying the government to kill our children in the hatred the government taught us? The mind boggles; especially for a mother who has borne the son that becomes a bullet for our government to play at targets with.

So here we were, talking about the beautification of America: 'Mrs Johnson,' the lady who held the floor was saying, 'you are right to beautify America. I never in my life saw so much filth anywhere as I see in my neighbourhood. I don't understand why people feel that they have to drop anything and everything right there on the sidewalk; where they pick it up is where they put it down. Can you tell me why the American folk are so dirty? Yes, Mrs Johnson, you are right to say "Beautify America".'

This lady was soon laid to rest so the afternoon could be got on with. Each lady named the area of her commitment before going on to say what and how her involvement caused her to be at the luncheon. The question on the invitation was constantly avoided. I raised my hand, as I had done already several times, to be told by Mrs Johnson that I would have my turn. I sat down and waited, getting more and more impatient. These women were not speaking from an honest heart, they were speaking from the razzmatazz of artificial protocol.

'I think we have missed out on something here today,' I said when Mrs Johnson finally gave me the floor. 'I thought the question was *why* is there so much juvenile delinquency on the streets of America?' Heads began to dip into laps. 'Not how to beautify America, but how to prevent the kids from getting into trouble when they don't understand why one or other of us parents are not there to console them in their time of need. Perhaps they don't feel it pays to be good in any case; the good boys are the ones who are given a gun to kill with in Vietnam. So the kids try to get a little stigma against them so they can stay home and be taken care of in jail; that's if they don't run away. I have met many of these runaway boys in various countries and here in America who have told me their feelings about our involvement in this unexplained war. They say, "Please Eartha, tell America we are not unAmerican or criminals – we just don't believe we should be involved in Vietnam." I am telling you what they have told me. I have also spoken to some of the parents of these boys, and they feel the same way. This is one of the reasons the boys smoke pot too, to sleep away their frustrations. Vietnam is the main reason we are having trouble with the youth of America. It is a war without explanation or reason. I have a daughter, but if I had a son, believe me, I would do everything in my power to have him live by the Ten Commandments and the lessons of the Bible: Thou shalt not kill, Thou shalt not steal, Do unto others as you would have them do unto you, and so forth. Our children are snatched from us before they have a chance to know life, taught to kill and if, by chance, they return, they are not retrained but simply thrown back into society. They are not given a job, or even examined to see if they might have an emotional or physical problem. They are not taken care of in any way. To beautify America, it seems, is to beautify her with jobs and less taxes and getting out of Vietnam.'

These were perhaps not my exact words, or all of what I said, but it was so in essence. Far off in a corner a lady got up and said, 'Miss Kitt, I'll have you know, I have eight sons and I would be glad to donate each one of them to Vietnam.'

'Then I don't see what I can say to you, or what this lunch is all about,' I said as I sat down.

'Just because there is a war going on,' Mrs Johnson said, rising to her feet, 'I see no reason to be uncivilized.'

I took it she was referring to me. We all sat down again, looking into the palms of our hands, as though the question of the day would be answered there. The lady sitting on my right with her head bowed put her hand on my knee and whispered, 'Thank you, Eartha, we would all like to say the same thing, but seventy-five per cent of the women here work for President Johnson.'

The lunch was suddenly over. I could feel a sensation of discomfort coming over me, a feeling of immediate ostracization. I had said what many obviously felt but were afraid to say. But the truth behind our children's problems was not to be told, not that day anyway. We were invited to show our support of the Johnsons in whatever they wanted to do. Be against them, and you're out of favour. I did not think we were there to play the privileged ones, but to give our honest opinions about the problem; not to approve of putting flowerpot band-aids on the poverty of America, but to find out *why* juvenile delinquency exists. I agree with America being beautiful, but jobs, less taxes, and no more wars like Vietnam could make it easier to achieve.

I had a limousine when I came, but now there was none. No limousine for Eartha Kitt. At the security gates I found a cab that took me back to the Shoreham Hotel where some of the representatives of the 'Rebels With A Cause' were waiting for me. They wanted to take me to see what the cry for help from them had achieved through my efforts. We went to someone's house where many of the community had gathered.

On the way I heard on the car radio, 'Eartha Kitt makes the First Lady cry . . .' I was stunned. 'What did he say?' I asked, not believing my ears. 'On the radio, what did he say?'

'You may not know it,' one of the Rebels answered, 'but you're a hero; you said what we all want to say. Yeah Kitt, you tell it like it is.'

The more he said, 'You tell it like it is . . .' the more I thought, isn't that the way it should be? The more we the people tell it like it is, the better the government will be. If we feel timid about how to express ourselves, or if we feel we do not know how to and simply follow the sheep that lead us off the edge of the cliff into oblivion, then we have no one to blame but ourselves, the people. If we put what we feel intelligently into words, we can rule the government that is to rule us.

We arrived at a house where a party was already in full swing. When I walked in, all quietly paid homage to my presence, which scared me a bit as I was still ignorant of the impact of my words at the luncheon. Everyone came to say hello and told me what an honour it was to have me there. To me it was the usual star treatment, albeit a bit exaggerated. Next to me on a sofa was a gentleman who turned out to be one of the Black Panthers: 'You see, you don't know what you did. You see how these people are behaving – they're like bees over the queen bee; they want to show you how proud you have made them. You said the truth, the truth of what we all want to say to the right man at the right time in the right place. You had that chance, you took it, and you did it for all of us.' I felt big and small at the same time; I had only said what came to me naturally – nothing had been planned – but I had seen the suffering of too many people all over my country, and having gone through this myself, I could not hold back because of protocol.

The people gathered around me; they sat on the floor whilst we talked of their frustrations at lack of jobs, high taxation, and the prejudice of Washington that represents the prejudice of the whole country. We talked of the unfairness of letting foreigners who come into the country get better treatment than those of us who are Americans; of the unfairness of the treatment of those who choose not to kill without a reason, and the unfairness of the last to get hired and first to get fired system. What is it all about? We sat and talked, we talked and sat. At about ten p.m. some of us decided to go to a restaurant, as we had been so busy talking about our problems that we had forgotten to eat.

'My daughter doesn't know where I am,' I said, 'I'd better call home.' I had missed the plane I was scheduled to return on.

'Get on the very next plane, Eartha,' said Evelyn, my mother-in-law's sister who was in my house at the time. 'Don't see anyone, don't talk to anyone. Keep your mouth shut and get out of Washington as fast as you can.'

'What's wrong, Evelyn?' I asked.

'Don't talk. Come home. Get out of there!' Evelyn screamed.

I could not imagine what all the fuss was about, but I hung up and called to find out when the next flight out was. The earliest I could get on was at about seven the next morning. One of the Black Panthers was with me all along. We had our dinner with my head more confused than ever, wondering what all the fuss was about. I returned to the Shoreham Hotel, and stayed up for the rest of the night arguing with the Black Panther that their way was not the right way, that Martin Luther King's way was my way.

'No, you must use violence against violence,' he argued.

'Violence causes the future to seek revenge,' I argued.

The Black Panther took me to the airport the next morning. I boarded the plane, sank into a seat, and went to sleep. I awoke at the sound of a male purser saying, 'Miss Kitt, we've arrived in Los Angeles. I think you might need these.' He handed me a pair of dark glasses.

33 Repercussions

I was ushered off the plane by the purser, who held my hand as the stairway was wheeled into place. The ground was covered with photographers, reporters, and God knows what. I looked behind to see what VIP they were waiting for but there was no-one else there – only me. The fuss was so great, the questions flew at me from all sides.

My boyfriend at the time, Doug Best, had come with his mother and father to meet me and they gathered round as if to say, 'It's all right, we're here.' I was comforted by this because I did not know what was going on. The press cameras flicked and flacked, the TV cameras whirred and purred. In my state of fatigue, I was pushed into a room, with the press crawling everywhere. Since I did not know what impact I had had in Washington, I barely said much in my confusion. Obviously Mr Best realized I was not aware of all that was going on or what had gone on, and he and his family led me to their car and took me to my home in Beverly Hills. There I was told how the TV stations were screaming, the radio was blasting, and the newspapers were screeching my name.

'Eartha Kitt made Lady Bird cry.'

'What is all the fuss about?' I asked them as we sat in my bar overlooking the swimming pool. 'All I did was answer the question of the day, "Why . . ."'

'Yes, Eartha, we know that,' said Mr Best, 'but obviously they didn't want to hear the truth.'

'Kitt,' said Doug, 'You're a sex symbol, you're supposed to be stupid, remember?'

I trembled in disbelief. I could not understand why we are told that we have freedom of speech and freedom of expression. Congress is ruled by the people; the President is only the President, but does he tell Congress the desires of the people and does he have the right to get rid of anyone who does not agree with him? I thought the American way is that you have a right to disagree. Like the man said somewhere in our history books, 'I may not agree, but I respect your right to disagree.'

I was alone inside of myself. I was hurting inside, I was crying inside. I had been rejected by my own government because I did not agree. 'I don't want to see that woman's face anywhere' President Johnson was reported to have said. I was afraid to watch the television news; no newspapers came to my house; no one called. I was afraid to call anyone and the few calls that did finally come in were answered by my housekeeper. I don't remember speaking to any one of my friends except Marjorie Meade, who asked me to apologize to our other friends, which I did not understand.

'Apologize for *what*? I did nothing wrong. President Johnson is wrong. Each one of us has children, Marjorie,' I said. 'How can you, a mother, go along with a war like Vietnam that your sons may be in at any minute? The American people are being prodded into accepting the escalation of something that is wrong. And you ask me to apologize?'

'We agree with you, Eartha, but you didn't have to say it in their home,' pleaded Marjorie.

'First of all,' I answered, 'I was invited to give my opinion about the problems of my country. That is what I was invited for, to give my honest opinion, not to sing songs. And, most of all, the White House is the house of the people. We the citizens pay the rent. And above all places, the truth should be heard in the house of the people, by the people, for the people.'

I was deeply amazed and perturbed by the way people were letting their sons be snatched away to be sent ten thousand miles, taught to abuse and kill. Then, when they were brought back home, to be thrown back into the family and the society without rehabilitation. We had no idea what kind of diseases they might be bringing back with them and they could not be entirely sane after such experiences. When I talked to the returned boys at the Montgomery Ward Hospital, they told me some of their experiences. I used to visit them while I was with *The Owl and the Pussycat*, and see them lying in net hammocks, too badly injured to move. Their stories were often too hard for me to take as I sat on the side of many beds, listening, asking simple questions to allow them to release their feelings. Their words always followed the same theme: 'What are we doing in Vietnam? Why are *we* fighting such a war? *They* don't understand why we came. They say we are burning up their country. Well, I guess that's what we are doing. When we can't find the enemy, we burn up the forest. No matter how much we burn, we still can't find them. I don't know what we are doing there. We shouldn't be there.'

Some of the boys spoke openly about their feelings; some were very silent. Their cry mostly was, 'Get us out of there!' But when the press accompanied me, it was a different story: 'Yes, we'd do it again. Anything for our country.'

When that mother at the luncheon got up and said, 'Miss Kitt, I'll have you know I have eight sons and I'd be glad to donate each one of them to Vietnam,' I was utterly horrified by her words. Obviously she had not seen any of the wounded returners. If she had, would she still have thought 'My country right or wrong'?

Mother McDonald was my one constant visitor, along with Marjorie. She would say, 'Yes, I agree with what you said. But did you have to say it?'

Martin Luther King called: 'We are proud of you, Eartha. You did what all of America wants to do. Thank God someone did it for us. You should really be the one to have the peace prize. We are proud of you, Eartha.'

I was so thrilled about this particular phone call that all went calm inside with the comfort of Dr Martin Luther King's words and, in a way, his sharing of the peace prize with me.

Since the time was nearing for my contracted engagement at the Ambassador Hotel in Los Angeles (about three weeks after the White House luncheon), I called the agents for the details of rehearsals and the etceteras of the contract.

'What contract are you taking about, Eartha?' asked my agent.

'The Coconut Grove contract at the Ambassador Hotel. I open there in a week,' I said, surprised at what I was hearing.

'There is no contract, Eartha,' said my agent.

'But I signed. . . .'

'Eartha, there is no contract,' said my agent. No explanation of any kind.

The Ambassador's Coconut Grove had lost, cancelled, or just ignored the contract. I feel funny about this hotel. It was there that Bobby Kennedy was shot, perhaps in the very same kitchen I used to travel through to get into the room to do my shows. I sat at home for some time with no contracts being recognized or no new ones being offered. Some kind of plague had hit my house and I became an untouchable. In the meantime, the news of me and the White House luncheon was going on and on. After the call from Martin Luther King, I began to pay more attention to the news and what the papers were saying. The young people were screaming all over America: 'Eartha Kitt for President.' People were fighting each other in bars all over the country; one would say 'She's right', the other would say 'She shouldn't have said it in the White House', and the fight would start. I took an engagement in Dallas, Texas, where the audience paid, as they said, to see the woman who stood up to Johnson. I was taken out for dinner afterwards and I learned that the Texan property owners had no love for Johnson.

In the meantime, President Johnson was making it obvious to all the media that I was out of favour. He didn't want to see my face anywhere –

ever. Out of sight, out of mind, out of work. Here started the erasing of Eartha Kitt. I became a prisoner in my own house. In my enforced loneliness I tried to analyze what was happening to me. My thoughts turned to Kitt. 'My baby, my baby!' 'It's all right, Eartha,' Evelyn kept saying to me, 'She's here. She's fine, Eartha, she's here.' 'I want to see her, I want to feel her. Why is she not here?' Then Kitt came through the door into my bedroom. She said nothing. She just laid her head in my arms for a moment and then wandered off to play. I thought that the normal warmth between us was missing. Something had gone wrong, and now it was touching my child. I could feel it but I could not see it. Oh God! Where did my world go wrong?

I had in my hand contracts for Los Angeles, Las Vegas, Detroit, Chicago, but it made no difference – all were cancelled. The only contract that was recognized and respected was the one with Mr Paul and his brothers, who owned the Plaza Hotel in New York, and through them I was still in the Persian Room. The Persian Room and I were great friends. The personnel, the maître d' and I were like hand-in-hand brothers and sisters. We knew each other, we migrants from the womb of other countries, other worlds, other cultures. My engagements at the Plaza were always interesting, with so many different cultures from all over the world; people were drawn in from everywhere by my repertoire of Hebrew, French, Spanish, Swahili and, of course, English songs.

One night the management asked me not to sing in Hebrew as there was a group of Arab dignitaries in for the show. My conductor, Maurice Levine, asked, 'Eartha, what are you going to do?'

'I'll think about it,' I said.

When the moment in my programme came for the Hebrew song, I turned to look at Maurice. Maurice looked at me with a smile that asked, 'What now?' It suddenly occurred to me that we were on neutral ground; I am an artist, I have no politics, no religion. We are not here to fight, we are here to entertain and be entertained. If I was to allow a management to delete all the songs in languages offensive to a particular group who happen to come into the room, I wouldn't have an act. I feel the same about the sports world, where athletes are denied entry into certain countries.

I heard myself saying, 'Ladies and Gentlemen, the management has politely asked if I would delete my next song because we have the honour of having some very important Arab dignitaries in tonight and my next song is in Hebrew. Since we are on neutral ground I am sure our guests would not wish me to change my repertoire because of them. It's about time we learned to get along anyway.' And my Hebrew song 'Kimitzion' brought the house down. We all had a great night, but I think the management was nervous until they saw and heard the whole audience react. Even more so the next day, when the flowers from both the Arab and the Jewish members of the audience with cards of 'thank you' and 'bravo' filled my suite to the brim.

The Plaza Hotel was always good to me. We were good for each other. The Persian Room was known as 'The Eartha Kitt Room' because of my continuous success there. Along with the Talk of the Town in London and El Rancho in Las Vegas, the Persian Room was my favourite. But the Plaza was sold to a Western corporation; El Rancho was burnt down mysteriously; the Talk of the Town wanted me to drop my percentages at the door, which to me was an insult because we were good for each other. I worked there for thirteen weeks a year (a record yet to be broken). The food was good quality, the service was wonderful and the shows were excellent. The ten o'clock follies of beautiful, glamorous girls, wonderful dancers, two orchestras – the whole show was theatre, and fun, with Mr Robert Nesbitt creating the lighting effects. Everyone had fun. Then the management told me I was making too much money from the door percentage. They wanted me to lower it. After three years, my contract was still the same. I paid all the expenses myself, even my transportation to and from England.

I have a special understanding with England – as with Scandinavia, Germany, Australia and Turkey. In Turkey it is because of the song 'Usku Dara' that the Turks tell me put them on the map because of the record's popularity all over the world. But with the clubs closing up and my government closing in around me, things began to change.

I did not know about the US government's policy at that time until 1974, when Seymour Hirsch of the New York Times called to ask me if they could print what they found in a CIA dossier which said I was on their list of disfavoured persons. I remember that I was about to leave my Beverly Hills home to take Kitt, a friend, and my St Bernard dog to the mountains to see the snow, when I picked up the phone and heard, 'This is Seymour Hirsch from the New York Times. We need your permission to print what we found in your CIA file.'

'CIA?' I asked, not knowing if I should be afraid or not.

Mr Hirsch said, 'Eartha, we know this is a lot of nonsense, but we need your permission to print it.'

I held the phone closer and closer to my ear in shock as I listened to what was in my CIA files: 'A sadistic, sex nymphomaniac . . . rude, crude, shrewd, difficult . . . one of six children . . . mother and father farmers in South Carolina . . . ran away from home at the age of sixteen . . . would do anything to get attention . . .'

I did not know if I should laugh or cry listening to this. I could not understand why the CIA would bother with investigating me only to fill my files with backyard gossip. I laughingly cried as I asked Mr Hirsch, 'What is this all about?'

According to the file, President Johnson had put me out of work in America in two hours. The FBI had been called first, apparently, to find something on me – anything to keep my face out of favour with the American public. According to the files, he called on the media to erase me. The FBI could not find anything subversive. Their file said, 'She is a good person. She's never been arrested for anything. Her only problem is she loves her country.'

Since this was not to President Johnson's liking, he then sent out the CIA to find something. Since a venue – or anyone for that matter – don't want the FBI or CIA coming around asking questions about a personality, I was considered a problem and was no longer hired by anyone in my own country except for one here and one there. From 1968 to 1974 I could not put my finger on why I was not being hired. I was suspicious that my phone was tapped. When I would ask a friend who was calling 'There is a funny noise on this phone, can you hear it?' my friend would say, 'Kitty, you're crazy. You're on one of your voodoo trips again', and we'd laugh, but the strange feeling that something weird was around me persisted.

When I returned home at times I felt a strange presence had been roaming around my house, though there was nothing I could put my finger on. Now, as Mr Hirsch was reading my files, I was finding the reasons for my feelings and why I had been erased from the American work scene; why I felt ostracized all those years. I gave Mr Hirsch permission to print anything and everything he and fellow journalist Jack Anderson found.

'I have nothing to hide and nothing to be ashamed of,' I said. 'Print it all.' I thanked Mr Hirsch and hung up the phone, stunned.

My daughter came to me, 'Momie, are we going to the snow?' she asked. 'Momie, are you all right?'

'Yes, Kitt, we're going to the snow, and Momie is all right,' I answered while my soul was singed in hurt with the question, 'What did I do wrong?'

As I drove to the mountain snow with no answer except 'You thought they wanted to hear an honest opinion,' thoughts came back to me of what President Johnson had said at the luncheon: 'I want you all to go back to your communities and tell them what a wonderful family you have here in the White House. You are all very lucky to have been invited here today. You are the privileged few . . .' His words flew around my head like the swallows returning to Capestrano. Now I had nowhere to go and little money in the bank. Worry about the future began to envelop me.

Work was very little or none at all. How am I going to keep my child? Start thinking, Eartha. No agent wanted to touch me, and even if someone wanted to offer me work they would not be able to get in touch because my phone is private. Of course no one ever thinks of calling the unions we are obliged to pay. The optimistic attitude I have always had, together with the ability to laugh at my own problems, has always been a great asset, but this was not a laughable situation. Still, as I always said to Kitt and my accountants, 'Don't panic, something wonderful will happen.' It usually does. Don't panic. My house in Beverly Hills became lonely now, just as I myself was. I felt more lonely than I ever had before. Thank God for Kitt.

34   South Africa and Catwoman

Then, in 1974, I was offered a contract in South Africa. I was doubtful about going to South Africa for a moment, but being the curious cat that I am, and feeling the artist should have no boundaries, I accepted. It would be an interesting education for Kitt as well as me. I hired an English teacher from Manchester who could help me keep Kitt up on her French. All papers were sought and arrangements made. Lionel Blair and his group were to appear with me so we were the first integrated show that I know of that went into South Africa for a three-month engagement.

Our first show was in the black areas, where it seemed to us there were just as many whites. My champagne-drinking number called 'The Charleston', which is all in French, calls for a waiter to bring on an opened bottle of champagne and one glass. The law in South Africa prohibits a white from drinking from the same glass as a black person. Since our company stage manager was an English white, he and I drank from the same glass and it was then passed along the front row. Blacks and whites were drinking from the same glass no matter what theatre we played. On many nights I opened an extra bottle to play this game with more and more people, breaking the law at every turn.

Kitt and I were able to raise money to build schools for black African kids by going to certain department stores every Tuesday and Thursday to sell an autograph on a replica of a brick. I dug up some ground for a school just outside Durban. The newspapers and the media, as well as this chain of department stores, were all behind us.

We were living in a very luxurious Hollywood-type suite just across the highway from an amusement park in Durban. I was very busy with interviews so Kitt and her teacher went to the park on their own one day. On their return Kitt said. 'Momie, I want *you* to take me to the park.' I had some hours before the next interview so off we went, me all made-up for my next session with the photographers. We were having the time of our lives: the little bumper boats, the little train rides and then the bumper cars. The cars ran out of tokens and stopped. The English teacher went to replenish us with tokens. When an Indian caretaker came over to my car and asked, 'Are you European?' I said, laughing, 'No, I'm American.'

'No, I don't mean that,' said the Indian caretaker, who was the same colour as I am, 'I mean, are you European?'

'No,' I said again. 'I'm American.'

I could sense that the Indian was a bit nervous: 'No, I mean . . . I mean are you coloured?'

Teasing him, I asked, 'Do I look coloured?' as I looked at the same colour tone he and I shared.

'Well, yes, you do,' he said.

'Well then, I guess I'm coloured,' said I jokingly.

'Then I guess you will have to leave,' the Indian said. It did not hit me until his last words were spoken that the park was for whites only.

'Come on, Kitt, let's go,' I said.

'But Momie, there are no signs here they say no coloureds allowed,' Kitt said, holding onto my skirt. 'What are you going to do, Momie?' asked Kitt, knowing her mother well.

'Don't worry, Momie will think of something,' I said, feeling like a dog who should have been on a leash.

The English teacher caught up with us saying nothing, but understanding what had happened. As I held my daughter's hand crossing the boulevard, Kitt was still asking, 'Momie, what are you going to do?'

'Don't worry, Momie will think of something,' I was still saying.

The moment I reached my hotel suite the phone rang to tell me of my next interview session. Inevitably a photographer would want to photograph me with some well-known scene in the background. The obvious one would be the amusement park. I bided my time until a photographer asked me to step out onto the balcony to pose with the amusement park at the back.

'That's funny,' I said. 'You want to show a scene of the park I was just thrown out of.' The interview then began to circle round that subject, making headline news for the evening and most morning papers.

The owner of the amusement park came to the theatre with his wife, then into my dressing room with flowers and champagne: 'I am so sorry, Miss Kitt, but they did not know who you are,' said the owner, who happened to be Jewish. 'It's not me,' he went on, 'I only care about the colour green, which is money.' I listened patiently, saying nothing as he went on, 'This stupid government forces us to do these stupid things. Our hands are tied. We can do nothing.' He went on apologizing.

'Yes, yes, I know, I know, but it takes fifteen thousand rands to build a school room for black children. May I have your cheque, please?'

So instead of getting angry, I made my embarrassment pay off.

At a fancy Cape Town dinner party with dancing after, I noticed all the whites were being served by the blacks and having a great time dancing. I pulled the black waiters and waitresses onto the floor and blacks and whites had a great time partnering each other.

Since the black areas such as Soweto have no theatre, we put the shows on in the cinema. The crowds came in all through the show thinking I was a movie and would start over and over again. They sent gifts of chickens, sheep and so forth down the aisles to me as a token of respect. Of course I could not take the animals, but one day in Johannesburg the hotel management called: 'Miss Kitt, I think you'd better get down here – we are having a problem.'

When I reached the lobby it was filled with several different tribes, who had brought so many animals and birds you would think it was Noah's Ark. Since my suite was the penthouse where I already kept my pet doves that I carried all over South Africa, I did take some of the chickens, not wanting to insult them. I got the permission of the hotel management, who supplied me with facilities to keep them during my stay, and when I left I gave the chickens to the cleaning boys of my suite, but carried my doves with me – four white doves.

I went to the copper mines and met Miss Oppenheimer at her home on various occasions with different tribespeople present. We had long discussions on the problems of South Africa and what we could do to eradicate Apartheid. These meetings were illegal but to hear the whites' and the blacks' sides of things was very educational; to hear for myself what people were doing amongst themselves to ease relationships. In 1974, to me, South Africa was the way it was in South Carolina during my childhood, only by a different name. Racial prejudice – it brought back the pains of my childhood in the South, especially when I saw the face of a young black girl waiting at the stage door to see the international star who was the same colour as she was but who had so many more opportunities and benefits. We stood in silence, looking at each other. Me in my privileged state and she probably wondering how she could be in my place.

I went into Soweto with a friend to see how the people of Soweto and places like it live. A dirt floor, a light bulb hanging from the ceiling – a place of very little comfort. A pot of something like stew on the primitive stove full of fatback. I walked through the muddy streets to see for myself the conditions in which they lived. No different from South Carolina except here at least there was electricity. In the streets of South Africa – Durban, Cape Town, Johannesburg, wherever – blacks walked in a world of their own and whites lived in a world all their own, as though the other did not exist. Same as it was down South. The blacks had to be in their areas before the sun went down, and not out before the sun came up.

In Cape Town there was a theatre that had been built from the tax monies of all the people but that only allowed whites. Kitt broke the barrier. She was taken there by some friends – all knew who she was but welcomed her and said nothing. Those who came to my show with cards to show their race found no guards asking for these cards. Since we were considered honorary whites, we broke all the barriers of Apartheid until Margot Fonteyn and Joan Fontaine came to South Africa. They both gave shows in a particular venue, but when my time came I was refused a permit because there was no black toilet. This threw the government into a quandary. They argued among themselves, it was said in the newspapers, and meanwhile the whole country was laughing at their government's stupidity. Cartoons of Joan, Margot and myself were all over the papers, while editorials discussed the issue of how two other international stars could play in this venue but not Eartha Kitt.

My show with Lionel Blair and his group – who were wonderful to work with – was only supposed to last for a few weeks, but over three months later we were still there playing games against Apartheid. I was meeting people from all sides who were seeking non-violent ways to eradicate Apartheid, in my hotel rooms and dressing rooms. A group of youngsters gathered outside my dressing room at one theatre, threatening to picket me. Coming to South Africa, they said, condones the system. I asked them to come to my dressing room.

'Sit down, let's talk,' I said. 'Why do you say I am condoning?' I asked, adding 'Have a glass of champagne.'

'Because you're here,' said they.

The leader was an American student. When I asked him questions, he knew very little about South Africa or the internal problems. All he knew was the word 'Apartheid'. He had had problems of his own in the States, and here he was the leader of the group, wanting to make a point.

'If I am condoning Apartheid by being here, then what are *you* doing here?' I asked.

'I came over to help these people,' he said.

'How?' I asked. 'By causing illegal situations where some of you can get killed and you get your name in the papers for your friends in America to see?' He dropped his head. 'Why don't you open your eyes and see what we have done by coming here?' I calmly asked him. 'Would you like another glass of champagne?'

He and those with him sat in my dressing room sipping on a glass of champagne. We compared what I had achieved against Apartheid with what they had achieved – which was nothing, except to try and prevent artists from coming to South Africa. We had talks until show time when I invited all of them to come in and see the show. They did. We met afterwards and talked again.

'You have an integrated show,' the American leader said.

'Every little bit helps subtly, doesn't it?' I asked.

The American youngster looked at me and I looked at him, understanding the different ways of making people think.

'We had a wonderful time,' the American leader said, and they left with no animosity.

I never had a problem with them from then on. I had seen this kind of thing before in Burma – students who came from communist areas, already fully educated and then planted in the schools in Burma to stir up the other students.

The success of our tour and the fact that it was a glamorous, classy event made Apartheid just a little bit weaker. I visited the Indian families for meals, the coloureds for meals, the blacks for meals, the Jews and the British for meals, and we talked. At each home, the kitchen is where I got more information on the feelings of all people than anywhere else. In Cape Town I invited about ten or twelve African 'maids' who worked in people's homes to have lunch in my hotel. On their arrival I had to go downstairs to bring them in. They were too afraid to enter the lobby. The management and I practically took them by the hand to bring them into the restaurant. The same as it was in New York when my black friends would not come through the front door of the Plaza Hotel. The owner and I had to go to the front door to fetch them. (They would not have been surprised to discover that I was once refused registration in a hotel in St. Louis.)

'This is the white man's world,' they would say. 'We can't go in there.' With the lunch we had some champagne – 'My kind of champagne,' I said to the maître d', who brought the cheapest he could find. After much to-ing and fro-ing, he finally brought Moet et Chandon.

'We never had champagne before,' said one of them. They all looked around in amazement, whispering to each other. After the lunch we went to my suite, sat on the floor and talked. I was on the top floor. The hotel is by the sea. As they looked out of the window, one said, 'I've never seen my country from so high up.'

They stayed until it was time for me to go to the theatre, after some had called in to their jobs asking permission to have the afternoon off. When I spoke to their 'boss' lady, they were given the afternoon off, leaving more time to talk. Fun was had by all, and the thoughts and problems that troubled them were spat out. Kitt and her teacher sat in on the talks, each of us learning from the other. It was the same cry as that of the blacks in America, except in South Africa Apartheid is legal and racial prejudice in America is not, at least not now. But because of the hangover from slavery, in many areas it is still a 'gentleman's agreement', as was the case with the Jews. I learned a lot and felt a lot of the undercurrent of something happening to change the thinking of the people about Apartheid. Things were on the move from all sides except that of the government, and even the government was in some turmoil.

On my return to America, I was asked to appear on *Good Morning America*. Barbara Walters was the interrogator: 'Eartha Kitt, how could you above all people go to South Africa?' she began before I could even say 'good morning'. I let her go on and on, then reminded her of what we were still going through in our own country.

'For the same reason we went to Selma, Alabama, with Martin Luther King,' I answered. 'Don't you remember, Barbara?' I asked. 'We had black toilets and white toilets, "whites-only" water fountains and restaurants blacks could not go into, and hotels blacks could not live in. And even today black people have a hard time getting into certain unions. Blacks couldn't even get into the army until President Roosevelt realized they couldn't be seen at night when the war was on. Then they formed the black army corps.'

She seemed to soften a little at this. She tried to interrupt me, but I went on: 'Even now blacks have a hard time getting into certain jobs, as we women do. I am sorry if you were never touched by this. You don't know what you missed.'

When I returned to the Plaza Hotel after *Good Morning America*, the phone started ringing – 'Right on, Eartha!' said my friends.

The years of jobs here and there with the continuous struggle to keep my head above the dirty waters was kept from Kitt as much as I could. It's hard enough to bring a child up in any part of this world without harassing her with problems she could not do anything about anyway. But if there were fewer presents at Christmas and birthday times, I explained that Momie didn't have enough money to get Kitt just what she wanted but pointed out that at least we were healthy. We had our home and food on the table and that's enough of a present for anyone. Sometimes Kitt would look at me not knowing exactly how to answer.

'Momie, are we rich?' she asked one day at dinner.

'Yes Kitt, we are very rich. We have each other.' I answered. I don't think she knew exactly what I meant by that. After all, she was going to the best schools from one end of the world to the next; she was associating with children from all cultures; I drove her to school in a big Cadillac car. I suppose it was obvious to her that we were not poor, but she had no idea how I had to pull the pennies together, or that at times I had to make the government wait for my taxes to keep us and our world in bread and butter. I don't think anyone knew what I was going through except the accountants, who were very often careless, causing more problems than at times were necessary. I felt the American government took eleven years or so out of my earning powers and I owed them nothing anyway. As a matter of fact, I still feel this way. I could have sued the government for all the harassment they caused me after the White House lunch but I did not have ten thousand dollars to put down for a lawyer to take a case that might have cost me more than I bargained for with the risk of not winning. Then too it would have taken years to prove what they had done to me. And many witnesses would be called, and I am sure many would not want to have been involved. So I went about my life and Kitt's, hanging from a rope on the magnolia tree of survival – in silence.

These are the times when the vultures move in. The jobs that were offered to me took advantage of my position of 'she needs money . . .', paying me well beneath the price they knew I was worth. 'She's in trouble', 'She hasn't been on the scene in a long time', 'She hasn't had a record'. The part of Catwoman helped a little, but not enough to make me 'in demand' again. I loved doing Catwoman. It was great, great fun, but the two actors who played Batman and Robin took their characters so seriously that they became the characters in real life. They forgot that the significance of Batman was Zap! . . . Pow! The rest of us did play the characters for fun, but the job was serious and the professionalism is evident when you look at the reshowings of the programmes. Cesar Romero, who played the Joker, was and is extremely professional and I was very fortunate to play alongside him.

I was asked one morning if I knew how to drive a manual car. 'Why are you asking me this question?' I asked, not letting on that I knew nothing about manual drive. I was taken to a hangar. The funniest car in the world was sitting there looking at me with an 'I dare you' expression.

'This is the first time Catwoman has had a car,' the stage manager said to me, 'and it's the first shot on camera tomorrow morning at eight. Think you can handle it?' he asked.

'Show me how it works, please,' I said.

The car had wing doors which opened up instead of out. You got into the car by lying down, put the key into the ignition, put your foot on the gas, the car pulls itself into proper position and off you go.

'How do you steer a car with a wish-bone steering wheel?' I asked jokingly.

'With great care,' was the answer. We laughed.

The man took me for a ride around the outside of the studio lot and back. 'Think you can handle it, Eartha?' he asked.

'See you in the morning,' I said. When I got home, I called a car rental place. 'Do you have a Volkswagen I can rent?' I asked. They said 'yes'.

'Can you deliver it to me at three a.m.?' I asked.

'Lady, nobody is awake at three o'clock in the morning, let alone up to deliver,' said the voice on the other end of the phone.

'I really wish you could do this for me. You see, I'm Eartha Kitt and I'm doing Catwoman in the Batman series tomorrow and I have to drive a manual car by eight a.m., but I don't know how to.'

'Lady, you mean to tell me you want us to rent you a car you don't even know how to drive?' I'm sure the voice on the other end thought I was calling from the insane asylum.

'I'm going to learn how to drive it by the morning,' I said.

'You can't learn how to drive a Volkswagen in a few hours,' said the voice.

'Especially if you don't have one,' I said, 'that's why I need to rent one.'

There was silence from the other end. 'You wouldn't want me to blame you for me not getting this part, would you?' I teased.

'Watcha say ya name is lady?' the voice asked.

'Eartha Kitt.' There was silence.

'And you're doing what?' The voice softened.

'Catwoman.' There was silence.

'Do you mind giving me your phone number?' he asked, letting me know he was going to call back to be sure it was me. I gave him the phone number, asking 'Now please don't pass this number on to anyone.'

'Yes, ma'am.' He hung up.

In five minutes or so the phone rang: 'Is this Miss Eartha Kitt?'

'Y-e-e-e-s.' I drew out the 'yes' in a teasing manner.

'Okay, Miss Kitt, we'll have it at your house at three a.m., but I want you to know we don't usually do this kind of thing, especially to someone who doesn't know how to drive,' said the voice.

'Oh, I know how to drive,' I said, 'I just can't drive a manual.'

'Are you gonna have a licensed person teach you?' the voice asked.

'Yes,' I said, 'Aunt Evelyn.'

'Aunt Evelyn,' he said.

'Yes, Aunt Evelyn, my aunt-in-law.'

'Okay, you got it.' He hung up.

At three a.m. Evelyn was at my house and so was the Volkswagen. We signed all the papers and insurance documents. As they drove off in their accompanying car, the man said, 'I hope it comes back in one piece. Lotsa luck.'

Evelyn and I drove up and down Sunset Boulevard with no traffic to get in the way for three hours – on the sidewalk, on the lawns, on the embankments, zig-zaggedly until I got the gist of it, but at times we were laughing so hard I could hardly see where I was going. I was so proud of myself when I finally mastered it that I made a wrong turn onto the street leading to my house and guess who was parked around the bend? A motorcycle cop. One of those Texas-type handsome blue-eyed blond sun-tanned Californian should-be-in-the-movies cops. I could not escape – caught in the act.

'May I see your licence, please?' he asked, looking at me in my Aunt Jemima bandana outfit jogging suit.

I handed him my driver's licence.

'Do you usually drive over embankments to make your turns?' he asked.

'Well, you see, officer, I'm Eartha Kitt and I have to drive a manual by eight o'clock this morning because I'm playing Catwoman in the Batman series and this was the only time I had to learn. You should see the car they are making me drive. It's absolutely crazy! The car has cat ears and cat eyes for the front lights and a wishbone for a steering wheel, and even whiskers . . .' I went on like a nervous cat on heat.

'Okay, okay, okay. Catwoman, eh?'

'Yes, I've done one segment, and today . . .' I blabbed on.

'All right, Miss Kitt, you can go. My eight-year-old son would never forgive me if I told him I gave Catwoman a ticket.' He left and I drove off without getting the ticket.

I drove to the studio in the Volkswagen, practising all the way for security. No traffic this early, so I didn't have to worry about other cars on the road. When the time came for the cat-car scene, the only trouble we had was getting Cesar Romero's tallness to fit into the car. A few tries with him folding himself in half and we made it. Zoom zoom zoom, off we went for the car scene: it was only five seconds long, but the challenge was worth it.

Time passed in its usual uncertainty, when I received a call from Geoffrey Holder in New York, asking me if I would be in for the next few days. 'Yes, I will be around,' I answered.

'There is something I want to talk to you about,' Geoffrey said. 'I am flying in to Los Angeles tomorrow and would like to drop in on you, my dear.'

'Okay, Geoffrey, I'll be here,' I said, anxious to know what he wanted to talk to me about. I had not seen or spoken to him in years and years. I had known him from the Dunham days. I knew he had directed and choreographed *The Wiz* and was very successful. He was riding high now and was in demand. But what in the world could he want to talk to me about? I walked the house from one end to the other, after looking in on Kitt to see if she was asleep and all right. The housekeeper, Mrs McCoy, was in the family room watching television next to Kitt's room. I didn't want to interrupt her intensity in watching her programme, so I walked through my fifteen-room house, changing things around, dusting, petting my cats and dogs, picking at the plants, wondering what in the world Geoffrey Holder was going to talk to me about.

35 Kitt Grows Up

I wasn't tired enough to sleep. My mind was too busy thinking and wondering. I took a sauna, went for a swim in the lights of the pool, took a shower, washed my hair, and still couldn't sleep even though I went to bed with the television on – an old movie, my favourite programme, Channel 28.

I woke up with the news telling me the problems of the world and the sound of birds tweet-tweeting in the air. Kitt came flying across my bedroom and landed at the foot of my bed as she usually did. 'Hi, Momie,' she greeted me softly. We lay there for a while with her cuddled in my arms. I started to think about how grown-up she was becoming. She was not a baby any more. She was now about sixteen. I started to recall when she took me to the pharmacist to buy her the things that made me know she had become a teenager; thirteen she was when I started to realize the time was getting closer when I was going to have to give her up to the love and care of a man. I think a kind of jealousy came over me then. She was not a baby any more. This was a full-grown woman I was holding in my arms. I felt the jealousy in me of the man that would be in the place I was in now. It was a year or so before, I remember, that Kitt called me from her girlfriend's Jackie's house, 'Momie, come and pick me up.' They had gone to a school party the night before. I knew there were always some parents or grown-ups from the school to watch over the children, so I was never too worried about these parties; though as a mother, I guess I was anyway. But I always told Kitt I trusted her, and I did. 'Momie, come and get me, but I must tell you, Momie, I'm sorry. We did not get home to Jackie's at the time you asked me to,' she said.

I held my breath as I asked, 'What time did you get back?'

'Well, you see Momie, I know you asked me and Jackie to be home not later than eleven o'clock . . .' she hesitated a bit.

'Kitt, what time did you get back?' Be calm, mother, I said to myself, let the child explain.

'W-e-e-e-ll' – the 'well' was drawn out in a slightly higher voice. When she does this, she is usually trying to make a serious situation a laughing one so that I can be more easily forgiving. 'Well, you see Momie, it wasn't really our fault' – she started to talk a little faster.

'What time did you get back, Kitt?' I asked a little sharply.

'Two o'clock in the morning?' she answered, more in a question than a statement.

'Two o'clock in the morning?' I asked. Don't get upset, mother, it's already done, being upset will not change the time.

'Momie, it wasn't our fault. We had no transportation and the boys had the car. We couldn't leave without them,' she said in a calm excited way.

'You could have called a cab,' I said.

'We had no money.'

'You could have called me.'

'They kept telling us they were leaving in a minute, but the minute turned into being another minute, and then another hour . . .'

'Never mind Kitt,' I said calmly, 'I'll be right over.'

I got in my car and drove to Jackie's, furious all the way. Not at Kitt particularly, but at the thought that boys would put girls in a position of not being obedient to their parents. They had the car so they were in control. The nerve.

When I picked Kitt up, I said 'We're going to buy you a car right now. You'll never be put in a position like that again. How dare those boys think because they have the car they can keep you out all night like you don't have to obey your mother.'

Kitt said nothing but her body language told me she was getting a bit excited about having her own car. I drove to several second-hand places along the boulevards of Los Angeles. We found a second-hand manual, something she liked, for four thousand dollars.

'But Momie, I don't know how to drive a car,' she whispered.

'I'll teach you,' I said. All the paperwork was made up with everything in my name. (Kitt was too young to drive alone so an older person with a licence would have to be in the car at all times, which I was aware of. But at least she would be learning how to be independent of such a situation again.) I called her father to meet us at the car dealer to check the car out in case the man was selling us a lemon. Bill drove the car around, okayed it, and drove her and the car to my house. Kitt's driving lessons started the next day and she has had a car ever since. But now the expensive kind. God, did that lesson cost me a lot! But I must say, Kitt is very sensible with driving. One day she made such a stupid mistake going through the narrow gates of my driveway that I made her back the car up and do it again.

'But Momie, I can't,' she pleaded.

'Yes you can, Kitt. Do it.'

I never saw such panic on her face but she backed the car up without a mistake and drove in again without a mistake and she never made that mistake again.

So many little pictures of bringing her up came to mind in the short while we were lying there, watching the news. The time she was about seven or eight and we had to leave on a plane to London (probably to make *The High Bid*); I had bought her what I thought were great knitted dresses from Marks and Spencer some time back – great for comfort, great for travelling. I had taught her how to pack her suitcase: all you don't use right away at the bottom, all you need right away should be on top; all should be packed as though you are going to use the suitcase as a closet. Everything should be right at hand. When you open your suitcase, you don't even have to hang anything up, you know exactly where everything is. We had done that the night before because the plane was leaving early.

I laid out one of these knitted dresses, shoes, stocking, a coat, all matching. When she awoke she came to my room. I was putting on make-up.

'Getting ready, Momie?' she asked.

'Yes, why aren't you?' I asked.

'I don't know what to wear.'

'I've laid everything out for you,' I said, 'there on the chaise.' Kitt looked at it and returned to her side of the house. Mrs McCoy was making breakfast. I could smell the egg, toast and coffee coming across the ninety-five-feet-long living room. Kitt returned with coffee for me.

'Why aren't you getting ready, Kitt?'

'Do I have to wear that?' she asked, looking at the laid-out outfit.

'Yes, Momie wants you to wear that. It doesn't wrinkle, so when we get off the plane in London you will look neat and tidy for the photographers,' I said in my motherly tone.

'But I don't want to wear that,' she said.

'Then you'll have to think of a good enough excuse for me to accept,' I said, 'for you not to wear it.' Kitt went to her room. She returned to my room.

'Not ready yet?' I asked.

'I don't like the colour of that outfit,' she said.

'Not a good enough excuse, Kitt,' I answered.

'But Momie . . .' I looked at her. She left. She came back.

'Momie, that dress is not pretty.'

'Not a good enough excuse, Kitt. When you think of a good enough one I'll accept you not wearing it,' I said.

Kitt must have given me at least eleven excuses that I would not accept. Finally she took the outfit and left, coming back with the whole kit and kaboodle on. She looked at me and said, 'Good enough?' I was on the floor with laughter. I never saw an outfit look so horrible. The dress was entirely too big, too long, and completely out of shape. So wrong I had to say, 'Good enough.' Kitt went to her room and returned looking like a child just stepped out of a fashion magazine. She won.

I used to practise stimulation of her brain in quick thinking. Just before she went to sleep, she had to tell a story that would include everything she saw on the wall of her room, from one corner to the other, including a spot, an insect, spider webs, cracks, small shadows, anything that was there. Without using ands, buts, uh-ums etc. The story had to flow, make sense, and be quick. She got so good at this she could beat me. We had a lot of fun getting this far in life, and now here I was holding a full-grown woman in my arms who was about ready to take her wings and fly. I drove her to school that morning, slyly looking at the make-up, not wanting to tell her as I always did, 'Too much make-up.' I never wanted her to wear make-up. 'You're too pretty for make-up, Kitt. You don't need it,' I'd say. 'Besides, make-up can ruin your pretty skin. Keep it clean, it will age more slowly.' Of course I could not be too firm about this since her peers were all wearing make-up. Yes, Kitt is a woman now. All the baby years are gone.

Geoffrey Holder came to my house that afternoon. Tall like a king, he walked in and bent over to greet me with a kiss. 'Eartha darling, long time no see.'

We did our long-time-no-see cordialities. I took him into the bar which is a glassed-in, bright room overlooking the pool area of bougain-villaeas, orange and lemon trees and magnolias – my favourite area. Geoffrey did not sit down. He stood over me like a lion about to devour a small prey. He had brought a sketch book under his arm. He laid it on the coffee table and opened it to show me his sketches.

'These,' he said, pointing to a few pages, 'are what I designed for you.' The sketches were more like paintings than designer sketches; beautiful paintings of men and women in African or Arabian garments.

'They are beautiful, Geoffrey,' I said, not understanding what it was all about.

He kept me in suspense for a while and then finally asked, 'Do you like them? The ones I designed for you, I mean.'

'Yes, Geoff, they are beautiful, but . . .'

'I'm doing a show called *Timbuktu*, based on *Kismet*, and I want you to play the Queen Saleem-la-loom.'

He was still standing. I looked up at the giant figure and said, 'You mean the part Marlene Dietrich played with Ronald Coleman in the movie?' She was the only female I really remembered playing that part, though I did remember Alfred Drake playing the part of the King of Beggars in *Kismet* on Broadway some years previously.

'Yes,' said Geoffrey, 'We start rehearsals in about six weeks. I want you as the Queen.'

I looked at him in silence. He had no idea what was going on inside me. I was so elated that there were tears of happiness running like a brook over my heart.

'I know it's not the leading character, but everything centres around her,' Jeffrey said anxiously.

I already had the whole picture woven in my mind like a spider weaving its web. Back on Broadway. A chance to be on the scene again in the eyes of the American public, to show them I'm still here. 'That sounds exciting, Geoffrey, I'd love to do that part.' I tried to hold the tears of excitement in check. But I also realized that often these projects do not materialize. Wait until a contract comes and then let the tears flow. 'Calm down, Eartha,' I said to myself. Then too, I may be rejected by the producers and investors if they feel I am still a bad risk because of my stand against Johnson's Vietnam escalation. They might think by casting me it would scare away the American public. Geoffrey left with my okay to accept. I picked Kitt up from school wanting to tell her about perhaps going to New York to do a Broadway musical while she drove us home, but I held back until dinner time when I asked her what her feelings were about going to New York for a while. Even though she was sixteen I still did not want to be away from her for any great length of time. She would definitely have to go with me – with her agreement, of course. Kitt was glad to be going to New York, making it easier to accept what might be a long time away from our home.

Geoffrey Holder called back some days later to say the contract was coming through. I prepared myself for New York and the musical *Timbuktu* went into production.

The sketch Geoffrey had drawn for my entrance was an oversized bowl that would be carried by four dancers with me in it. 'I've always wanted to be supported by one man,' I said to Geoffrey. Nothing more was said about this one-man desire until one day in a rehearsal at the Minskoff Theatre, during the lunch break, when in came a man with muscles like a bull. 'That's it,' I said. Jeffrey introduced me to him: Tony Carol – Mr Universe, Mr World, Mr Body Beautiful (if you go for muscles), the sepia Arnold Schwarzenegger. We practised during the lunch break to see how it could be choreographed for Saleem-la-loom to make her entrance in the hands of one man. We achieved it. When the cast returned, it was done to the applause of all.

I know there was some trepidation that Eartha Kitt as one of the stars in a Broadway show might not be too kosher because of her (famous or infamous) stand with the Johnsons. And to be honest I was nervous about this myself; but as soon as the audience saw my head above the cast in the Saleem-la-loom entrance on opening night, it started to applaud so loudly one could barely hear the music. As soon as I was let down, slowly stepping on one of the dancer's backs saying 'I'mmm here', the audience was so excited the applause stopped the show. I was laughing inside so much I could have cried in my joy at the public's acceptance, to the point that I could hardly start the song Mr Farester and Mr Wright wrote for me, called 'In the Beginning Woman'. I was home and I was glad.

Timbuktu opened in Washington where President Carter greeted me with 'Welcome home, Eartha' when we were invited to the White House for the opening of the Ford theatre and the cameras and TV stations made a special issue of my presence.

We were in Washington about three months then New York, where the opening night audience really went crazy when I said, 'I'mmmm here!' I got nominated for the best actress in a musical for *Timbuktu*.

My career should have shot up from there but for some reason not much happened after a run of two and a half years. I had no agent representing me at this time. Agents were calling asking to represent me, but they all wanted ten per cent of something that was already there – nothing much for them to work for. Usually they sign you up exclusively, take ten per cent of what you are already doing, and do nothing to advance your career. My stand has always been, I'll give you ten per cent of what you do for me, not what I'm doing already that you had nothing to do with. Most of the time the artist gets the job for the agent, not the agent the job for the artist.

At any rate, time went on. Kitt stayed in New York at the apartment I had rented, and became an undergraduate at Columbia University, where she was studying law. She was getting more and more interested in boys but I trusted her, having faith that she would take care.

I had to pull one of Kitt's friends up, though. She was kept out into the wee hours of the morning without phoning to let me know where she was. When I saw the friend whom she stayed out with I asked, 'Why would you keep my daughter out so late?'

'Kitt is not a child,' he said, 'she has a mind of her own.'

'I agree with you, but she has been taught to call to at least tell me where she is,' I said, like the mother Kitt knows.

The friend began to argue with me. 'Oh, you're so old-fashioned,' he said. 'The children don't ask their parents how long they can stay out, or where they can go any more,' he argued.

'Do you have sisters?' I asked.

'Yes,' he said.

'How old is your youngest sister?' I asked.

'Seventeen,' the friend said.

'How does your mother react when your seventeen-year-old sister stays out late and your mother does not know where she is?' I asked.

'She has a fit,' the friend said.

'What makes you think I am any different?'

We looked at each other.

'Kitt is seventeen,' I said. I assume the friend figured that since Kitt's mother was in show business she could not possibly care about her child as much as his mother did about her child.

I was lonely when *Timbuktu* went on tour and I had to leave Kitt behind. I was kept busy with the show and public relations – interviews, personal appearances and the like – moving from one city to the other, one hotel bed to another. It could never feel like home without my own personal belongings around me. I took Numi my little poodle who kept my sanity in control. It's amazing how an animal can make you feel so needed, so wanted, so loved and so unpressured. I rarely went anywhere without Numi – restaurants, opera, fancy places no one would ever think of taking a dog into. She was always in my handbag. The only time she made a noise was when I went to see one particular play, where the denouement had a mother killing her children. Numi said 'Yip' at that point.

As long as we were together, Kitt and I were both happy. A picture of her was always in my mind. I recall when she was about three, an offer came to me for a South American rest/work tour; one night a concert followed by a few days of rest. A paid working vacation. I left Kitt at home with a certified nurse, the housekeeper, and caretakers; I was always a bit nervous that something might go wrong, but with a certified nurse present how could it? Besides, my mother-in-law would be in and out. 'Rest, Eartha, take your mind off the baby,' my musicians who travelled with me would say. How can a mother take her mind off her baby?

We were in Bogota, Colombia. I had a television show the next morning. As I bathed before going to bed, I saw a vision of little Kitt. Her arms were held out to me; I could hear her voice, 'Momie'. The vision was so clear and strong, I repacked my bags, ordered a taxi to take the first plane home, and eleven hours later – after an agonizing five-hour stop-over in Panama – I was in Los Angeles. When I walked in the door, little Kitt put her arms out to me and said, 'Momie'. When I picked her up she was so hot with fever I could hardly hold her. I called the doctor and he came over immediately. After examining her, he said, 'Eartha, if you had been one day later, Kitt would have been deathly ill.' The nurse thought all babies have fevers so it was not serious. Needless to say that nurse was never to be seen again.

Kitt stayed in New York with my trust that she could take care; she was also looking for an apartment for us to settle in eventually. We were taken advantage of by an interior decorator who was supposedly decorating an apartment Kitt had found in one of those modern fandangled buildings I am not fond of because they lack personality. We were also ripped off by a lawyer who gave me a bill for some forty-five thousand dollars of telephone calls; I thought he was putting my earnings from *Timbuktu* away for a rainy day only to find it all gone. At the end of the tour of *Timbuktu* I found myself scrounging again. An offer here, an offer there – Australia, England, or a few places in America. And no recording contract could be obtained anywhere.

Jacques Morali came along and offered me a contract to make a disco record. He and Bruce Villanche wrote 'Where Is My Man?' which became a gold record in Sweden. (I did not know this until I walked into the office of Scorpio Records in Paris where I saw it hanging on the wall of Henri Belolo's office.) The album, I am told, especially 'Where Is My Man?', was a huge success, but no royalties were paid to me in the four years we worked together. I didn't enjoy making the record but at least I was in the charts again, riding back into popularity, which I am extremely grateful for. Flying to Paris to promote the records with jet-lag, settle into the Georges Cinq Hotel, make-up on at seven a.m., all day runabout doing TV, radio and personal appearances, off to Germany or Spain or Italy where I was accused of being drunk, thrown back into my hotel room until the following morning, up again to repeat the same routine, even at times to be followed to see if I was being a bad girl. I guess since many disco entertainers have earned this sort of reputation, all are thrown into the same bag and are assumed to have the same habits. Especially by those who are ex-something; they are the first to point a finger.

No one knew what I was going through emotionally – my time of life was changing biologically and was giving me a very hard time. I had been told by Doctor Golenternek in Los Angeles never to take even a birth control pill because I was born a prancing pony, ready to take off at any time. A birth control pill would drive me through the ceiling. I happen to be the one in a million that cannot take the risk of any stimulation at all. I tried birth control pills once and I did go through the ceiling; even a diet pill sends me mad. So when I felt the pangs of the bio change I took a brandy and an aspirin. No, I wouldn't take the oestrogen shots because the doctors said I would have to come back every three months for a check-up because oestrogen shots can perhaps cause cancer.

So I was in a catch twenty-two, because I had no idea where I would be every three months to have this check-up and, too, why put myself in a position of risking cancer when aggravation alone can cause it. It could turn out to be like my daughter's experience. She was given a shot by her doctor to counteract an allergy; the serum came from horses, and now she is allergic to horses. The cure can sometimes be worse than the symptom.

I went along my way keeping my problems to myself. There was no one to talk to about them. Anyway, who would understand, and why bother others who could not do anything about them? A doctor only says, 'Take a pill and call me in the morning.' After my stint with Doctor Miracle, I never wanted to see a doctor again.

Kitt had found an apartment of her own in New York where she settled down, after a period of living in several apartments on her own – sometimes in the same building, with me in one apartment and her some floors below. Now she had found one she thought would be ideal for her to be in for a while and she decorated it beautifully. She had gone through a few boyfriends but none I really liked much, except one whom Kitt thought was a bore. The one I liked was well brought-up, intelligent, kind and considerate. His parents were European, had a good sense of humour, were kind, considerate and good conversationalists. Kitt and he even went on a student trip together in Europe. I felt comfortable that he would take good care of her. She called often to say where they were and that all was fine.

With one of her boyfriends I had to bite my tongue and hold my breath until it was all over. He was much older than Kitt – his children were her age. This was obviously a period when she was looking for a substitute father. His past reputation was not in the least kosher. I am sure Kitt got my silent message that this was not kosher for her either, but as calmly as I could I bided the time until it was over.

Then there was another who used her to smuggle dollars out of Spain, putting Kitt and her girlfriend in a very risky position if they had been searched by the customs. When they arrived in the apartment back in New York, they unloaded thirty-five thousand dollars from their bras, panties, boots, and God knows where else, laughing their heads off as I looked at them and said, 'Do you know what would have happened to you if you were searched?'

'Oh mother!' Kitt's usual reply.

'You would have been picked up as international whores or for being in narcotics.' My heart was bleeding that she did not think before she took such a chance – both of them in fact.

The anger I had in me at the sight of them laughing as they stripped for the boyfriend who took such advantage of two young girls made me want to kill. I hope you can see what kind of person you are dealing with, I thought to myself, though I never said it out loud.

I was in Washington doing some shows when Kitt called me on the Friday of my last week at the club. 'Momie, wouldn't it be nice if I drive to Washington on Friday, see your last show on Saturday, and we can drive back together on Sunday?' she said excitedly.

'That's a great idea, I'd love that, Kitt. It would be fun.'

So there I was, waiting for her to walk in the door of my hotel room at any minute, or call. Seven p.m., no Kitt and no call; eight p.m., no Kitt and no call. Just as I was about to walk out the door to go to the club, the phone rings: 'Hi Mom! Guess where I am?' I held my breath. 'I'm at Heathrow. I'm on my way to Madrid. Isn't that exciting? Blah-Blah (the name of the boyfriend) said he wants me to come to Madrid right away. He wants me to meet his parents.'

The blood ran hot through my veins. The tricks men can play, especially on young girls. 'Is Jocelyn with you?' I asked calmly, knowing there was no point in showing anger or disappointment. Kitt was at Heathrow, what was there to do but wait with baited breath until she returns? At least Jocelyn was with her; she was not alone. She had taken heed, therefore, to my 'Don't go anywhere without Jocelyn' routine.

Kitt was all excited at the prospect of meeting the boyfriend's parents, thinking 'When the boyfriend wants you to meet his parents he's getting serious' – but it was only a way for him to get more dollars out of Spain. He had sent them a first-class ticket for the way over, but sent them back on a 'cattle ticket'. They were exhausted when they got back – they walked into the apartment looking like two cats escaping from the animal catcher.

Kitt was annoyed; I could see, but did not want to point it out. She did not want to admit that she had been used. More proof of this came when she called the boyfriend's lawyer to come and pick up the money. 'I'd keep it if I were you,' I said, 'after someone putting you on a chopping block of hell.' I thought of all the men who told me I was beautiful, who used me like some pawn then walked off for some reason. While I had been an ugly duckling I could somehow protect myself, or was somehow protected from the abuse of men's macho egos. But as a beautiful woman I was trusting, naive and helpless. Being beautiful had made me a prey for hunters to conquer; my whole life had been spent dodging hunters to escape being conquered. Kitt being beautiful was now walking on the same path. I feared for her.

So there I was, saying 'If I were you I'd keep it. What's he going to do? Report it?' I was half joking, but only half.

Then when the lawyer picked up the money there was a question of a discrepancy in the amount. I said nothing, only hoped that she was learning how easy it is to be duped into being made a fool of in all innocence.

The affair was over in no time flat, nothing more to be said. But mother was accused of interfering when she asked the boyfriend a few days later at 'Club A', 'Why would you use my daughter in such a way?' He nervously got up and walked away in guilt, never to be seen again.

'Kitt, you are too wonderful to let anyone use you foolishly,' I always told her. 'You are beautiful, wonderful, and intelligent. I know what Momie has put into you; don't let anyone take it away.' I would add, 'Your values are much more than dollars that do not make sense.'

'Oh mother!' was Kitt's usual reply.

I was at Kitt's apartment one evening, staying overnight because I had to catch a plane for Paris the next morning. I had driven in from Connecticut where I had bought an old (1773) house which I intended to refurbish in the future. It was a two-hour drive from Kitt's apartment. I cannot let myself pay astronomic rents in a big city like New York. The country is what I love – space, animals and trees, gardens and freedom from the city jungle. Plus something I can call my own, that I can show (at least for a moment) after my efforts.

Tired and weary of the tour I had just finished and with the prospect of the trip to Paris, I was lying down in thought on the sofa listening to Kitt expound on her adventures in decorating her apartment, which was now just about finished, and on her episodes in the building's health club. The doorbell rang. Kitt opened it and a young man entered, looked straight at me and headed in my direction with his hand held out for mine.

'Momie, this is Charles, Charles, this is my mother.' Kitt performed the niceties. How do mothers know these things? What makes a mother feel this is it, this is the one? This is the one that will break the tie and take my baby from me. A tear fell from my heart the moment I felt his presence, the moment his hand touched mine. I knew she was gone. The moment his eyes met mine, the wedding ring was squeezing my soul. His eyes were pleading for acceptance.

I said nothing to Kitt though I could see in her body language and the manner of her talk after he left that this *was* it. I left for Paris the next morning. On the plane my fingers worked into my tapestry the emptiness that was beginning in me.

'Don't judge by first impressions,' Mother McDonald used to say to me.

'Mom, I'm never wrong,' I used to say to her, 'but we'll wait and see. My instincts are never wrong.'

36 'All By Myself'

The trip to Paris seemed longer than ever before. I could not sleep; I could not eat. I drank soda water all the way. My duties started the next morning – TV, personal appearances, and the etceteras of promotion, after a day of choosing clothes from Balmain. It's terribly hard to find a wardrobe to my liking these days since everything seems to be designed for the Arabs to buy. Everything is so overdone and expensive; I don't even think the Arabs would buy them, and I am told that the French can't afford to buy their own any more since the prices are set for the Arab money. A plain simple luxury is hard to find.

Fluff and fuss is the mode of the day – flash and fury in every turn, even in the entertainment world, perhaps especially in the entertainment world, where laser beams and smoke can make anyone a star in flash and fury. Gladly the theatre has not yet been saturated with it, but it is sneaking in.

The phone rang one evening in my suite at the Georges Cinq: 'Momie, sit down,' the voice said with a smile in it. I did not have to sit down as I waited for the words. 'Are you sitting down, Momie?' I said, nothing. Pulling every muscle in my body as tightly as I could, I braced myself against, 'Charles has asked me to marry him.' Her voice was ringing the bells of her glory. My whole being sank. 'Momie? Are you there? Why don't you say something? Charles asked me to marry him, aren't you happy for me?'

I was silent. Be calm, Eartha, hold on; you knew this was coming, it had to come one day. At least he seems like a good person. He seems solid. He's a lawyer, so he's a good risk as a provider. But I was looking for fault; I was determined to find fault, not necessarily with Charles Shapiro, but with the figure he represented. Finally, I came up with, 'his eyes are too close together', irrationally satisfied to have found a fault. I realize now how trivial it all was. They've only known each other for a few months, I kept thinking. I don't know him at all. Well, at least she's not going to be living with him illegitimately – she'll have a legal partner. At least she's not marrying him because she's pregnant – it's all above board. So much went through my mind before I said, 'Are you happy, Kitt?' trying to hide my hurt of losing her.

Kitt must have the instincts of her mother: 'Momie, I thought you would be happy for me. Aren't you happy for me, Momie?'

'If you are happy, Kitt, that's all that matters,' I finally said, almost to myself. If I'm supposed to be happy, then I guess I am, was my state of mind.

'Just think of it this way, Momie: you're not losing a daughter, you're gaining a son,' Kitt laughed.

If I wanted a son, I would have borne one, I thought to myself. 'When is the wedding?' I meekly asked.

'We haven't quite got to that point yet, Momie, but it will probably be in June. A June wedding is what I always wanted. Oh yes, and Mom, you know the bride's mother pays for everything – so get prepared. I want my wedding to be the talk of New York.'

When I hung up the phone my head reeled with anger and happiness at the same time, in confusion. Was I angry or happy for her? Or was the resentment of her being taken away from me stronger than all the feelings? Or was I numbed by it all?

No, I wasn't angry, I wasn't happy. I was confused by what my feelings should be, so I became numb and almost felt nothing at all. Not only does the stranger come in out of nowhere and take my baby from me, but I have to pay for it as well? Whoever thought of that idea? I stood by the window looking onto the patio of the Georges Cinq for a long time, remembering the fun times Kitt and I had had together. The whole world of places we had been; the games she had played on me, and me on her.

The time she was about eleven – I had gone into Watts, the poor area of Los Angeles, to take care of the kids I was trying to help with physical therapy through dance. I went there every Saturday when I was in Los Angeles for a two-hour class and talk with the children and parents. When I returned home, Kitt and one of her friends who had come to visit had baked some cookies. 'Momie, we have a surprise. Look what we did.'

Cookies were everywhere: all over the stove, the kitchen counter, and almost as many on the floor. Mrs McCoy was watching TV soaps or something. 'Momie, try one, they are delicious,' Kitt said. The cookie was so hard I could not even make a dent in it, though I kept trying (without giving myself away to the child, so as not to discourage her). Then their little faces broke into laughter – I was being put on by both of them. We all had a good laugh, except when I went into the bar and saw all the alcohol had been mixed together, the bottles half empty, and a bowl of mixture sitting on the counter with everything but the kitchen sink in it. I asked, 'Where was the housekeeper all this time that you were playing with the bar, Kitt?'

'Watching television,' came the reply.

'Did either of you drink this stuff?' I asked.

'No.'

I believed them because neither gave that impression.

'Whose idea was it to play this game?' I asked.

Kitt's friend admitted guilt. Since she was two years or so older than Kitt, I called her mother, told her what influence her child was on my child and banned her from visitor's rights for a year, or until she was better disciplined. It turned out that child had been a problem at every house she visited, and was running out of visiting rights everywhere.

The patio of the Georges Cinq looked as wounded as I felt. The copper roof was green with age and lack of care. Neglect was showing; the potted plants were withered and the umbrellas over the garden tables were folded to wait for spring. The painting on the face of the building was dried from the rain and sun etching the lines of wear more deeply. The beauty of the building had saddened with time and abuse. This building I had known since I was a very young girl, that I admired so much and loved, now showed me what time perhaps had done to me.

You may be wanted, but you're not needed. I lay down with my eyes open to the ceiling making pictures of Kitt playing and laughing; of her stumbling to find her walking mobility; of her first phone conversation with the operators at the Carlton Towers Hotel near Sloane Street, London, trying to make sense at eleven months old. She took her first real walk across the room on this day and went straight for the telephone, making just sounds, no words. We finally had to put the phone out of reach. I remembered the time she climbed onto the window sill at the Plaza Hotel in New York and was looking down on the traffic below as I came into the room and calmly removed her and the furniture she had aided herself with. And the time she had every petal from my opening night chrysanthemums strewn from one end of the room to the other, and I played the mother plant that cried over her lost children as I picked up each petal, replacing it near the almost naked mother plant. Kitt never touched the plants again except to hug and kiss.

I remembered when I had to put a 'Please do not disturb' sign on her at the beaches in Puerto Rico because no one would leave her alone – the little blonde-haired blue-eyed golden-complexioned child had to be touched by everyone, leaving us with no peace. And how I would feed her with bananas, mashed potatoes, and food I chewed up myself to nourish her because I hated packaged or canned foods for babies; I didn't trust them because I did not know what was in them. Then everyone thought what a strange mother I was to feed the baby, then lay her down on my mink coat on the floor in the corner, give her her bottle of freshly squeezed juice, then feed myself. The swimming lessons at nine months old, the ballet classes, the equestrian lessons, the ice-skating lessons at five a.m. and school at nine – all this came flooding back to me. And the stages of rebellion when nothing I did was right; when she became Miss Know-It-All.

And the analyzing of her paintings to see if she had a problem, talking to the teachers about her behaviour and her school marks. And the boyfriends whom I often spoke to in the wee hours of the mornings who would call just to talk when they broke up with Kitt. Now she's going – completely. What do I do with myself now? I knew there was no turning back. Kitt is not the type to say yes to marriage and change her mind. He did not give me that impression either. I knew she would go through with it. And I'm asked to *pay* for a stranger to take my baby away from me? When I thought of this I laughingly cried myself to sleep.

My commitment in Paris was work and more work; I was in a quandary with myself but went about it as though all was well. The video to 'I Love Men' was a five-day to ten-day event.

I returned to America and continued with concerts etc., living alone in my Connecticut house, making a living quarters of the old barn where I was again taken advantage of by the contractor and the cottage is still not right. If you're not on the scene to watch at all times, it can be money down the drain. A woman alone . . . 'Momie, you must be in New York to help me choose my gown. We have to choose the floral arrangements. I need a deposit for the Pierre Hotel to secure the room – everyone wants to get married in June. The only date left is the thirteenth of June. I need a deposit to hold it. Momie, I need a deposit to hold the orchestra – it's the same orchestra that played for the royal family. Momie, you have to help me choose the guests. Don't you think we should have the wedding videoed? Shall I invite Daddy? . . .'

The questions, the demands, the requests. Kitt had no idea, nor had anyone else, of how I was bleeding inside. A million pins in a pin cushion could not explain my feelings. I did all that was requested of me with dry eyes. The fact that I had to keep working to make the deposits until a piece of property was sold was never mentioned. I knew what I had to do and just went ahead and did it. I did it by selling a piece of my insurance and taking from one account to put into another for the deposits to be at hand. I was borrowing from one savings account to another with the help of my accountant, Art Robbins, to see that all went well for Kitt's marriage, until monies came in from selling a building in Los Angeles.

Kitt wanted me in New York at her beck and call when it was getting closer and closer to the day, getting annoyed at me when I was not available. The list of those she and Charles wanted to invite was long enough to fill Grand Central Station – at least it was to me, at two hundred and fifty dollars a plate. 'You must cut down, Kitt,' I would say.

'Whom shall we cut?' she would ask.

Knowing nothing about Charles' family, I could say very little, but a cousin seven times removed to me was ridiculous, on his side or on Kitt's side. After long debates over the list I omitted most of the friends whom I had not seen in years. Kitt's father was there, and her stepbrother Chad. Bill quietly came up behind me and said, 'You did a good job' in a whisper. Only the spirits must have held me back from putting my heel in his you-know-what as I hurriedly took myself away from his bad spirit saying, 'No thanks to you, you bastard.' No one heard me but two of my best childhood friends, Morgan and Marvin Smith, who teasingly said, 'You want us to put him away?'

I grabbed a glass of wine and hid myself behind a wall where Norene found me to say, 'You don't like him touching her, do you?'

'Every time he goes near her I want to vomit,' I said. To see them dancing together with a smile of pride on his face made my skin crawl. When Kitt had asked me if she should invite her father, I said, 'Yes, of course, if that is what you want,' wondering if she was going to.

'Do you think I should ask him to give me away?' she asked.

'That's up to you, Kitt. After all he is your father, no matter what.' I eased the situation with my reply.

'I think you should give me away, Momie. Daddy gave me away when he refused to pay child support.'

As I looked at Bill, analyzing how proud he was to be Kitt's father, I also looked at the members of his family who had come. I could see the streak of what Mother McDonald told me about. Not one of them, she said, lifted a finger to help Gramma in times of need. Mother was the eldest of those left out of something like sixteen children. Every time another was born she had to work harder to help the family as well as give up something. According to Mother McDonald, the rest of them did not feel it necessary to help her with their mother since she was very wealthy. The same attitude was adopted by Bill with me and Kitt.

I had an engagement up to two weeks before the day of the wedding. 'Momie,' Kitt requested nervously, 'I want you to be with me to help me take care of the last-minute plans.' There was nothing important that was not already done. I really wanted to scream out loud to rid myself of the pain that was burning inside. I came home, bought a bottle of Dom Pérignon champagne and, as the saying goes, cried in my beer and emptied myself of all tears. I moaned, groaned, and died a thousand times over champagne from my silver goblets until no tears would come any more.

When the time came for me to walk Kitt down the aisle, I was strong, daring myself to drop one tear. The Gods held me straight down the aisle that was a thousand miles long. I brought her into the world and now I was giving her away. No pain can be so great as that of this moment; no love can hurt so much as that of a mother for her child, and no love can be more rewarding when the child turns out as wonderful as Kitt. I felt proud of myself for doing such a good job and the Gods for helping me, but the giving of her to someone who probably will never know the values she and I have put into one another, the give and take between us, the sharing, the loving, and the time in patience and fortitude to see that hurts are as few as possible – that is too painful.

The vows made to each other, both in Hebrew and in English almost brought tears to my eyes but, standing directly in front of Kitt who was watching me for strength, I dared not let a tear drop. When I had to step aside on the arm of the father-in-law-to-be I almost screamed. The vision of my mother came to me as I saw her on the arms of the man she walked off with, leaving me in the yard of the family she gave me to.

When Charles stomped on the glass to break it in the vows, he might as well have stomped on me. That is the hurt I felt. As the glass shattered into several splinters, I was that glass. I prayed to the Gods to hold me tight, to keep me strong. The ceremony was over – again I had to rewalk that thousand miles into nowhere. Charles' father took me by the arm trying to pull me into the reception room where all were gathered for photographs. I pulled away from him to run into the ladies' room where I emptied the tears that were about to overflow the ducts. I was screaming inside myself. I wanted to leave, to be alone, to cry alone. I had a strong desire to jump into my jeep and drive home to Connecticut. Putting on a false face has never been my forte. Ann Grayson, Morgan and Marvin Smith and Gloria consoled me, but even they did not know me at this moment. I could not eat the two hundred and fifty dollar dinner, and I could not drink the wine. I ordered a bottle of Dom Pérignon but it was consumed by a guest sitting next to me. I was walking in a zombie-like state, numb from wounds of hurt.

Kitt came to my table now and then to see if I was all right. I was surprised that Charles did not. As a matter of fact, I don't remember seeing him at all after the wedding ceremony. Perhaps I had erased him completely from my mind. During the ceremony I only saw him vaguely as I was transfixed on Kitt, but I kept seeing the glass he had stomped on, smattering it into bits, feeling it was me. I wanted to go home to wallow in my wound.

From time to time I excused myself into the corridor or a place I could hide to release my hurt. I saw Bill looking for the men's room. He was so frail – like the wounded soldier he had spoken to me about when he was wounded in the Korean war. I could not look at him. He tried not to see me as I said 'What goes around comes around.' I could not have any feelings for him and though I did not wish him harm, I could not help but think that God has his ways. Now you are hurting and I feel no sorrow over it. All the hurts you have brought on others are now sticking like swords in your soul. If only you had played fair.

The wedding was a huge success. Fun was had by all including Mr Lenon, the band leader, who said, 'I've played for a lot of weddings but this one was the most fun.' As the evening drew to an end, I found myself, like a zombie, asking those I cared for the least to leave. There were a few who had crashed the party. How they got in I had no idea until Kitt told me how someone had cornered her into sending an invitation without checking with me. I saw a few leeches whom I said nothing to as I did not want to spoil any of these moments for Kitt, but when I watched the petals of the fifteen-thousand-dollar plants and flowers wilting, my hurt was exacerbated.

The evening finally came to a halt. After everyone left, I stood at the door looking back on the room that had been so extremely beautifully decorated in simple luxury. The tables were now strewn around in ragged memory; the candles were dimming as the melting wax dripped onto the tablecloths; the bouquets of flowers stood alone in sorrow, not to be taken home; and I recalled every note I sang to afford them, only to be thrown in a garbage bin. The bits of food left on the plates that I wished I had had in the days of hunger when I picked the garbage cans of Manhattan and slept on rooftops and hoped my one nickel would keep me on the subways from one end of New York to the other for a night. I felt empty. I was empty. Well, Eartha, you did it, I said to myself. You paid for a licence to have her and you paid for a licence to lose her. You did it for your daughter. Remember, you haven't lost a daughter, you have gained a son. The words rang in my head.

The room was lonely; it looked like the empty theatre after the curtain goes down, the audience has gone, the cast has gone, and only a work light is standing on the empty stage, revealing something past, waiting for the next act to begin. I was a mother when I came in. What am I now? What is my title? What is my purpose? What am I supposed to do now? Where am I to go? I recalled dancing with Mr Shapiro Senior. There was a body I was dancing with, but I could feel no spirit. No matter whom I danced with, I could feel no spirit. I was completely disconnected from everyone – my soul had left my body to stand and watch, observing all that went on. I wanted to love the evening, I wanted to love and enjoy my daughter's happiness, but I was not there. I was in a world all by myself, in search of a place to land my soul. I was looking at the faces of those I knew from childhood – Gloria, Ann,

Marvin, Morgan. But only in my body could I feel and touch them; they were all in a haze. I was in another place looking down on it all.

Bruce Hubbard sang beautifully, forgetting the words, which made me laugh the only time that evening.

'Aren't you happy for her, Kitty?' Ann Grayson asked.

'If I'm supposed to be happy then I guess I am,' I said. 'I'm not happy for myself.'

'Kitty, she's beautiful, she's wonderful, and she's happy,' said Gloria.

'But I'm not,' I said.

'You did a great job,' said Morgan Smith, 'he's a lucky guy, her husband.'

Morgan or Marvin (I can't remember which, they're twins) said, 'Yes, just think, if we had married you, look what we would have had.' I couldn't laugh at this because it was too true. If they had married me I would not have had Kitt even though Kitt at one time said, 'Momie, it would not have mattered whom you married, I would still be your daughter because I chose you to be my mother.' With this in my head I was going upstairs when I met Kitt and Charles by the elevator. We went to the bridal suite. I changed clothes, bade them goodnight as Kitt said, 'Thanks, Ma, we couldn't have done it without you,' and left the Pierre Hotel looking like the original bag lady. I got into my jeep and went to Kitt's apartment to look at the ceiling of pictures that formed in memory of the night.

I returned to the hotel the next morning to pick them up – they were waiting on the sidewalk. The wedding gown was hanging on the rain drain on the side of the hotel; the train of the gown had so much material a box could not be found to accommodate it. We shoved and squeezed and squeezed and shoved until it could be squashed into the back of the jeep to be taken to Kitt's apartment where it hung on the wall (there was not enough space in the closets). It remained hanging on the wall of their apartment until they moved into a house in Scarsdale about a year later.

37   'I'm Still Here'

I drove back to my house in Connecticut, alone in the jeep and almost in a daze. I did not want to remember the wedding, but the pictures of the event kept floating in my head. I wanted to cry but could not, though a tear or two trickled down my cheeks. The car almost drove itself, like a trained horse who knows its way home. The thoughts of 'What am I to do with my life now, what am I to do with myself, what does the future mean for me, what purpose do I have now she's gone?' came flooding to me. He has taken her from me. Again, I am given away as though I never existed. I could see her eyes watching me as I stood alone watching her during the ceremony.

You've been here before, Eartha, you can be here again – alone. You cannot possess the child, you cannot own the child, you can only bring it into the world, give it the best chance you possibly can to survive on its own, and let it go. It's all very intelligent to realize that and prepare yourself for when the time comes, but there can be no preparation for the emotional hurt, no matter how intelligent one is. And that hurt never goes away. It subsides, it calms down, but at this moment the hurt was too great for my emotional sanity.

On the road nearing my house I stopped the car to look at one of my favourite scenes – the rambling hills of beauty that seemed so serene, where God seems to take a stroll from time to time. The beauty of the sunset that was forming now, the sound of birds who keep me company, especially in the evenings and the long mornings – I wished I could get lost in all this until the hurt subsided. I reached my house, where my dogs Numi and Mati greeted me with screeches of happiness in welcome. I went for a long walk in the pine hills with the dogs. The deer tracks made me curious as usual; the deer path I always followed in interest to know their hiding places, wondering how the mother deer feels when one of her babies gets shot down. No loneliness ever struck me so hard as on this walk. It might have been akin to the feeling I had when I saw my mother walking away from me, after leaving me with that family in the South. There was nothing to talk about; there were no words for this feeling of hurt. I walked by the running brook where lots of baby trout were seeking a means of survival. Everything was making sense but me.

I finally sat down at my desk and wrote what I was feeling as best as I could find the words. Then I cooked all the pickings I had gathered from the garden until no pots were left to cook in. I tapestried my hurts on the canvas, working on until my eyes burned with the salt of my tears and fatigue. And finally to bed, with my cats and dogs.

I was home for some days going through the same act with a bottle of Dom Pérignon champagne helping me to empty myself, until I had to fulfil a contract. I picked up Numi and Mati, my music and gowns like the gypsy bag-lady I have been all my life, feeling like the given-away child standing in the yard watching my mother walking away on the arms of the black man.

Some weeks before Kitt's marriage I had an engagement at the Ballroom in New York. The emotional inbalance started coming on then, but I did not understand exactly what was happening to me, though I knew the idea of Kitt getting married had thrown me out of kilter. The feeling was strange and weird. I drove every day and night the two hours to New York and back to Connecticut. The drive was good for me; just me, the dogs, and my loneliness. Thank God the show was extremely successful. No one knew how I was bleeding inside. My sense of humour was sharp, my dramatic songs were controlled. I was able to hold the reins to channel my confused state of mind.

I decided one afternoon driving into New York to take a short cut through the Bronx and got so lost in my fuzzy state of mind that I had to ask directions from a cab driver whom I waved down. The cab driver was so shocked that it was me that he ran into me with a slight bump. Not a scratch was on either car, but he made me drive to the authorities to report the accident. I had lots of time left to get to the Ballroom so I went along. The authorities were only a block or so away. I waited in a room while papers were supposedly made out while the driver ran all over the building telling everyone, 'Look what I caught!' Like a tigress in a cage I sat as a parade passed along asking for an autograph. The joke was over, I was sent on my way, but somehow I went north instead of south. My mind was so fuzzy when I realized it was too dark for me not to have arrived at the club, that I looked up and saw I was three-quarters of the way home. I could not believe the car had automatically steered me home. Now I was ashamed. No one would believe this. I drove on home, called the club to say I was okay and would make up for it by doing an extra show.

The club manager, Scottie, said it was okay. 'No problem, Eartha, as long as you're all right.'

The next thing I knew, there was a knock at the door. The police: 'Your daughter was worried about you. She called us to see if you're okay,' said one.

'Thank you, I'm okay,' I said. But I wasn't okay. I was not there, I was completely out of it and couldn't do anything about it. I was grateful the

Gods brought me home. I fiddled and faddled around the house, moving furniture, changing the paintings from one wall to the other, scrubbing the floors, vacuuming the rugs. I polished the silver, cleaned the closets, picked at the plants, cleaned the bird cage, and cried until my head ached. Then the dogs and cats and I finally lay down.

I called a limousine to drive me to and from work for the rest of the engagement. The limousine also drove me to the airport when I had to go abroad. I took a plane to wherever my contract was to land me and I went on with my life with no one the wiser. The hairdresser and make-up person, Ted Jenkins, who noticed I was a little non compos mentis at times, never said much except, 'You're upset over Kitt, aren't you?' and let it go. Dayrel Waters, the pianist-conductor, did his job and went about his business. Sometimes after Ted had made me up and I was ready to go on, I'd look in my mirror and say, 'What am I doing here?' Ted would just look at me and say, 'Well, you have a show to do, Eartha,' and on I went. This was at the Roosevelt Hotel in Los Angeles where I had accepted an engagement for two weeks. Thank God it was successful. Leonard Feather, the jazz critic of all times, said, 'There is nobody else quite like Eartha Kitt in show business. She is the ultimate actress-singer-comedienne.' I don't usually read the reviews, but Ted made me read this one. I think Ted knew I was in need of an uplift, since I was staying in the hotel suite, not wanting to see anyone or go anywhere. After I had paid my respects to my friends in Los Angeles, I just wanted to be alone.

Leonard Feather's review did indeed give me a lift, as did the others. They had no idea of my state of mind. I was begging inside to be wanted, to be needed, to be necessary, to be loved, to be hugged. I needed that praise more than at any other time of my life – a psychiatrist could not have done anything for me.

I started to feel a bit more worthwhile and then Cameron Mackintosh came to see me about going to London to do a show called *Follies*. I had never seen *Follies* and all I knew about it was the song 'I'm Still Here' that I had taken and rewritten for myself. I had been sent legal letters from Sondheim requesting that I sing his words and not mine. This was therefore some card Fate was throwing me.

I jumped at the opportunity. I would have a unit around me; everything would be taken care of; I did not have to think about doing everything myself; I would be in one place for a while to settle my mind, to pull myself back, hopefully to being me again and being busy. I was too out of control in my mind to be on my own travelling from place to place, packing and unpacking. I was weary and tired of being the bag-lady I have been all my life, so London and *Follies* would save my soul.

I arrived in London, settled in at the Shaftesbury Theatre and the show got underway to wonderful reviews in the most influential London newspapers. My interpretation of the song 'I'm Still Here' made the critics say 'Run to Eartha', but I was still trying to run away from myself. Things hadn't changed overnight, but I was exorcising a lot of ghosts as I sat day after day in my dressing room writing my memoirs.

Meg Johnson, a member of the *Follies* cast, would often pop in to say hello. She'd sit and talk about how lucky she was that her cancer had been arrested and that she has a wonderful daughter whom she cherishes, just as I cherish mine.

'I know that you feel that your daughter has gone, Eartha,' she would say, 'but she hasn't, you know. She will always be your daughter.' I began to believe she was right.

Because of the wonderful critical and audience reactions to my performance in *Follies*, Ian Alberry asked me to do a one-woman show during the spring of 1989, *Eartha Kitt in Concert*. I was terrified as I'd never done a one-woman show before. What if the audiences didn't like me? What would I do? When rehearsals started I was happy but my nervous tension got worse. I had to try and channel my fear and use it constructively on stage. The previews started with me still panicking, 'Oh God, are they going to reject me?' On the second night of the previews they almost did. The subconscious devil of my mind got stronger than the conscious part and I almost didn't make it, but the rhythm of the applause soon brought me back to my senses.

The actual opening night came and I was so nervous I was sure I would never remember anything. But when the curtain came down, all was well and I realized at last that life is fine again. I felt in control.

Charles and Kitt came over to London to see the show. The marquee displayed my name in the largest letters to be seen in the West End and the critics were saying, 'Pure magic', 'The Sorceress of song', 'Spellbinding, erotic and superbly performed', 'Silk and Suede'. Though I was ecstatic about the praise, it meant much more to me when Kitt said, 'Momie, fantastic!' and Charles said, 'Unbelievable, you're great!'

I know now that you can never possess another person. I have learned to be glad that Kitt chose a man with his feet on the ground and a responsible attitude to life. Charles truly adores her and they should live happily ever after. The fight was, and is, within myself. Charles is good for Kitt and she for him.

The conflict between Eartha Kitt and Eartha Mae continues but nowadays Eartha Kitt always wins. She is the stronger, the breadwinner. I'm still here, and my one-woman show will go on, with both of us interpreting life as we feel it. Thanks to the public for keeping me here – still. The only family I know is the audience, Kitt, who makes me so proud to be her mother and now Charles.

Index